Strategy, Organization and the Changing
Nature of Work

Strategy, Organization and the Changing Nature of Work

Edited by

Jordi Gual

Professor of Economics, IESE Business School, University of Navarra, Barcelona, Spain and Research Fellow, Centre for Economic Policy Research, London, UK

and

Joan E. Ricart

Professor of General Management, Chairman of the General Management Department and Director of the Ph.D. Program, IESE Business School, University of Navarra, Barcelona, Spain

Edward Elgar

Cheltenham, Uk · Northampton, MA, USA

658.4012
S89892

Published by
Edward Elgar Publishing Limited
Glensanda House
Montpellier Parade
Cheltenham
Glos GL50 1UA
UK

Edward Elgar Publishing, Inc.
136 West Street
Suite 202
Northampton
Massachusetts 01060
USA

A catalogue record for this book
is available from the British Library

ISBN 1 84064 713 2

Printed and bound in Great Britain by MPG Books Ltd, Bodmin, Cornwall

Contents

List of figures   vii

List of tables   viii

List of contributors   x

Preface   xii
Carlos Cavallé

1 Introduction: Strategy, Organization and the Changing
  Nature of Work   1
  Jordi Gual and Joan E. Ricart

2 Employment Contracts, New Organizational Forms and
  Competitive Advantage for Continuous Innovation   5
  Joan E. Ricart and Carlos Portales

3 Strategic Human Resource Management and the New
  Employment Relationships: a Research Review and
  Agenda   47
  Carlos Sánchez-Runde

4 Employment Security, Employability and Sustainable
  Competitive Advantage   79
  Sumantra Ghoshal, Peter Moran and Christopher A. Bartlett

5 The New Deal with Employees and its Implications for
  Business Strategy   111
  Peter Cappelli

6 Business Strategy and Employment Systems in Spain:
  an Empirical Analysis   124
  Carlos Portales

7 The Adoption of Innovative Forms of Organizing in
Europe and Japan in the 1990s   169
Andrew Pettigrew and Silvia Massini

8 Impacts on Employment of New Forms of Organizing:
an Evaluation from a Knowledge Requirement Perspective   201
Rafael Andreu and Sandra Sieber

9 The New Employment Relationships: the Dilemmas of a
Post-downsized, Socially Excluded, and Low Trust Future   215
Paul R. Sparrow

Index   241

Figures

2.1	A summary of the chapter concepts and relationships	9
2.2	Employment system	12
2.3	Exchange relationships between the firm and its employees	23
2.4	From employment exchanges to employment contracts	25
2.5	Employment contracts	29
2.6	Strategy types	34
2.7	Contingent employment contracts	35
4.1	Employment security and competitive advantage	88
4.2	Employability and competitive advantage	90
6.1	Strategy typology	131
6.2	Contingent employment contracts	146
6.3	Porter's competitive strategy index	152
6.4	Speed/variety–quality/brand name	154
6.5	Innovation index	155
6.6	Classification of firms in the sample	156
7.1	New forms of organizing: the multiple indicators	173
8.1	Knowledge processes leading to knowledge integration, flexibility and competitive advantage	208
8.2	Jobs on the rise and jobs on the decline	211

Tables

3.1 Summary of individual-based models   53

3.2 System-based models: summary of formal elaborations   55

3.3 System-based models: summary of substantive elaborations   57

4.1 Alternative integrated models of firm strategy and the
     employment relationship   85

6.1 Ideal profiles of WO, HRM practices and other
     organization characteristics   138

6.2 Sample distribution by size   148

6.3 Country of origin in the sample   148

6.4 Industry distribution in the sample   149

6.5 Matrix of rotated components   150

6.6 Construct validity of Porter's competitive strategy index   152

6.7 Construct validity of innovation strategy index   155

6.8 Correlation between our own classification of firms
     and hierarchical cluster analysis   156

6.9 Center of ideal type employment systems   157

6.10 Center of final cluster representing employment systems   158

6.11 Distance between centers of ideal type employment
     systems and centers obtained from a cluster analysis
     of the sample   159

6.12 Relationship between competitive strategy and
     employment systems (number of firms in each category)   160

7.1 Incremental and radical changes in European and
    Japanese organizations, 1992–6 (%)   178

7.2 Incremental and radical changes in European and
    Japanese organizations, 1992–6 (%)   182

7.3 Types of corporate structure in European and Japanese
    organizations, 1992–6 (%)   184

7.4 Increasing emphasis in organizational structural types
    in European and Japanese companies in the period
    1992–6 (%)   185

7.5 Increasing emphasis in organizational structures
    in European and Japanese organizations: intentional
    choice or random adoption?   186

7.6 Individual organizational innovations with regional
    and business contingencies in Europe and Japan 1996   187

7.7 Similarities and differences between European and
    Japanese organizations   189

9.1 Past and emergent forms of psychological contract   223

Contributors

Professor **Rafael Andreu**
IESE Business School, University of Navarra, Barcelona, Spain

Professor **Christopher A. Bartlett**
Harvard Business School, Harvard University, Boston, US

Professor **Peter Cappelli**
The Warton School, University of Pennsylvania, Philadelphia, US

Professor **Carlos Cavallé**
Dean of IESE Business School, University of Navarra, Barcelona, Spain

Professor **Sumantra Ghoshal**
London Business School, London, UK

Professor **Jordi Gual**
IESE Business School, University of Navarra, Spain and CEPR, London, UK

Professor **Silvia Massini**
Manchester School of Management, UMIST, Manchester, UK

Professor **Peter Moran**
INSEAD, Fontainebleau, France

Professor **Andrew Pettigrew**
Warwick Business School, University of Warwick, Coventry, UK

Professor **Carlos Portales**
School of Business, Pontificia Universidad Católica de Chile, Santiago, Chile

Professor **Joan E. Ricart**
IESE Business School, University of Navarra, Barcelona, Spain

Professor **Carlos Sánchez-Runde**
IESE Business School, University of Navarra, Barcelona, Spain

Professor **Sandra Sieber**
IESE Business School, University of Navarra, Barcelona, Spain

Professor **Paul R. Sparrow**
Sheffield University Management School, University of Sheffield, Sheffield, UK

Preface

Job creation has been an area of priority research at IESE since 1992, when the school launched its annual conferences designed to give impetus to the notion that job creation should be seen by governments as a key objective of economic and social policy and by companies as a key strategic trait.

By 1990, unemployment in Europe was running at the already worrying rate of 8%, but was considered a chronic problem in only a few countries (Spain, for example). Few imagined that throughout the 1990s the average unemployment rate in Europe would increase above 11%, reaching 10% in countries as important as Germany.

In the early 1990s, government officials and business leaders tended to underestimate the rigidities inherent in European labor markets and their potentially negative impact on job creation. True, some pointed to the United States' more fluid and flexible job market as a model to be emulated, but meaningful reform of labor laws and markets was deferred.

If IESE was sufficiently concerned about the problem of unemployment to call for a new focus on job creation at a time when most countries in Europe enjoyed nearly full employment, it is because we were seized with the problem of chronic Spanish unemployment. Some 20% of the Spanish workforce was at serious social risk and IESE was concerned to call attention to the crisis.

We intended at the outset to sustain the initiative over a 10 year period to better understand the roots of the problem, to seek out the best thinking of some of the world's leading authorities in the field and to make steps, however modest, toward putting the issue at the top of the corporate, public policy and media agendas. We aimed to come up with concrete recommendations that could be applied to Spain and other countries marked by chronic unemployment.

In the intervening years, the crisis of unemployment became not merely a Spanish problem, but a European one. Unemployment became a hot political issue and governments and corporations came under scrutiny for their commitment to social responsibility. A spate of articles on how to deal with the crisis appeared in the press and there was much debate about American and other models of job creation.

By 1996, publicists and opinion leaders began to speak of a New Economy marked by unimpeded, non-inflationary growth, vigorous rates of job creation and stability in workforce pay scales. This state of affairs went hand-in-hand with the technological revolution, globalization and widespread deregulation of industry. Many wondered if this would constitute the definitive model for dealing with the problem of unemployment.

These developments placed the issue of job creation at the top of the agenda for policy makers, business leaders, journalists and others. A consensus began to emerge that labor market rigidities brought about mainly by legislation were only one aspect of the problem. The key to sustained job growth came to be seen as new professional competencies on the part of employees that would allow firms to respond flexibly to technological change and the demands of increasingly global markets. Unprecedented competition and market turbulence called for new talents, new sources of creativity and intellectual capital.

Business schools such as IESE were among the first to feel the effects of the new job market. This stands to reason as business schools are important sources of talent for major corporations and new business ventures on a global scale. Their career placement activities for MBA students have changed markedly in recent years as corporate clients increasingly seek graduates with a daunting range of talents, knowledge and personal qualities. Great store is set by global outlook, strategic thinking, general management knowledge, technological savvy, leadership talent and the ability to speak a variety of languages. Such demand for employees of wide competency is not limited to MBA graduates. It is felt with varying degrees of intensity throughout the world of hiring at all levels of corporate work.

Meeting such exacting demands for talent on such a vast scale is a tall order. In fact, there is a growing imbalance – both quantitative and qualitative – between the demand and supply of qualified talent. Many companies today are having a hard time meeting their hiring goals. The shortage of high-tech specialists in Germany and the United Kingdom is a case in point.

The problem, in many respects, has also to do with the demographic crisis in the Western world. Europe is experiencing negative population growth. The United States circumvents the problem through regulated immigration, a policy that may, for historical, political and cultural reasons, be better suited to the US than to Europe. European immigration laws tend to impede the hiring of talented people from other parts of the world.

For their part, corporations are being forced to redefine their strategies and their organizational structures to take into account what may prove to be long-term job market shortages.

The practice of hiring someone to do a set job for many years on end, even a life-time, is increasingly a thing of the past. Instead, corporations must offer people the means to develop competencies they need now, and new, unforeseen ones they may need tomorrow in a continual process of professional development. They must take steps to see to it that people can enjoy productive and creative professional lives, while supplying themselves with a workforce capable of meeting the challenges and opportunities of a rapidly evolving global economy.

I do not mean to propose any prescriptions for the problem of employment in our time. I leave that to the many fine specialists in the field who have contributed to this book. I merely mean to put the matter in historical perspective and give some notion of how the world of employment has evolved since IESE launched its job creation initiative.

I find this an excellent and though-provoking volume that I hope will shed light on a theme of vital significance for people everywhere. For it is in work that people find happiness and fulfillment and meaning.

I should like to express my gratitude to all who contributed to the writing and production of this volume.

Carlos Cavallé
Dean of IESE Business School
Anselmo Rubiralta Professor of Business Administration

1. Introduction: Strategy, Organization and the Changing Nature of Work

Jordi Gual and Joan E. Ricart

As we enter into a new century the challenges that are being confronted by the industrialized world are shifting dramatically, with unprecendented changes in multiple dimensions of business and social life. New technologies, global markets and increased competitive pressures mean that companies have to reinvent themselves, constantly reappraising their competitive strategies, rethinking the way they organize business activities and developing new forms of professional careers and new employment relationships.

These changes are profound and not just another management fad. They are starting to take place at the level of individual businesses, but have serious implications for society at large. Changes in organizational forms, work practices and employment contracts affect key social relations, since much of a person's life (from professional education to retirement) is structured around his or her job and the working relationship. The new forms of employment and work within firms (team group, outsourcing, multitask, temporary employment and others) also have an impact on other social institutions such as the family and are likely to affect broader social and political processes.

This book collects the revised papers presented at the V Conference on Job Creation that IESE organized in June 1999. These contributions provide an interdisciplinary assessment of some of the key changes that modern businesses are experiencing as they adapt to the pressures spurred by new technology and competitive markets. The papers in the book do not attempt to gauge the broad social impact of these changes, but rather they focus on the more manageable problem of tracking down how firms adapt their competitive strategy to changes in the market environment, and how these strategic realignments translate into organizational changes within the firm and in new ways to handle the relationships with employees and collaborators.

The eight articles in the book draw on several strands in the business literature and, appraised as a whole, they constitute a first step towards an integrated assessment of how firms adapt their organizations and employment relationships as a result of (or in line with) market-driven shifts in business strategy.

The contributions in the book are scheduled in a systematic fashion, gradually developing an analysis of how the new employment relationships have come into place, what they mean for employment relationships and organizations, and what are the consequences for employers and employees.

The first two papers, by Ricart and Portales, and Carlos Sánchez-Runde, provide an in-depth analysis of the relationship between strategy and human resource practices.

Ricart and Portales present a framework which explores the links between some commonly accepted dimensions of strategy analysis and alternative "stylized" employment contracts. The authors also provide some discussion of the organizational implications of these changes in business strategy and work relationships. The paper by Sánchez-Runde provides a tight link between the innovative approach of Ricart and Portales and the traditional literature in the strategic human resources management (SHRM) field.

A second set of three papers, by Ghoshal, Moran and Bartlett, Cappelli, and Portales, constitute a detailed theoretical and empirical analysis of the new employment relationships that have evolved in recent years, as firms have adapted to market and technological pressures.

Ghoshal, Moran and Bartlett develop the concept of organizational employability as a key component in the innovation strategies deployed by firms. This employability concept contrasts sharply with the market employability idea discussed by Peter Cappelli in his contribution. For Ghoshal and his coauthors, organizational employability is intimately linked to the ability of firms to sustain competitive advantage, and has profound implications in terms of the internal organization of the firm and the employment contracts. The market employability concept presented by Cappelli focuses on the outside opportunities available to employees and on the portability of skills. It appears as a concept which is specially suitable to social and economic environments such as those in the United States, where lightly regulated and tight labor markets may favor the development of this type of relationship.

The paper by Carlos Portales provides an empirical assessment of some of these ideas through a careful look at the evidence, on the basis of a representative sample of Spanish firms. His work provides evidence that firms do indeed attempt to align their human resource practices (and in particular the type of employment contracts) with their overarching business strategies. This is an innovative piece of empirical work, which provides a first building block in a research program that tries to assess the link between strategy, organizational form and human resource management practices in a variety of institutional country-specific settings.

The last three papers in the book, by Pettigrew and Massini, Andreu and Sieber, and Sparrow, present a set of complementary analyses which study the consequences of the new employment agreements that are being adopted by firms.

Pettigrew and Massini emphasize the organizational implications. They do so through a careful look at how firms in Europe and Japan have adapted their organizations to the changing requirements of international competition and technological progress. They find that Japanese and European firms are changing the way they organize their businesses, even if they do not appear to be following similar development paths. In particular, European firms appear to be more active in developing horizontal linkages. Remarkably, much less change and heteroegeneity is perceived in terms of human resource practices, which, one could argue, may be lagging organizational changes.

Andreu and Sieber consider the implications of the new employment deals in terms of the development of organizational knowledge. They argue that knowledge-based competitive advantage can only be sustained if firms are able to combine technical excellence and external employability with the development of organizational "glue" which fosters internal employability and job stability.

Finally, Sparrow provides an alternative perspective by considering what the implications of all these organizational changes are from the point of view of the perceptions, expectations and attitudes of individuals. This much neglected psychological perspective must be a prerequisite for a broad-based assessment of the management implications of new work relationships.

The contributions that have been prepared for this volume provide an initial assessment of the complex changes that technology and new organizational forms imply for the nature of employment. To understand fully the broad implications of these changes we need to develop a framework that encompasses the interaction between the strategic reactions of businesses to a changing environment, and the restrictions imposed by social institutions in terms of the organizational changes that can be adopted. Moreover, this model of strategic and organizational change, and what it implies for jobs and the job relationship, has to be contrasted with data, as some of the papers in this volume start to attempt.

A key theme of this book is that we are living a transition age, where some concepts which have played a key role in society and in business culture, such as job security, are no longer valid. The new concept of employability embodies the direction of change that we are witnessing, both at the theoretical level and in business practice. Nevertheless, employability is a complex concept. As the papers by Cappelli and Ghoshal, Moran and Bartlett show, the employability concept if understood as market employability can lead to individualistic behavior and diminish dramatically the social role of the firm, possibly contributing to other disgregating trends already present in the Western world. At the opposite end, organizational (or group) employability stresses the competitive advantage achieved by increased social interaction and paves the way to an employability concept that supports the pivotal role of firms in modern societies.

It is not the objective of this book to provide an assessment of the extent to which alternative employability concepts more closely approximate the patterns of employment relationships that are developing in advanced economies. This is a complex research program and we hope that this volume provides useful first steps along the right path of analysis.

This research program is not only intellectually fascinating, but also extremely important in a practical sense since, as we stressed above, the social and political implications of the new employment relationships that are beng developed are rather large.

Part of the academic research should be directed at strengthening an integrative view of these problems, bringing together the perspectives of human resource specialists, strategy experts and scholars in the area of organizational change. This conceptual work must be actively complemented by a comparative study of experiences across the world, focusing in particular on the comparison between the US, Europe and Japan.

This book, through a combination of theoretical and empirical research papers from several business disciplines, attempts precisely to open the way for this kind of research work. We will feel gratified if it promotes further interest and research in this area.

2. Employment Contracts, New Organizational Forms and Competitive Advantage for Continuous Innovation

Joan E. Ricart and Carlos Portales

2.1 INTRODUCTION

In recent years managers across industries have emphasized in firm's results the increasing impact of the workforce and the way it is managed. In an impressive number of conferences, articles and interviews top managers stress the critical role that people play in their organizations. Managers are increasingly aware that since other sources of organizational success have become less important, what remains as a crucial and differentiating factor is the people, their knowledge, capabilities and effort to deliver results. Along the same lines, several scholars have begun to argue that employees can usually fulfill the required conditions to be considered a unique source of competitive advantage (Wright and McMahan, 1992; Pfeffer, 1994, 1998). Employees can add value to the firm's production processes and services, in many cases they are difficult to find and replace, and competitors may have difficulties in replicating or substituting their contributions (Barney, 1991). In addition, a substantial and rapidly expanding body of evidence shows that the way in which firms manage their people can have strong overall performance effects (Arthur, 1994; Huselid, 1995; MacDuffie, 1995; Dunlop and Weil, 1996; Osterman, 1997).

Through a wide variety of human resource management (HRM) policies, work organization (WO) practices, and other organizational arrangements, firms implement and support their business strategies. The strategic perspective through which these policies, practices and other organizational features are being both studied and utilized in practice has developed a fairly new field called strategic human resource management – SHRM – (Schuler and Jackson, 1987b; Wright and McMahan, 1992). The purpose of this perspective is to analyze the role that several of these practices and organizational aspects play in the successful implementation of different competitive strategies. In addition, this study discusses the impact on performance that an adequate "fit" (Govindarajan, 1988) between HRM policies, WO practices and other organizational arrangements and specific business strategies they intend to support.

Within the field of SHRM two main debates exist. These discussions are presented here and further developed in section 2.2. A first important issue to take into account is whether it is more appropriate to study individual practices and their impact upon performance (Kerr and Slocum, 1987; Sonnenfeld and Piperl, 1988; Cutcher-Gershenfeld, 1991) or, instead, HRM policies, WO practices and other organizational characteristics should be analyzed as a system of mutually reinforcing activities (Wright and Snell, 1991) – which in this study we label employment system (ES) – that collectively affect firms' results. We follow this second path and, in contrast to the great number of studies that investigate the relationship between individual practices and organizational performance, HRM policies, WO practices and other organizational traits are studied as a system of mutually supporting practices that collectively affect firms results.

Within this systemic view, however, a second and probably more fundamental debate arises. Two main different modes of theorizing, the best practices or high performance work practices – HPWP – (Pfeffer, 1994, 1998) and the contingent perspectives (Schuler and Jackson, 1987a) have been employed to explain how ESs affect company performance. The HPWP approach states that there are certain "universal practices" that, irrespective of the company's strategy or characteristics, are more effective in achieving competitive success through the way they manage people (Osterman, 1994; Pfeffer, 1994, 1996; Huselid, 1995; Huselid and Becker, 1996; Ichniowski *et al.,* 1997).

The other theoretical view, labeled the "matching model" (Boxall, 1992), the "behavioral perspective" (Wright and McMahan, 1992; Lado and Wilson, 1994) or the "contingent perspective" (Miles and Snow, 1984; Dyer and Reeves, 1995), argues that most organizational practices and activities should be matched to the organization's specific business strategy in order to be effective (Schuler and Jackson, 1987a; Baird and Meshoulam, 1988; Milgrom and Roberts, 1995). In this study we follow this second path, the contingent view toward SHRM. We argue that certain bundles of HRM policies, WO practices and other organizational traits are more appropriate – lead to better performance – in implementing some business strategy than others.

Several authors have proposed theoretically derived ESs (Miles and Snow, 1984; Kerr and Slocum, 1987; Osterman, 1987; Sonnenfeld and Peiperl, 1988, Arthur, 1992; Delery and Doty, 1996). These ESs are usually defined in terms of a number of policies, practices, and other organizational characteristics. In section 2.3, building on the work of some of these researchers, we choose a few of these policies, practices and other characteristics to offer a more comprehensive typology of ESs than the currently existing ones. Five different ESs, each one composed of a number of these policies, practices and other characteristics, are described.

Employment systems, however, are only one element shaping employees' behavior and performance. Among other factors, this study emphasizes the role of individual needs in shaping individuals' performance. Individuals assess the degree to which their needs are being satisfied by the company through their set of HRM policies, WO practices and organizational characteristics. In section 2.4, drawing from exchange theory (Homans, 1961; Blau, 1964), we argue that firms influence employees' behavior through the policies, practices, and other organizational arrangements contained in the ESs they have in place. At the same time, ESs are a main source of satisfaction of employees' different types of needs. Firm and employees, then, establish a series of exchange relationships (Organ, 1990; Cardona *et al.,* 1999). The nature and type of exchange relationships that take place between employer an employees are described in section 2.4.

The rich array of possible exchanges create, in turn, a variety of potential employment contracts between the firm and its employees (Rousseau and Wade-Benzoni, 1995). These contracts define what the company obtains from the employees and what they give in return. The firm and its employees exchange services (e.g., certain level of output, hard work, loyalty) for some form of compensation (e.g., pay, personal development, sense of identity). This work explains what particular HRM policies, WO practices and organizational arrangements would be required for a successful creation and implementation of different types of exchange relationships and employment contracts. The policies and practices are grouped, in turn, in different employment systems. Three different type of exchanges are defined: economic, work, and social exchange relationships that shape the employment contracts. In these exchanges, employees expect that their economic, intrinsic and social needs are going to be satisfied through the firm's policies, practices, and organizational arrangements that make up particular industrial relation system. Conversely, the organization expects in exchange that these policies will influence employees' behavior, which in turn will lead to high performance.

Through a specific ES a firm tries to provide its employees the technical skills, knowledge, abilities, and the desired behaviors required to successfully implement their particular competitive strategy. In exchange, employees' needs can be satisfied through these HRM policies, WO practices and some other organizational characteristics. People in an organization will tend to show high levels of performance if organizational policies and practices also permit them to meet some of their own most important needs through membership and work in the organization. (Schein, 1988). The different exchange relationships that exist and the many possible theoretical combinations of them may lead to several distinctive employment contracts. Considering these multiple possibilities and also drawing from previous work on employment contracts (Rousseau, 1995; Ghoshal *et al.,* 1996; Pfeffer, 1998), in section 2.5 we propose a typology for employment contracts. These contracts are defined in terms of both the ESs and the compounding exchange relationships supporting the contracts.

Later on, following a contingency approach, it is argued that certain employment contracts are more suitable for companies competing through different strategies. In section 2.6, we present a typology of business strategies. This typology is based on two different dimension. The first one is associated with the type of efficiency – static or dynamic – firms try to pursue. The second one is associated with Porter's strategic typology, emphasizing a product/market dimension. We distinguish among strategies of both static efficiency and either low costs or differentiation. In contrast, a different type of employment contract would be required to support firms facing the consequences of a deconstructing business landscape where competition is based on differentiation but where, at the same time, dynamic efficiency and innovation efforts firms make to generate new competitive capabilities (Ghemawat and Ricart, 1993; Tushman and O'Reilly, 1997).

Finally, some conclusion are drawn from our discussion. In particular we address the sustainability of different combinations of strategies and employment contracts. We also discuss the impact of the political, social and institutional contexts on the different types of employment contracts. In Figure 2.1 we present a summary of these arguments that will be further developed along this study. The chapter in this text by Carlos Portales, "Business Strategy and Employment Systems in Spain: An Empirical Analysis," is an empirical test of the existance and contingency of the employment contracts developed in this chapter.

2.2 DEBATES IN THE FIELD OF SHRM[1]

Firms usually support the implementation of their business strategies through a particular ES, which in turn comprises a wide variety of HRM policies, WO practices, and other organizational arrangements. It is not coincidence, then, that a first debate within the field of SHRM has to do with the issue of whether is it more appropriate to study individual practices and their impact upon performance or, instead, that HRM policies, WO practices, and other organizational arrangements should be analyzed as a system of mutually reinforcing practices – ES, as we have labeled them – that collectively affect firms' results. Within the systemic view of HRM, however, a second debate arises. Two contradictory modes of theorizing, the high performance work practices (HPWP) and the

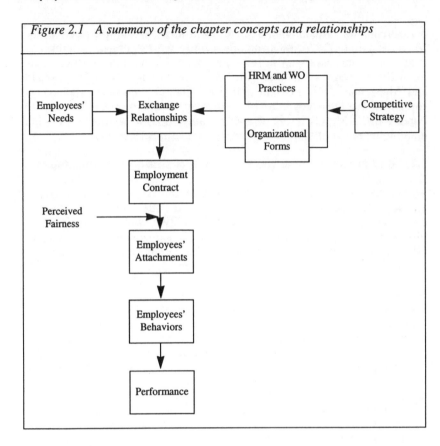

Figure 2.1   A summary of the chapter concepts and relationships

contingency perspectives, have been employed to explain how ESs affect company performance.

2.2.1 One practice or many?

In this study, HRM policies, WO practices and other organizational traits are studied as a system of mutually reinforcing practices that collectively affect firms' results rather than on a piecemeal basis. There are many reasons for adopting a systemic view. First, measurement of the impact of one single practice may dramatically overestimate its contribution to firm performance (Milgrom and Roberts, 1995; Wittington *et al.*, 1998). As both recent research (Arthur, 1992; MacDuffie, 1995; Osterman, 1987, 1994) and conventional wisdom predict, high performance firms that adopt, for example, one particular practice are more likely to implement others that are mutually consistent with the first one so that their joint effect on performance is considerable. Second, from a managerial perspective, the fragmentation of HRM, WO, and organizational arrangement systems may lead to an unnecessary waste of resources since different practices may mutually neutralize each other, rather than reinforcing one another (Wright and McMahan, 1992; Wright and Snell, 1991). Following this recent "systemic", in our study we will focus then on the impact of systems or bundles of HRM policies, WO practices and organizational features rather than on the effect of individual practices, on firm performance.

2.2.2 Best practices versus contingent view of strategy implementation

Within the systemic view of SHRM two theoretical lines of research try to explain what particular type of ES may be better suited to influence employee behavior and performance. The HPWP view is very much in line with the work of Peters and Waterman's *In Search of Excellence* (1982), which argued that the most successful companies were guided by a few common management principles. Later, within the field of HRM, Walton (1985) and Guest (1987, 1990) were the first to introduce the idea of managing by best practices. In particular, they emphasized the need for a skill and relational model of labor management in the workplace.

Recently, the works of Pfeffer (1994, 1996) have supported this vision, arguing that a set of HRM policies, WO practices and other organizational characteristics – incentive pay, above-market compensation, employee ownership, wage compression, job security, symbolic egalitarianism, high levels of training and development, cross training, promotion from within the company, selectivity in recruiting, cross functional teams, and information sharing policies (Pfeffer, 1994) – are the most appropriate to support any company strategy. These policies, practices and organizational characteristics will develop flexible and committed employees who will be prepared to work efficiently in any competitive scenario. At the same time, these practices do not have to be contingent on an organization's particular competitive strategy, including a low-cost one (Pfeffer, 1994: 27), since a well-paid, highly motivated worker will not only do a better job but also with a higher productivity rate (Pfeffer, 1994: 35).

Furthermore, the "best practices" perspective has received some empirical support. Ichniowski *et al.,* (1997), Arthur (1994), Huselid (1995), MacDuffie (1995), and Dunlop and Weil (1996) have found a positive correlation between the level and intensity of HPWP adoption and firm performance. Some of these studies were carried on in very particular business settings while others display important measurement weaknesses.

In contrast, the contingent view argues that if ESs influence employee's behavior and that if specific employees' behaviors are required to implement different strategies in order to achieve superior performance, then ESs should systematically vary with organizational strategy (Walker, 1980;

Miles and Snow, 1984; Schuler and Jackson, 1987b; Purcell, 1989; Peck, 1994). The notion that firm performance will be enhanced by alignment of the ES with a firm's competitive strategy has gained considerable currency in last few years and in fact underlies a big portion of the recent scholarship in the field (Begin, 1993; Butler *et al.,* 1991; Cappelli and Singh, 1992; Jackson and Schuler, 1995; Schuler, 1992; Wright and McMahan, 1992).

Moreover, a developing empirical literature suggests that firms do indeed attempt to match ESs with competitive strategies (Schuler and Jackson, 1987a; Martell, 1989; Arthur, 1992; Sivasubramaniam, 1993). For example, Jackson *et al.,* (1989) found that firms pursuing a strategy of innovation implemented HRM specific practices that were broadly consistent with that approach and different from the ones firms competing in other ways were using. Similarly, Arthur (1992) found that steel minimills adopting a strategy of differentiation emphasized employee relational ESs, while cost leadership strategies were supported by transactional-oriented ESs. Finally, Martell (1989) and Snell and Dean (1992, 1994) found that human resource management practices varied systematically with type of manufacturing system, individual job characteristics, and firm environment.

In this study we follow a contingent approach toward SHRM. In line with many researchers we argue that high levels of performance need a match between the personal characteristics, skills, behaviors, and work conditions of employees with the nature of the business they are in. Similarly, we recognize, as many managers do, that for different business strategies – cost leadership, differentiation by quality, and differentiation through innovation among others – they need quite different people to run them (Fombrun, 1982). Different types of business, we suggest, also require different skills in terms of their quantity, quality, and breadth. At the same time, specific competitive strategies require particular employee behaviors to vary in dimensions such as creativity, cooperation, risk taking, task focus, responsibility and flexibility to change, among others.

Finally, as several authors have suggested (DePree, 1986; Schuler, 1987), we argue that different work organization practices and other organizational arrangements allow employees to develop their activities in ways particularly well suited to their strategic requirements.

2.3 EMPLOYMENT SYSTEMS

The many HRM policies, WO practices, and other organizational features that have a role in the strategy implementation process can cluster together into different types of employment systems. These ESs in turn, will shape particular type of employment contracts, as we will see later in section 2.5. In this section, we propose a typology of five of these ES systems. Based on the work of many SHRM authors (Miles and Snow, 1984; Arthur, 1992; Delery and Doty, 1996) and other researchers in organizational theory (Ghoshal and Bartlett, 1996; Pfeffer, 1998; Whittington *et al.,* 1998) we selected several of these policies, practices and features (Figure 2.2) to derive our ES typology. The practices and policies selected are the ones considered in the literature as the most influential over employees' effort and performance.

Figure 2.2 Employment system		
HRM policies	WO practices	Organizational characteristics
• Selection • Appraisal • Compensation • Promotion • Training	• Skill variety • Task identity • Task significance • Decision making on the job • Job design • Job rotation	• Allocation of decision rights - decentralization - delayering - horizontal linkages • Information flows • Social bonds

A very large number of these ESs can be theoretically plausible by combining values for each variable. However, we constrain our analysis only to those theoretically derived systems that make "business sense," that is, those described in current research work and at the same time being adopted in practice.

From this set of policies, practices and organizational characteristics, we can describe five different and internally coherent ESs. Previous work has described only a few of them. Our work makes a first contribution here: by simultaneously describing under a common framework five different ESs, five major types can be distinguished in the contemporary literature.

Two ESs have been described extensively in the literature. Through the first one, the transactional system, firms buy their needed skills on the open market. Staffing is based, therefore, on arm's length contracting. Career paths are limited and narrow. Appraisals are designed to measure performance. Compensation is performance based, reflecting output more than position or organizational tenure. At the same time, pay is strongly determined by market considerations. Their cost cutting orientation forces these companies to continuously compare their payroll expenses with their competitors'. Similarly, the organization terminates employees' contracts (including managers') as labor demand fluctuates over time. For this reason turnover is not excessively avoided. At the same time, limited training is provided (Walton, 1985; Dyer and Holder, 1988). Firms implementing transactional systems offer very specifically and narrowly defined jobs, few chances for mobility, low levels of empowerment and decision making on the job over things such as job design and the sequence in which tasks are developed. At the organizational level, this system is characterized by low levels of decentralization, many echelons in the chain of command and few horizontal linkages and information flows given the strong emphasis on functional specialization. Similarly, social ties between the organization and its employees are usually weak. These types of ES closely resemble the buy (Miles and Snow, 1984), performance-based (Kerr and Slocum, 1987), control (Arthur, 1994), and the market (Delery and Doty, 1996) type systems.

A second form of ES has been labeled the relational system. Selecting and recruiting are done primarily at the entry level. Careers are developed on the basis of organizational requirements over time rather than being a function of the occupation a particular person holds at a particular moment in time. Appraisal systems have also an internal rather than external focus; behavior and process are given more weight than results. Compensation policies are expected to emphasize internal consistency rather than market characteristics. Firms implementing this kind of systems also provide employees with long organizational tenure, trying to retain them for a long time. For this same reason these firms are also reluctant to terminate employment. Consistently with this long-term orientation toward employees, companies following a relational orientation invest heavily in employees through extensive training and development in firm-specific skills, expecting employee development and long-term returns in exchange (Walton, 1985; Dyer and Holder, 1988). Skill variety, empowerment, and power over decision making on the job are greater compared to transactional systems. At the organizational level, higher levels of decentralization and horizontal linkages and information flows are found in relational systems. The number of layers within the organization is high and similar to transactional contracts. Social bonds are extremely important in this system since in order to obtain internal consistency from its employees firms need to develop a strong sense of identification with organizational values.

Balanced systems represent a third kind of ES. They blend elements of the two previous ones. Under this kind of ES firms tend to hire both from inside and outside the company. Thus, there is some room for career paths within the organization. Appraisals are design to measure both performance and behavior. Compensation policies mix shorter-term output based incentives with an emphasis also on payments based on employees' behavior and commitment to corporate values. At the same time, market pressures and comparisons with salaries in other companies are not so important as they are in the case of transactional systems. Similarly, the organization tries to maintain some continuity among a certain number of its employees. Therefore, employees' contracts are not massively terminated as labor demand fluctuates over time. For this reason turnover is, up to some degree, avoided. At the same time some training is provided usually combining both general as well as firm-specific skills (Walton, 1985; Dyer and Holder, 1988). Firms implementing balanced systems offer quite challenging jobs, characterized by a considerable level of job rotation, autonomy, and teamwork. Allocation of decision rights is shifted more towards the bottom levels of the organization and personal and informational horizontal linkages are emphasized. Social bonds between the firm and its employees are not stressed a great deal since although the company relies on its internal labor market it also uses the external market quite heavily to hire new employees.

During the last decade, however, many firms have realized that transactional, relational, and balanced systems are no longer the only appropriate alternatives to support their competitive strategies. Organizations particularly affected by the waves of increased globalization, intensification of competition, and revolutionary technological changes have been looking for new forms of organizing and the corresponding new ways of managing their human resources. Pettigrew and Massini (Chapter 7 in this book) present an emprirical overview of the adoption of new ways of organizing in Europe and Japan in the 1990s, new forms that have wide implications for employment. As a result, two new forms of ES have appeared. They have in common their emphasis on the employability of their workforce. They differ, however, on several other features.

Under what in this study is labeled a "market employability" system organizations offer, for concrete and short periods of time, market-based pay, challenging jobs and interesting assignments. Knowledge and skills acquired on the job, in turn, will help people build and upgrade their general skills that will be useful elsewhere. In contrast, this system offers neither promises for long-term careers nor training, given the short tenure employees have in the organization and the impossibility of recouping investments made in employees' training and development. Instead the only promise is that the work and the general skills acquired on the job will help to make the people more employable if and when they have to leave. As a result, social employer–employee ties are weak since the organization doesn't look out for the employees' interests any more. The employees need to look after them by themselves, taking individual responsibility for their career development (Pfeffer, 1998).

A second form of employability can be distinguished among the "new" ESs currently adopted by firms. What in this study is called the "organizational employability" system corresponds to a contractual form that offers, like the market employability system, extremely interesting jobs characterized by high levels of variety, empowerment, and decision making power on the job and at all levels in the organization. These great amounts of responsibility over company activities and results given to employees is also facilitated by high levels of decentralization and few layers between lower levels and upper echelons in the organization. At the same time, since companies implementing this system hire people with general skills they need to compensate them with market level salaries. In contrast to the market employability system, however, firms provide the best training in general skills and development resources, and an environment committed to providing opportunities for personal and professional growth (Tichy and Sherman, 1995). Therefore, instead of going to the outside market for the required combination of general skills they need, these firms develop their own internal market of general skills and keep them inside the organization. The general skills that make people employable outside the company also make them more adaptable and valuable for different tasks and needs within it, thereby making it easier for the company to use their expertise more flexibly and in higher value jobs. At the same time, the compromise for continuous on-the-job training and general education is an incentive for people to stay in the organization. Employees could possibly sell their general skills in the market to another company, but in the long run, they may run the risk of "falling victim to the next round of skill obsolescence in a company that does not have the same commitment to adding value to people" (Ghoshal and Bartlett, 1997). The combination of skills is essential in these organizations. This is why horizontal linkages, information flows and social bonds are strongly emphasized by organizational employability systems.

Although the employment system adopted by firms can have a strong impact on employees' behavior, other factors may also intervene and shape their efforts and performance. HRM policies, WO practices, and organizational characteristics are, in fact, only one part of a more complex relationship in which both the firm and its employees are involved. Other factors may influence employees' behaviors at work as well. Some authors, for example, have stressed the role of dispositional factors – personality, temperament – and professional background on individual behavior (Organ, 1990).

In this study, we are particularly interested in the role played by employees' motives in their behavior at work. Increasingly, organizational researchers are recognizing that employee behavior and, consequently, performance, is not just an organizational issue. Individual needs are also an equally important part determining their behaviors and performance (Mathieu and Zajac, 1990). Organizational experiences play an important role as determinants of employees' behaviors because they evaluate the degree to which their needs are being satisfied by the company through their set of HRM policies, WO practices and organizational characteristics. Some research suggest that employees will show high levels of performance only if organizational policies and practices also permit them to meet some of their own most important needs through membership and work in the organization (Schein, 1988). Moreover, some empirical work supports the idea that employees' motives may have an impact on individuals' effort and performance at work (Van Dyne *et al.,* 1995; Cardona *et al.,* 1999).

The motives and needs of employees should be related to the incentives and rewards offered by the organization through their ESs. Thus, in order to be successful in its attempt to support a particular business strategy through the implementation of a series of policies and practices, those policies and practices should, at the same time, satisfy employees' needs and motives. In order to understand employees' behavior and performance, we need to look at these exchange relationships (Homans, 1961; Blau, 1964) that are taking place between employees and the organization.

2.4 EXCHANGES IN THE WORKPLACE

Employee behavior may well be the result of a series of exchange relationships between them and their employer. Through the implementation of a particular ES the organization obtains hard work, high performance and employees' loyalty, all things that help to support its business strategy. The firm's ESs are aimed at responding to those employees' needs and shaping their behavior in order to implement and support its competitive strategy. Through the implementation of ESs, firms expect employees to be highly motivated, willing to make sacrifices for the organization, try to enhance the corporate image, be loyal, and keep organizational secrets (Schein, 1988: 23).

In exchange relationships, employees expect their basic needs and motives to be satisfied by the policies, practices, and other organizational characteristics incorporated in the ES. Employees are paid a salary, and they may also receive benefits, certain privileges that go with a job, and guarantees that they will not be fired unexpectedly. Employees can also be offered challenging work and to receive feedback on how they are doing. Opportunities for self-actualization and further learning may also exist in the company. Employees, at the same time, expect organizations to provide an appropriate social context and common goals. An organization, then, can provide or increase employees' sense of membership, identity, dignity and worth. Moreover, particular individual needs or motives will cause employees to engage in different exchange relationships with the firm.

Employees may exchange with their organization when the relationships appeal to their motives. Employees' perception of fairness, that is, that their needs are reasonable well satisfied by the organization's policies, practices, and other characteristics, will increase their attachment to the organization and, therefore, greater levels of performance should be expected from them. When individuals perceive their experiences in the workplace as motivating, their attachment to the organization is strengthened, and they are more likely to reciprocate with more effort and with behaviors that maintain their exchange relationship with the organization (Mowday *et al.*, 1982).

Much confusion exists, however, about the nature of the different exchanges that take place at work. Several authors have studied the different type of exchange relationships that take place between a firm and its employees (Rousseau, 1995; Cardona *et al.*, 1999). Drawing from previous work (Pérez-López, 1993), three type of motives are identified: extrinsic, intrinsic, and social. Each of these motives may lead, respectively, to three particular types of exchange: economic, work, and social exchanges. Therefore, different types of exchange relationships appeal to different motives, and these different motivating perceptions, in turn, may strengthen different kinds of individual attachment to the organization (Cardona *et al.*, 1999).

In this chapter three types of exchange are described. In section 2.5., in turn we will explain how different combinations of these exchanges can make up several employment contracts.

2.4.1 Economic exchange

In an economic exchange some form of economic compensation is exchanged for time at work (Schein, 1988: 99). This form of exchange is essentially a calculative involvement (Etzioni, 1961). The organization is buying the services and obedience of the employee for economic rewards (Schein, 1988: 54). Employees engage in economic exchanges when this transaction appeals to their need for extrinsic rewards, that is, those rewards that the employee expects to receive as a result of his or her work (Pérez-López, 1993). Economic exchanges assume, then, that employees are extrinsically motivated.

Two types of extrinsic needs have been found across many studies (Lawler, 1994): (1) existence, and (2) security needs. According to Maslow (1954), individuals have needs for such things as oxygen, hunger, thirst, and so on. Later on, Alderfer (1972) gave them their most commonly used denomination: existence needs.

In other studies these needs were more specifically job related and were identified as the basic working conditions employees encounter in the workplace (Herzberg, 1966).

Security needs are, in general, related to the needs for safety (Maslow, 1954), stability, and the absence of pain, threat or illness. In an organizational context they are usually associated, according to Schein (1975, 1978), with the guarantee of continued employment, a stable future, and the ability to provide comfortably for oneself and one's family through achieving a measure of financial independence. Herzberg (1966) also linked security with individuals' need for an appropriate salary and benefits.

Companies can satisfy extrinsic motives in many ways, particularly through the implementation of certain HRM practices. Compensation is, according to several authors, one of the most important in this respect. Pay appears to have the ability to satisfy not only the existence needs but also security and some social needs. For example, Lawler and Porter (1963) report that the more a manager is paid, the higher is his security – and the satisfaction of some of his or her social needs. This statement means that when a person is trying to satisfy either security or social needs, pay will be important. It is not difficult to see why pay has the ability to satisfy a number of needs. Pay can be used to buy articles, such as food, that satisfy existence needs, and high pay also earns a certain amount of social recognition needs (Lawler, 1994: 44).

Promotion is another reward that most organizations have to offer to satisfy employees' extrinsic motives. Promotions generally bring with them increased responsibility, greater task complexity, and higher pay; they are therefore compounded in their impact. They represent a fusion of the rewards the organization can offer and the opportunity for advancement can be highly motivating. Promotion, of course, has to be linked to performance in the eyes of organization members if it is to have a motivating effect. Georgopoulos *et al.,* (1957), in their study of over 600 workers in an appliance factory, found a significant relationship between productivity and the belief that poor performance would hurt one's chances for promotion.

2.4.4 Work exchange

In a work exchange the opportunity for professional achievement and learning is exchanged for high productivity, high quality work, and creative effort in the service of organizational goals (Hackman and Lawler, 1971; Hackman and Oldham, 1975, 1979; McEvoy and Cascio, 1985). Employees engage in work exchange relationships when this transaction appeals to their need for intrinsic rewards, that is, the personal satisfaction resulting from the interaction between the employee and the job itself (Cardona *et al.,* 1999). Work exchange assumes, then, that employees are intrinsically motivated by their need to grow and sees work as growth producing. At the same time, desirable outcomes both for the person, in terms of needs satisfaction, and for the organization, in terms of high productivity, high quality work, and creative effort, will result only if the company implements the appropriate WO practices in order to offer enriched jobs.

Employees' general intrinsic needs for professional achievement and learning can be translated into three specific job related ones:

1. meaningful work;
2. sense of responsibility;
3. need for competence.

First, the employee needs to experience the job as meaningful, worthwhile, or important (Schein, 1988). This motive has also been characterized as the need for achievement (McClelland, 1961; McClelland and Burnham, 1976), growth needs (Alderfer, 1972), or self-esteem needs (Maslow, 1954). Firms can offer meaningful work to employees through a variety of WO practices. Through skill variety, jobs require employees to perform activities that challenge a variety of their skills and abilities. Skill variety and complexity is strongly associated what the need for self-actualization (Maslow, 1954), that is making maximum use of all one's talents and resources. In particular, job rotation, both within an employee's area and across units, can help provide skill variety. Meaningful work can also be obtained by providing task identity, that is, jobs that need completion of a whole and identifiable piece of work – doing a job from beginning to end with a visible outcome.

Through teamwork, for example, employees can achieve the required task significance since they are usually implemented to allow a group of employees to develop a whole product or component. Finally, task significance, meaning jobs that have a substantial and perceivable impact on the lives of other people either within the immediate organization or in the world at large, are another way to give meaning to employees' work (Schein, 1988: 89).

Second, employees need to have a sense of personal responsibility in their job (Schein, 1988). In other studies this motive is associated with strong needs for independence, power (McClelland, 1961, 1976), or supervision over the employee's own work (Herzberg, 1966). A company, in turn, can make employees responsible for their work through WO practices that emphasize job designs characterized by high levels of autonomy, independence, and participation in decision making (Schein, 1988: 89).

Firms can also satisfy employees' need for responsibility through high levels of autonomy at work with particular organizational forms. In particular, the so-called new organizational forms (NOFs) can provide employee freedom, independence, and discretion in scheduling work and determining how the work will be carried out. Decentralization – both operational and strategic – delayering fewer hierarchical levels, and the existence of horizontal linkages are three of the most important distinctive aspects of NOFs which in turn can help provide high levels of autonomy for employees.

Finally, employees have a need for competence, which in turn means they want to have the necessary skills and abilities to do their job. Many large organizations abound with HRM practices, especially training and development programs designed to help people develop their skills and abilities. Sometimes people do enter these programs in the hope of obtaining a raise or promotion, but on other occasions they do it only because it contributes to their self-development.

2.4.3 Social exchange

In social exchange relationships social need satisfaction is exchanged in return for employees' loyalty and hard work (Schein, 1988). It is possible to classify social needs[2] in two broad groups: extrinsic social needs and altruistic needs. The first group is characterized by the need for belongingness and self-esteem (Maslow, 1954). Need for belongingness includes the need for affection, love, relatedness (Alderfer, 1972), or affiliation (McClelland, 1961, 1976). Whyte (1948) has shown that being a member of a closely knit social group seems to motivate people to work well. People who belong to such groups presumably associate more rewards with going to work (for example, the satisfaction of social needs) than do people who are not group members. They enjoy the companionship they obtain at work, and they look forward to finding out what the people at work have been doing. To miss work means to miss out on one day's events in the life of the group. Often, the social part of work can become more important than the performance aspects, so that people come not so much to work as to see their friends (Lawler, 1994).

This first group of social needs also includes a second type called social esteem (Maslow, 1954) or recognition or respect (Herzberg, 1966) from others. Social esteem needs are associated with the employee's acknowledgment of the results of his work. Thus, from the employee's point of view, feedback would be desirable. Feedback will be provided by the company through appraisal practices if the worker gets information about the effectiveness of his or her efforts, either directly from the work itself (such as when a quality test is run by the worker on the work) or from supervisors, co-workers, quality-control inspectors, or others in the work-flow (Schein, 1988: 89).

Both the need for belongingness and social esteem are extrinsic needs, in the sense that their source of satisfaction comes from the employee's environment. They are different, though, from economic needs, given the specific type of motives they satisfy and the different type of extrinsic reward that satisfies them. In the case of social needs, extrinsic rewards satisfying those needs come from the social context surrounding the employee. In contrast, in the case of economic motives, satisfaction comes from monetary or monetary related rewards.

Organizations can help satisfy employees' need for belongingness by developing cohesive social groups. Many WO practices influence whether groups will form. For example, the physical design of the work area is controlled by management and has a strong influence on group formation. The simple act of dividing a large room into small rooms with six people in each encourages group development. Similarly, if work is laid out so people can talk, it encourages group development. One organization found that it could reduce turnover in some production jobs by placing the machinery in a way that allowed the employees to walk together and talk, whereas previously they were always walking in different directions (Lawler, 1994). Organizations also influence group formation by their job rotation practices. If the organization rotates people frequently, it is easier for them to shape both formal and informal networks within the organization. Organizational forms that promote horizontal linkages among employees may be a third way by which the organization can influence the formation of social groups. By promoting employee access to several other people within and across different areas, through communication systems for example, firms can avoid isolating employees from each other and help create social ties among them.

A second group of social needs can be associated to individuals' altruistic motives which in turn are represented by the benefits the employee expects the group or organization to receive from his or her work and cooperation. Employees may have a need to cooperate and be useful to their peers and to the organization in general, without purposively having in mind the self-benefit. Contrary to the first type of social needs, in this case the satisfaction of the need is not extrinsic, but, in contrast, intrinsic to the individual. Satisfaction of altruistic motives goes from the individual to the group and not the other way around. Altruistically motivated behaviors are also different in nature from intrinsically motivated behaviors. The distinction between intrinsically and altruistically motivated behaviors is usually ignored in the literature. It is true that both are self-rewarding, but it is also true that they are self-rewarding for very different reasons. Intrinsically motivated behavior is self-rewarding because the behavior is interesting or enjoyable for the individual, whereas altruistically motivated behaviors are self-rewarding because the individual perceives the behavior as making an important contribution to others (Schwartz, 1977; Batson, 1991).

When individuals perceive transactions as altruistically motivating compared to alternative options, they are likely to develop an attachment to the organization. People who are attached to the organization by an altruistically motivating exchange are likely to reciprocate with behaviors that maintain their social exchange relationship with the organization, such as helping co-workers who are new in the department or volunteering for things that are not formally or even informally required. If employees can expect gratification of some important emotional needs through participation in the organization, they become morally involved in the organization. Such involvement in turn permits the organization to legitimately expect loyalty, commitment, and greater identification with the organizational goals (Schein, 1988: 64).

In exchange for altruistically oriented behaviors, employees expect the firm to provide an environment in which they can obtain satisfaction of these motives. Since altruistically motivated employees expect the group or organization to benefit from their work and cooperation, the organization in turn should provide an adequate organizational setting for their employees. The company needs to give content and meaning to that organizational setting for those altruistically motivated behaviors to make sense and to motivate the employees. For this reason, organizations need to go beyond the creation of groups through linking mechanisms. They need to provide something else: a shared purpose. In Barnard's (1938) terms, "willingness to cooperate, except as a vague feeling or desire for association with others, cannot develop without an objective of cooperation. Such an objective we denominate the 'purpose of an organization'" (p. 86).

A purpose, however, does not incite cooperative activity "unless it is accepted by those whose efforts will constitute the organization" (*ibid.*) We may say, then, that a purpose can serve as an element of a cooperative system as long as the participants do not recognize that there are serious divergences between their own purposes and the organizational purpose, which is the object of cooperation. Hence, an objective purpose that can serve as the basis for a cooperative system is one that is believed by the contributors (or potential contributors) to it to be the determined purpose of the organization. There is, then, something like simultaneity in the acceptance of a purpose and willingness to cooperate.

Organizations, consequently, should provide not only a purpose, but one in accordance to their individuals' goals and values. People with altruistic motives are particularly sensitive about the content of organizational purpose and the fundamental values that explicitly or implicitly arise from that purpose. Employees care about how the firm relates to its environment and also how the organization treats its own people. A common set of values can help shape a coherent and attractive institutional context. By creating an alignment between the convictions of its members and the overall purpose of the firm, social bonds achieve continuity in the employment relationship through mutual attractiveness (Ghoshal and Moran, 1996).

This alignment, however, does not arise spontaneously. Besides policies, practices and other organizational arrangements, leadership is required to align organizational and individual goals and values.

The limitations imposed by both the context and individuals – the uncertainties of the outcome of cooperation, the difficulties of common understanding of purpose, the delicacy of the systems of communication essential to organization, the dispersive tendencies of employees, the necessity of individual assent to establish the authority for coordination, the great role of persuasion in securing adherence to the organization and submission to its requirements, the complexity and instability of motives, the never-ending burden of decision – where the moral factor finds its concrete expression, spells the necessity of leadership, the power of individuals to inspire cooperative personal decision by creating faith: faith in common understanding, faith in the probability of success, faith in the ultimate satisfaction of personal motives, faith in the integrity of objective authority, faith in the superiority of common purpose as a personal aim of those who participate in it (Barnard, 1938: 259).

So far, we have explored three types of exchange relationships between the firm and its employees: economic, work, and social exchanges. A summary of the different exchange relationships and their constitutive elements is presented in Figure 2.3.

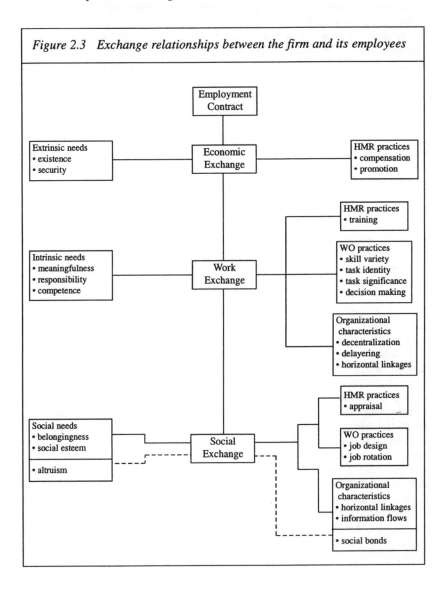

Figure 2.3   Exchange relationships between the firm and its employees

2.5 EXCHANGE RELATIONSHIPS AND EMPLOYMENT CONTRACTS

The set of mutual exchanges operating at all times gives form to an employment contract between employees and the organization. An employment contract is an exchange agreement between employee and employer. The contract may include written terms (e.g., union agreement, job offer letter), orally communicated terms (e.g., promises of training, support, and best efforts), as well as other expressions of commitment and future intent (e.g., tradition, custom, and culture) (Rousseau, 1995: 1–2).

The nature of what is being exchanged within employment contracts can vary significantly among different types of contracts. Some employment contracts emphasize certain types of exchanges, while in others the content of what is being exchanged is very different. This different emphasis is what really distinguishes, then, one type of employment contract from another. Thus, different emphases on particular types of exchanges can shape different types of employment contracts. In this section we theoretically derive five possible employment contracts from the multiple possible combinations of the different types of exchanges we discussed in the previous section. Later on, we describe the most commonly found employment contracts by looking at the different exchange relationships that constitute each of them. We show how the theoretically derived employment contracts coincide very much with contracts found in the literature. Finally, we suggest, it is not coincidence that to each of the strategic types we describe in section 2.6 corresponds one of the five specific supporting contracts we analyze in this section. There is some logic, after all, behind the contingent arguments developed in this study.

In Figure 2.4, the eight possible combinations of the three type of exchanges discussed in section 2.4 are shown. As we argue, from these combinations five possible employment contracts arise. Case 8 is a non-viable case since none of the three types of exchanges is part of this possible contract. Similarly, case 6 is also non-viable given that social exchange is the only type of relationship taking place between employees and the firm. We argue that for social and work exchanges to take place, a minimum level of economic exchange should exist to make the relationship between employer and employee possible and sustainable. Case 1 is clearly influenced by transactional ESs. It emphasizes economic exchange and it is closely related to transactional contracts that are discussed later in this section. Cases 2 and 3 appeared to be supported, respectively, by market and organizational employability. They both emphasize economic and work exchanges. Among other features, these contracts provide market-based pay and extremely interesting jobs in which employees can maintain and upgrade their general skills that make them more "employable" outside the firm if they need or want to quit. The main difference among them is that in case 3 social exchanges are not important. In market employability contracts, all the general skills required are bought in the market place and when new ones are required employees are replaced by new ones with the required set of abilities. We think cases 4 and 5 should be combined in one single contract. It is difficult to think that case 5 would be sustainable in the long run because of the low economic exchange in this possible contract. For any contract to be sustainable it requires a minimum of efficiency and financial performance. In fact, we believe that at least a medium degree of a given level of exchange is necessary to consider the next level of exchange.

Otherwise its existence is threatened. If case 4 then is merged with case 5, we could end up with a possible contract in which both economic and work exchange have relative importance – not as strong as in cases 2 and 3 – and high levels of social exchange. This potential employment contract seems to be strongly supported by committed oriented employment systems and closely resembles the relational contracts that appear in the literature. Finally, cases 4 and 7 could be combined to get a fifth potential employment contract. In this type of contract, economic exchanges have a small role. Its sustainability is, therefore, questionable. Work and social exchanges, however, can have a certain role. Balanced ESs might be supporting this type of contract. Moreover, it can be argued that this type of employment contract is similar to the balanced contract described in the literature (Rousseau, 1995).

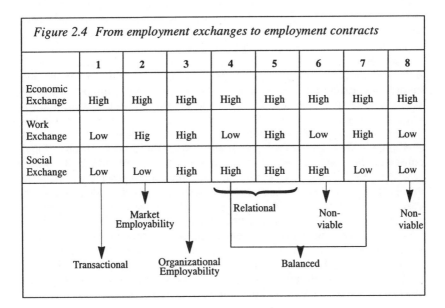

Figure 2.4 From employment exchanges to employment contracts

	1	2	3	4	5	6	7	8
Economic Exchange	High	High	High	High	High	High	High	High
Work Exchange	Low	Hig	High	Low	High	Low	High	Low
Social Exchange	Low	Low	High	High	High	High	Low	Low

Market Employability

Relational   Non-viable   Non-viable

Transactional   Organizational Employability   Balanced

Traditionally what researchers have focused on in the study of employment contracts have been referred to as transactional and relational (Macneil, 1985; Rousseau, 1989). Transactional contracts are closely related to the transactional employment system. They emphasize, primarily, economic exchange. These relationships are charaterized by a fair day's work for a fair day's pay. They comprise "short-term monetizable agreements with limited involvement of each party in the lives of the other" (Rousseau and McLean Parks, 1993: 10). Economic exchanges are the only ones considered in transactional contracts. Employees under this type of contract perceive the economic conditions offered by the company – salary and bonuses – as fair. They also perceive fairness in the economic conditions offered by the company as fair vis-à-vis external conditions such as alternative jobs outside the organization and the costs involved in changing jobs (Allen and Meyer, 1990). Work and social exchanges are less important in transactional contracts. Among other things, jobs are generally narrowly defined, the level of required skills is low, and minimum training is provided. Employees for the most part work for the salary. Either their intrinsic and social needs are not very strong or they expect the job to help them in "building up their CVs". In contrast, they are not interested in the experience that the job itself or the company can offer at the moment. In transactional contracts, then, a policy of continual recruitment of people looking for a "ticket punch" is maintained, creating a well-defined employment relationship that allows both the firm and the employee an easy exit (Rousseau, 1995). Social exchange has a very limited role in transactional contracts. As we saw in section 2.3, internal recruitment as well as efforts in communication and socialization are very limited. Employees, on their part, have little expectation of staying there for a very long time.

A second type of contract, relational contract, is strongly associated with relational employment systems. It focuses on open-ended relationships involving considerable investments by both employees (company-specific skills, long-term career development) and employers (extensive training). Such investments involve a high degree of mutual interdependence and barriers to exit. Relational contracts are based, fundamentally, on social exchange. Work exchanges are more important than in transactional contracts, but not as important as in the case of employability-based contracts. Employees have moderate economic needs since they consider this exchange of lower wages – compared to the market – in return for job security as a fair trade-off. Work exchange is relatively important in relational contracts – certainly more than in transactional relationships. Employees' intrinsic needs are usually satisfied by moderate levels of skill variety, task identity and significance, and power over decision-making. They value the job characteristics that relational contracts offer, but only up to certain degree since the work conditions and characteristics are always firm-specific and therefore they are not so useful in other working contexts. Similarly, relational contracts imply a moderate need for training on the part of employees given that these programs are also restricted to firm-specific abilities. Social exchange is, undoubtedly, the most important exchange relationship supporting relational contracts. Employees hope their needs for belongingness, social esteem and altruism will be highly satisfied. They expect to keep a lifetime employment relationship with the company. When people leave the company it is usually during their first years and mainly because they don't fit the culture (Rousseau, 1995: 101). Similarly, those who stay spend a long time in lower-level positions before advancing up the hierarchy. Firms, in this sense, try to provide an adequate social context fostering people's interconnectedness and communication and through extensive socialization programs, strong objectives, and corporate values.

Balanced contracts, clearly in connection with balanced ESs, are a middle-of-the-road relationship between the transactional and relational contracts. For these reason, in balanced contracts all three types of exchanges exist but at a moderate level. Employees have a pecuniary attachment to the company, and they consider market salaries in the assessment of the fairness of the economic relationship they have with the organization. At the same time, however, they are willing to accept compensation levels offered by the company that are usually a bit lower than the market in exchange for some degree of stability and career opportunities which the firm provides. Thus, employees taking part in balanced contracts like to stay with the company, but at the same time are open to interesting opportunities that may appear in the labor market. Work exchanges are also relatively important in balanced contracts. Employees engaged in balanced contracts have a high degree of creative performance, a long-term focus, and do not excessively avoid risk taking in their job. In exchange, companies implementing this type of contract offer jobs and training that allow employees to develop skills which can be used in other positions within the firm, give them more discretion, use minimal controls, allow and support experimentation (Schuler and Jackson, 1987: 339). These conditions often result in feelings of both enhanced personal control and morale and commitment to themselves and their profession, leading, in turn, to perceived fairness in the work relationship. Balanced contracts also emphasize a certain level of social exchange. Employees have a relatively high-level desire for cooperative and interdependent behavior. Firms supporting their strategies through a balanced contract promote policies, practices, and organizational arrangements such as personal and informational horizontal linkages and encourage employees to offer suggestions for new and improved ways of doing their own job or products. These policies, practices, and other characteristics enhance greater commitment to the employing organization and perceived fairness in the social exchange relationship.

Through market employability contracts, very much in connection with market employability employment systems, firms offer greater pay for performance, more challenging jobs, and development of employee skills that will keep them employable in exchange for hard work and greater risks and responsibilities. Employees have to undertake to manage their own careers (Cappelli, 1999; Cappelli, Chapter 5 in this book). Market employability contracts, then, are heavily based on economic and work exchanges, while social exchange is not considered in these type of employer–employee relationships. The highly qualified employees whom firms usually hire would increase their economic attachment to the organizations if they perceived that their skills are paid at the corresponding market levels or above it. In order to attract and retain highly qualified people, companies, in turn, provide strong economic incentives to employees. These highly skilled employees working under market employability conditions are probably the best paid in the industry. Work exchange is a key component of market employability type of contracts. In these relationships, individuals care about professionally rewarding jobs, such as jobs that help them learn, satisfy their curiosity, or develop them intellectually and emotionally (Cardona *et al.,* 1999). Their work attachment to the organization results from a perception of fairness in their work exchange relationships with the organization. In response to these needs, and in order to achieve variety, shorter product cycles and dynamic efficiency, companies offer probably the most interesting and challenging work employees can find in the industry (Cappelli, Chapter 5 in this book). High job rotation, extensive teamwork, and higher degrees of autonomy are common features of market employability contracts. Social exchange, in contrast, has a limited role in such contracts. Employees do not stay in organizations for too long. Market forces increasingly impose the need for greater organizational flexibility. Constant changes in the market place require continuous rearrangement in firms' products and technologies. As a result, many companies change their people every time a new set of skills and capabilities is required. A good number of employees are employed on a project basis, often moving from firm to firm as they finish one project and go on to the next (Laubacher and Malone, 1997). Under this type of contract, employers are no longer responsible for meeting employees' social needs. Individuals have to look for other sources like professional associations, college alumni associations, unions, fraternities, clubs, neighborhoods, families, and churches, where they can satisfy those needs. These external sources could provide meeting places, either actual or virtual, where workers with similar interests and experiences might gather on a regular basis to trade stories and share advice. They are also likely to become the primary institution with which those employees come to identify and a place where altruism can be develop.

Finally, in organizational employability contracts, which are supported by organizational employability systems, firms offer high economic rewards – as in market employability relationships, challenging jobs, ample opportunities for enhancing the skills and capabilities of employees, in exchange for hard effort, superior performance, and loyalty. The difference with the previous contract, however, is that organizational employability organizes work around long-term relationships between employer and employee. This, in turn, makes it possible for companies to offer, in addition, high levels of training in general skills, social factors, networking, a sense of self-identity and an appropriate setting to develop altruistic behaviors. As in market employability contracts, economic exchange is important. Great compensation packages are offered to a workforce characterized by a high level of skills. Work exchanges are also crucial. These companies offer the most interesting jobs in their industries, in which employees can continuously update and enhance their current pool of abilities. In contrast to market employability, however, organizational employability provides high levels of training in general skills to their employees (Ghoshal *et al.*, Chapter 4 in this book). This is possible because, through a series of connecting mechanisms and social bonds, they can establish long-term relationships with their employees, even in situations of fast change and radical modes of innovation. Social exchange, therefore, is a distinctive characteristic of organizational employability *(ibid.)* These firms are bigger than the ones that usually adopt market employability and are almost self-contained in terms of the general skills they need to combine to deliver their products and services. As a result these large communities (Laubacher and Malone, 1997) can provide common goals and values that engage employees in long-term relationships. Individuals, in turn, do not need to go outside the company to satisfy their social needs. The company itself is a scenario where employees can meet their needs for a sense of belonging, self-esteem and altruism. Figure 2.5 summarizes the arguments we have developed in this section.

Figure 2.5 Employment contracts					
	Employment contracts				
	Transactional	Balanced	Relational	Market employability	Organizational employability
Economic Exchange	High	Medium	Medium	High	Medium High
Work Exchange	Low	Mediun	Medium	High	High
Social Exchange	Low	Medium	High	Low	High

2.6 COMPETITIVE STRATEGIES

Exchanges between employer and employees are part of the employment contract they hold. A critical choice which has to be made in this study is about which aspects of firms' competitive strategy are going to be taken into account. Several aspects of firms' competitive strategy have been used to test contingency theory arguments. This study examines the relationship between five specific strategic types and five corresponding particular forms of employment contracts. Competitive strategy is analyzed along two dimensions. The first one is its product/market approach and the second one is associated to the way firms develop their competitive capabilities in order to create a typology. To construct the product/market part of our strategy typology, Porter's (1980, 1985) distinction between cost leadership and differentiation strategies is used. Within differentiation strategies it is particularly useful to distinguish between firms that follow a differentiation through product variety and speed and those that pursue differentiation through quality and brand image. The work of Porter is one of the most widely used typologies to describe firms' product/market strategic dimension. According to Porter, value can be created in one of two generic ways: by reducing costs or by differentiating a product or service relative to its competitors. These two sources of value lead, in turn, to two basic strategies.

The first, cost leadership, is achieved by constructing efficient large-scale facilities, by reducing costs through capitalizing on the experience curve, and by controlling overhead costs and costs in such areas as R&D, service, sales force, and advertising. This strategy provides above-average returns within an industry, if it ends up building entry barriers to other potential entrants into the industry, as the firm lowers its prices below competitors' costs. Cost leadership is likely to be strong when the product is simple, and there are only a few easily ranked attributes that matter to potential customers. Cost-based strategies require managers to do whatever is necessary to drive down costs: move production to or source from a low-wage country; build new facilities or consolidate old plants to gain economies of scale; or focus operations down to the most economic subset of activities. These tactics reduce costs but at the expense of responsiveness.

The second business strategy type is based on differentiation. Through differentiation, firms try to position their products and services in a distinctive way, compared with its competitors. The differentiation may arise from many different sources. This chapter emphasizes two of them: (1) product variety and speed, and (2) quality and brand image. Some authors (Stalk, 1988) have argued that firms can compete through differentiation through variety and speed. They emphasize swiftness as an important organizational capability. Many companies compete with flexible manufacturing, rapid-response systems, and expanding variety. These types of strategies emphasize time-based competition with factories located close to the customers they serve and organizational structures enabling fast responses. Companies following these strategies concentrate on reducing delays and using their response advantages to attract customers.

A second source of differentiation considered in this study is quality and brand image. Following a long-term focus companies using this strategy try to build a brand image through the superior features and service they offer to customers. Quality enhancement means, in turn, a high concern for process, that is, how the goods or services are made or delivered.

The concepts of differentiation through either variety and speed or quality and brand image can be associated, somehow, to the notions of horizontal and vertical differentiation, coming from the industrial organization literature (e.g., Besanko *et al.*, 1996). Vertical differentiation occurs when a company makes a product better than those of its competitors. The typical consumer in this case is willing to pay a significant price premium for attributes that enhance the utility obtained from consuming the product. A firm that can differentiate its product by offering additional features – product quality, complementary goods and services offered with the product, and characteristics associated with the sale or delivery – may achieve an enhanced competitive position. Gillette, for example, was thinking of this effect when it launched its Sensor razor in 1990. It concluded that there was a significant number of men who were willing to pay a relatively high price for blades that gave a better shave than disposables or cartridges. Thus, vertical differentiation can be associated with the notion of superior quality and service, in Porter's (1980) terms.

Horizontal differentiation arises, in contrast, when a firm makes the product distinctive from those of competitors, which may involve making it better, more appealing, or more suitable for one class of potential customers, but making it worse, less appealing, or less suitable for other potential customers (Besanko *et al.*, 1996). Usually horizontal differentiation is likely to be strong when there are many product attributes that consumers weigh in assessing the overall benefit of that product, and there is substantial disagreement among consumers about the desirability of those attributes. Breakfast cereals, soft drinks, and automobiles are businesses in which horizontal differentiation is significant.

It is possible to relate horizontal differentiation, then, to the notions of variety in the product range and speed. Variety stresses the idea that each specific market segment would value a particular version of a firm's product, thus calling for variety in the firm's product range. Increasingly, however, this strategy of variety would need to be coupled with higher speed in product innovation. Products life cycles have shortened, and if a company wants to compete with variety, as opposed to superior quality, it makes sense to think that the quantity of new products launched on to the markets needs to be increased.

We prefer to stick to the concepts of speed–variety and quality–brand name because the concepts of horizontal and vertical differentiation imply consumers' assessment of a product's position regarding the speed–variety and quality–brand name attributes. These evaluations can be very diverse and subjective in nature and, therefore, difficult to operationalize in future empirical work based on our framework. We prefer, then, to consider the firm's strategic perspective – its intended strategy, if you want – leaving aside consumers' perception about the strategic positioning of firms implied in the concepts of horizontal and vertical differentiation.

Competitive strategy is also determined by the way firms accumulate resources and capabilities, as well as how they adjust over time to changing circumstances. Porter's (1980, 1985) strategic typology is in fact only one part of a firm's strategic picture. Implicitly underlying a company's market/product positioning there is a static view of strategy. A second strategic dimension considered in this study is the type of efficiency firms want to pursue. In particular, we believe that a firm's performance is also determined by the way in which firms accumulate resources and capabilities, as well as how they adjust over time to changing circumstances.

Both Miles and Snow's (1978) and Porter's (1980) strategic typologies are in fact only one part of a firm's strategic picture. Implicitly underlying a company's market/product positioning there is a static view of strategy. For example, one of Miles and Snow's (1978) three dimensions, the technical dimension, which refers to the technology and processes a firm uses to produce its products and services technical dimension, may capture some of the organizational learning aspects we refer to. Its content, however, has rarely been operationalized (Shortell and Zajac, 1990). Moreover, many of the learning aspects were not even taken into account by this typology. As Shortell and Zajac (1990: 829) asked:

> *What behavior should we expect of prospectors, analyzers, defenders, and reactors? Will a prospector move more aggressively against a new competitor than a defender? Are prospectors and analyzers likely to adopt innovation earlier than defenders? Does this timing depend on the type of innovation?*

In the case of Porter's typology, at a given moment in time the firm is either competing on the basis of low costs or is differentiated in key dimensions and can thus charge a premium over the prices charged by the firms with which it competes. We argue however that this traditional view of strategy should be complemented with a more dynamic perspective. Dynamics has to do, for example, with the process emphasized so eloquently by the economist Joseph Schumpeter, who argued that "the impulse of alluring profit," even though inherently temporary, will induce firms and entrepreneurs to create new bases of competitive advantage that redefine industries and undermine the ways of achieving advantage (Besanko *et al.,* 1996). This process of capability creation, development, and destruction has been usually called organizational learning.

We want to explore the relationship between employment contracts and the way firms structure their process of organizational learning and, ultimately, the impact of this relationship on performance. Two different organizational learning processes are available to a company. A central concern for organizations is whether they should emphasize the one type of learning which mainly consists in the exploration of new possibilities or, in contrast, whether they should concentrate on a second kind of organizational learning, which is based on the exploitation of old certainties and capabilities (Schumpeter, 1934; Kuran, 1988). Exploitation implies processes like refinement, choice, production, efficiency, selection, implementation, execution. Exploration, on the other hand, includes actions such as search, variation, risk taking, experimentation, play, flexibility, discovery, innovation (March, 1991).

Exploration and exploitation usually compete for the scarce resources a company has. As a result, organizations need to make explicit and implicit choices between the two. Companies often face several alternative investment opportunities, each characterized by a probability distribution over returns that is initially unknown. Information about the distribution is accumulated over time. Choices must be made, however, between gaining and using this information to search for improvements within the framework of existing beliefs about how the environment behaves and responds to organizational actions and, therefore, improve present returns through the current competitive position – static efficiency – versus getting and using new information to reconsider the beliefs themselves and, in turn, trying to improve future returns through new visions of how to compete – dynamic efficiency – (Ghemawat and Ricart, 1993), transformation (Pascale, 1991), or stretch (Hamel and Prahalad, 1993).

A classic example of this problem of balancing exploration and exploitation arises when companies need to decide between the refinement of an existing technology or the invention of new one (Winter, 1971; Levinthal and March, 1981). It is clear that exploration of new alternatives reduces the speed with which skills at existing ones are improved. It is also clear that improvements in competence at existing procedures make experimentation with others less attractive (Levitt and March, 1988).

Thus, in order to achieve either of these two kinds of efficiencies or a combination of both, when possible a firm needs to make explicit choices about alternative investments, specific organizational forms, and procedures. Organizational arrangements that promote static efficiency may be inconsistent with arrangements that promote dynamic efficiency.

According to Ghemawat and Ricart (1993) this is due to two reasons:

1. the pursuit of the two kinds of efficiency may not be consistent in their implications for individual organizational elements;
2. the requirement of consistency across individual organizational elements may reinforce the tension, forcing organizations to cluster into two relatively distinct archetypes.

This bidimensional approach toward strategy types may result in five different strategies (Figure 2.6): as a result, five strategic types arise from this two-dimensional and enriched view of competitive strategy:

1. cost leadership;[3]
2. differentiation through product variety and speed/static efficiency;
3. differentiation through quality and brand image/static efficiency;
4. differentiation through product variety and speed/dynamic efficiency; and
5. differentiation through quality and brand image/dynamic efficiency.

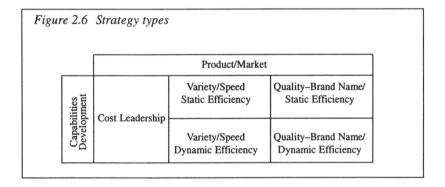

Figure 2.6 Strategy types

2.7 COMPETITIVE STRATEGIES AND EMPLOYMENT CONTRACT ALIGNMENT

Following a contingency approach, in this section we argue that an appropriate match between business strategies described in section 2.6. and the employment contracts mentioned in section 2.5 should lead to higher performance. Each particular business strategy, we suggest, should be aligned with a specific employment contract if firms want to achieve superior performance (Figure 2.7). Specifically:

1. firms following a cost leadership strategy would tend to be more oriented towards a transactional employment contract;
2. firms that pursue differentiation through product variety and speed/static efficiency strategy would be inclined to implement a balanced contract;
3. firms that pursue a differentiation through quality and brand image/static efficiency strategy would support their strategy by implementing a relational employment contract;
4. firms implementing a product variety and speed/dynamic efficiency strategy would prefer to adopt a market employability contract; and
5. firms following a product quality and brand image/dynamic efficiency strategy are likely to adopt an organizational employability contract in order to achieve superior performance compared with competitors in their industry.

Figure 2.7 Contingent employment contracts

		Product/Market	
Capabilities Development	Transactional	Balance	Relational
		Market Employability	Organizational Employability

Because the cost leadership business strategy typically involves producing relatively few commodity-type products at a lower cost, it is possible for firms following this strategy to break down the production process into relatively narrow, well-specified job tasks. There are a number of labor cost advantages associated with this work organization approach. First, the skill level requirements of employees needed to perform these tasks is reduced, which reduces the wage levels needed to attract and retain qualified employees. Second, the training costs for production employees are also reduced. Third, the combination of low skill requirements and low training investment reduces the costs of turnover for these firms. Production employees become more easily replaceable.

It is proposed that, under these conditions, firms' needs to promote employee involvement, information sharing, job security guarantees, and extensive employee benefits is greatly reduced. In fact, as Galbraith (1977) argues, stimulating innovative or creative employee behaviors through relational systems activities when, as in the case of high volume assembly-line operation, any deviation from standard performance can cause production bottle-necks, may be dysfunctional from the point of view of firm performance. The primary function of a transactional contract is, then, to reduce direct labor costs and other employment-related expenditures (such as outlays for training and employee involvement programs) (Arthur, 1992).

Strategies based on quality enhancement, brand image/static efficiency should be better supported by policies, practices, and organizational arrangements that help to ensure highly reliable behavior from individuals who can identify with the goals of the organization and, when necessary, have some flexibility and adaptability to new job assignments and technological change (Drucker, 1985; Albrecht and Albrecht, 1987). A strategy of quality improvement and strong brand image coupled with static efficiency often means repetitive and predictable ways of working. Relational contracts provide this desired stability by providing employees with very high degrees of job security and socialization initiatives. Incremental improvements in quality often means, however, some degree of change in the way the work is done. Relational contracts also allow changes in the processes of production and encourage workers to be more involved and more flexible than in firms following cost leadership strategies supported by transactional contracts. Relational contracts may provide a greater degree of flexibility in both the job and the use of production processes. They do this by fostering higher levels of employee participation in decisions relevant to immediate work conditions, and the job itself can be achieved. For example, employees can do things such as inspect their own work and review the work methods currently being used and correct them, in addition to running their daily tasks. Since innovations are developed around current products, services, and technologies, transactional contracts provide continuous learning by these same work organization practices and also through firm-specific training programs where new, but related, skills and abilities are learned. It is because of these types of policies, practices, and organizational characteristics that employees become committed to the firm and, hence, willing to give more. Under these conditions, the level of quality is likely to improve. Finally, through extensive socialization and by emphasizing the firm's common objectives and values, relational contracts foster employees' long-term commitment and attachment to the organization.

Firms following a strategy of differentiation through product variety and speed/static efficiency have to be flexible enough to shift production and organization resources to meet changing markets and customer demands. Under these conditions, it is proposed that employees must have the skill and training to perform a variety of different tasks in order to improve current products and technologies. Because it is more difficult to predetermine all production contingencies and situations, compared with cost leadership strategies, standardization is reduced and the level of uncertainty in performing production tasks increases. Production employees engaged in uncertain tasks are required to use some discretion in determining when and how to perform specific activities. Innovation is, however, incremental, which means that changes in products, processes and technologies are somewhat "predictable." Thus, we argue, a balanced contract is the most adequate to support strategies emphasizing variety, speed and static efficiency. These contracts may foster employees' creativity and innovation within the established organizational framework through balanced contracts that combine market-oriented aspects with policies, practices, and other aspects that promote employees' social and cultural attachment to the organization.

Business strategies based on differentiation through product variety and speed/dynamic efficiency, we argue, will be better supported by market employability contracts (Cappelli, Chapter 5 in this book). Firms competing in turbulent environments through innovation, product variety, speed, and dynamic efficiency which move away from vertical integration and emphasize outsourcing from third parties have better chances of achieving superior performance. In fast-changing competitive environments organizations usually try to be leaders in a few segments of their market. To support this type of strategy, these companies should become very flat and emphasize a narrow set of capabilities in which they can excel. These arrangements may result, in turn, in light cost structures and fast information and communication flows, two key components of product variety, time-to-market, and dynamic efficiency. In contrast, vertically integrated, as opposed to more delayered, horizontal firms, may result in high fixed costs and slow communication, which runs in the opposite direction of what firms need in those competitive situations (Saxenian, 1994).

At the same time, in order to realign their skills and develop new ones, companies need to hire their employees in the market, where a wide variety of capabilities may exist. Hiring highly qualified employees in the external market also helps firms stay at the frontier of new product development. Thus, the model of short-term employment relationships operating in some industries is likely to allow firms to develop a unique capability for innovation and flexibility. Moreover, these companies do not need long-term employment relationships because the rate of innovation in the product market and the pressure to rearrange capabilities within the firm make those relationships difficult to sustain.

Similarly, in market employability based contracts, sustaining product variety and speed/dynamic efficiency training is neither desirable nor necessary. Training is expensive and its cost difficult to recoup in a context characterized by very short product cycles. In market employability based contracts, then, employees should be responsible for their own training and skill development. Firms do not provide that. They hire either the best graduates from educational institutions and also they poach the required people from larger firms competing in more established positions and stable markets. Larger and more hierarchical companies operating in less turbulent environments have longer product cycles and can provide more opportunities for internal development and career tracks. Firms competing through variety and speed/dynamic efficiency usually poach these trained employees from them (Cappelli, 1999).

In employability based contracts, employees' attachment to the organization is weak. Employees usually satisfy their social needs outside the company. Even though market employability contract work is extremely well-suited to rapid innovation and dynamically changing markets, employees' social needs cannot be satisfied within the organizational boundaries. In market employability contracts between employer and employee, where all relationships are contractual, there is no room for social exchange. The individuals' need for belongingness, social esteem, and altruism are usually satisfied outside the firm. Independent organizations such as professional associations, college alumni associations, unions, fraternities, clubs, neighborhoods, families, and churches help to meet individuals' social needs. Among other things, these more stable communities provide a place for social networking, learning, and reputation-building, among other things. Probably their most important role is to provide individuals with a sense of identity and belonging and a place in which they can develop altruism.

Finally, we argue that firms supporting a differentiation strategy through quality and brand image/dynamic efficiency by implementing an organizational employability contract should obtain superior performance (Ghoshal *et al.*, Chapter 4 in this book). These contracts are better suited to firms driven by dynamic efficiency, which do not have the constant pressure of short product cycles and a wide range of products. Instead they establish long-term relationships with their customers, offering them high quality, service, and a superior brand name. Through organizational employability these firms obtain and develop the required advanced general skills (Ghoshal *et al.*, 1996: 19) and the many combinations among them they require to deliver the dynamic efficiency process and high quality their products need. In contrast to market employability, firms implementing organizational employability create an internal market in the required skills they need. Instead of going to the market they create their own pool of general skills inside organizational boundaries. Organizational employability offers employees high levels of job rotation, teamwork, involvement, autonomy, general training, and wages and benefits. In this way the firm attracts and motivates employees. Then, by providing connecting mechanisms, such as horizontal linkages, a common purpose and values, firms may foster the process of dynamic efficiency and quality they need to incorporate in their products. Moreover, these linkages and social bonds allow for a long-term relationship between employer and employee, since individuals find satisfaction of their three sources of needs within the company, lowering the probability that those people will leave the company. This logic of retention, however, is different from the case of relational contracts, where the company explicitly offers job security. In organizational employability, in contrast, people stay in the company because they are probably the best paid in the market, they have the most interesting jobs in which they can exercise and upgrade their current skills and abilities, and because they find a sense of belongingness, self-esteem, and a place in which altruism can also be developed.

2.8 CONCLUSIONS

Many of the strategic types supported by specific employment contracts are currently viable options for firms. Some of them, however, will probably be less sustainable in the near future. External forces, such as globalization and deregulation coupled with higher rates of market and technology changes, can make some of these competitive strategies increasingly outdated. We are probably going to see more companies that stress dynamic efficiency trying to come out with radically different products, technologies and ways of organizing (Pettigrew and Massini, Chapter 7 in this book). Cost leadership strategies and differentiation through quality on a static efficiency basis will probably have a hard time in the future.

As more and more companies start to compete on the basis of dynamic efficiency, however, "the new" employment contracts replace "the old" human resource, work organization and organizational paradigms. Some features of the old contracts such as excessively structured jobs, employee's low level of skills and high employment guarantees can no longer respond to the challenges placed by dynamic efficiency-based strategies. These new ways of competition, however, present new challenges to firms adopting them. High levels of coordination are required both within and outside the firm. Employees need constantly to develop new skills as their current ones may become obsolete. At the same time, increasingly less identification of employees with their organizations would raise doubts about the commitment of these employees to organizational goals and performance. The distinction between internal and external knowledge developed by Andreu and Sieber (Chapter 8 in this book) is completely relevant in this respect.

In particular, we have some indications of the impact of these new realities on firms and their employees. Low morale has been observed in companies competing through product variety and speed and dynamic efficiency. As these firms, in their constant search for new sets of capabilities, change their employees constantly, less commitment and even fear has been observed among a good proportion of the workforce

(Pfeffer, 1988; Cappelli, 1999). These phenomena, in turn, raise some doubts about the sustainability of some of the new competitive realities. Sparrow (Chapter 9 in this book) develops many of these issues from a psychological perspective.

One possible solution is the appearance of safety networks. But they are slow to develop, especially regarding the institutional context in which they need to arise. They are better for some low skilled employees but not for the highly qualified who will become an increasingly important part of the active population. Reliance upon and even fostering other sources of social support like professional associations, alumni associations, and small communities will be important in the future.

NOTES

1. Chapter 3 in this book by Carlos Sánchez-Runde goes over these debates in greater depth and detail.
2. These types of needs although extrinsic in nature are distinguished from extrinsic economic needs since the latter's source of satisfaction is economic rather than social.
3. Cost leadership and dynamic efficiency seem to be incompatible given the nature of the two strategies. While a cost minimization strategy enphasizes "doing more of the same" in order to achieve economies of scale and efficiency in processes, dynamic efficiency means risk taking and exploration of possibilities outside the current products, markets and operations domain.

REFERENCES

Albrecht, K. and Albrecht, S. (1987). *The Creative Corporation.* Homewood, Ill.: Dow-Jones-Irwin.

Alderfer, C. P. (1972). *Existence, Relatedness, and Growth: Human needs in organizational settings.* New York: Free Press.

Allen, N. J. and Meyer, J. P. (1990). The measurement and antecedents of affective, continuance, and normative commitment to the organization. *Journal of Occupational Psychology,* 63: 1–18.

Arthur, J. B. (1992). The link between business strategy and industrial relations Systems in American steel minimills, *Industrial and Labor Relations Review,* 45: 488–506.

Arthur, J. B. (1994). Effects of human resource systems on manufacturing performance and turnover, *Academy of Management Journal,* 37 (3): 670–87.

Baird, Ll. and Meshoulam, I. (1988). Managing two fits of strategic human resource management. *Academy of Management Review,* 13 (1): 116–28.

Barnard, C. (1938). *The Functions of the Executive*. Cambridge, MA: Harvard University Press.

Barney, J. (1991). Firm resources and sustained competitive advantage, *Journal of Management*, 17: 99–120.

Batson, C. D. (1991). *The Altruism Question: Toward a social-psychological answer*. Hillsdale, NJ: Lawrence Erlbaum Associates.

Begin, J. P. (1993). Identifying patterns in HRM systems: lessons learned from organizational theory. In J. Shaw, P. Kirkbride and K. Rowlands (eds), *Research in Personnel and Human Resource Management*, suppl. 3: 3–20. Greenwich, CT: JAI Press.

Besanko, D., Dranove, D. and Shanley, M. (1996). *Economics of Strategy*. New York: John Wiley.

Blau, P. M. (1964). *Exchange and Power in Social Life*. New York: John Wiley.

Boxall, P. (1992). The strategic HRM debate and the resource-based view of the firm. *Human Resource Management Journal*, 6 (3): 59–75.

Butler, J. E., Ferris, G. R. and Napier, N. K. (1991). *Strategy and Human Resources Management*. Cincinnati: South-Western.

Cappelli, P. (1999). *The New Deal at Work*. Boston, MA: Harvard Univeristy Press.

Cappelli, P. and Singh, H. (1992). Integrating human resources and strategic management. In D. Lewis, O. S. Mitchel and P. D. Sherer (eds), *Research Frontiers in IR and Human Resources*. Madison: WI: IRRA.

Cardona, P., Lawrence, B. and Bentler, P. (1999). *The Influence of Social and Work Exchange Relationships on Organizational Citizenship Behavior*. Unpublished manuscript.

Cutcher-Gershenfeld, J. (1991). The impact of economic performance of a transformation in industrial relations. *Industrial and Labor Relations Review*, 44: 241–60.

Delery, J. E. and Doty, D. H. (1996). Modes of theorizing in strategic human resource management: tests of universalistic, contingency, and configurational performance predictions. *Academy of Management Journal*, 39 (4): 802–35.

DePree, H. (1986). *Business as Unusual*. Zeeland, M: Herman Miller.

Drazin and Van de Ven, A. (1985). Alternative forms of fit in contingency theory. *Administrative Science Quarterly*, 30: 514–39.

Drucker, P. F. (1985). *Innovation and Entrepreneurship*. New York: Harper and Row.

Dunlop, J. T. and Weil, D. (1996). Diffusion and performance of modular production in the U.S. apparel industry. *Industrial Relations*, 35 (3): 334–55.

Dyer, L. and Holder, G. W. (1988). A strategic perspective of human resource management. In L. Dyer (ed.), *Human Resource Management: Evolving roles and responsibilities*: 1–46. Washington, DC: ASPA-BNA.

Dyer, L. and Reeves, T. (1995). Human resource strategies and firm performance: what do we know and where do we need to go? *International Journal of Human Resource Management*, 6 (3): 656–70.

Etzioni, A. (1961). A *Comparative Analysis of Complex Organizations*. New York: Free Press.

Fombrun, C. (1982). An interview with Reginald Jones. *Organizational Dynamics*, Winter: 46.

Galbraith, J. (1977). *Organization Design*. Reading, MA: Addison-Wesley.

Georgopoulos, B. S., Mahoney, G. M. and Jones, N. W. (1957). A path–goal approach to productivity. *Journal of Applied Psychology*, 41: 345–53.

Ghemawat, P. and Ricart, J. E. (1993). The organizational tension between static and dynamic efficiency. *Strategic Management Journal,* 14 Special Issue, Winter: 59–73.

Ghoshal, S. and Bartlett, C. A. (1997). *The Individualized Corporation*. New York: Harper Business.

Ghoshal, S. and Moran, P. (1996). Bad for practice: a critique of the transaction cost theory. *Academy of Management Review,* 21 (1): 13–47.

Ghoshal, S., Moran, P. and Bartlett, C. A. (1996). *Employment Security, Employability and Sustainable Competitive Advantage*, SLRP Working Paper, London: London Business School.

Govindarajan, V. (1988). A contingency approach to strategy implementation at the business-unit level: integrating administrative mechanisms with strategy. *Academy of Management Journal,* 31 (4): 828–53.

Guest, D. (1987). Human resource management and the American dream. *Journal of Management Studies*, 24 (5): 503–21.

Guest, D. (1990). Human resource management and industrial relations. *Journal of Management Studies*, 27 (4): 377–97.

Hackman, J. R. and Lawler, E. E. (1971). Employee reactions to job characteristics. *Journal of Applied Psychology Monograph*: 259–86.

Hackman, J. R. and Oldham, G. R. (1975). Development of the job diagnostic survey. *Journal of Applied Psychology*, 60: 159–70.

Hackman, J. R. and Oldham, G. R. (1979). *Work Redesign*. Reading, MA: Addison-Wesley.

Hamel, G. and Prahalad, C. K. (1993). Strategy as stretch and leverage. *Harvard Business Review*, 71 (March–April): 75–84.

Herzberg, F. (1966). *Work and the Nature of Man*. Cleveland: World Publishing Co.

Homans, G. (1961). *Social Behavior: Its elementary forms*. New York: Harcourt, Brace.

Huselid, M. A. (1995). The impact of human resource mnagement practices on turnover, productivity, and corporate financial performance. *Academy of Management Journal*, 38 (3): 635–72.

Huselid, M. A. and Becker, B. E. (1996). Methodological issues in cross-sectional and panel estimates of the human resource-firm performance link. *Industrial Relations*, 35 (3): 400–22.

Ichniowski, C., Shaw, K. and Prennushi, G. (1997). The effects of human resource management practices on productivity. *American Economic Review,* 87 (3): 291–313.

Jackson, S. E. and Schuler, R. S. (1995). Understanding human resource management in the context of organizations and their environment. In M. R. Rosenzweig and L. W. Porter (eds), *Annual Review of Psychology,* 46: 237–64. Palo Alto, CA: Annual Reviews.

Jackson, S. E., Schuler, R. S. and Rivero, J. C. (1989). Organizational characteristics as predictor of personnel practices. *Personnel Psychology,* 42: 727–86.

Katz, D. and Kahn, R. L. (1966). *The Social Psychology of Organizations*, 2nd edn.

New York: John Wiley.

Kerr, J. L. and Slocum, J. W. (1987). Linking reward systems and corporate cultures. *Academy of Management Executives,* 1 (2): 99–108.

Kuran, T. (1988). The tenacious past: theories of personal and collective conservatism. *Journal of Economic Behavior and Organization,* 9: 143–71.

Lado, A. and Wilson, M. (1994). Human resource systems and sustained competitive advantage: a competence-based perspective. *Academy of Management Review,* 19 (4): 699–727.

Laubacher, R. J. and Malone, T. W. (1997). Flexible work arrangements and 21st century workers' guilds. *MIT Initiative on Inventing Organizations for the 21st Century,* Working Paper 21C WP 004. Sloan School of Management, MIT.

Laubacher, R. J., Malone, T. W. and MIT Scenario Working Group (1997). Two scenarios for 21st century organizations: shifting networks of small firms or all-encompassing "virtual countries"? *MIT Initiative on Inventing Organizations for the 21st Century,* Working Paper 21C WP 001. Sloan School of Management, MIT.

Lawler, E. E. (1994). *Motivation in Work Organizations.* San Francisco, CA: Jossey-Bass.

Lawler, E. E., and Porter, L. W. (1963). Perceptions regarding management compensation. *Industrial Relations,* 3: 41–9.

Levinthal, D. A. and March, J. G. (1981). A model of adaptive organizational search. *Journal of Economic Behavior and Organization,* 2: 307–33.

Levitt, B. and March, J. G. (1988). Organizational learning. *Annual Review of Sociology,* 14: 319–40.

MacDuffie, J. P. (1995). Human resource bundles and manufacturing performance: organizational logic and flexible production systems in the world auto industry. *Industrial and Labor Relations Review,* 48 (2): 197–221.

Macneil, I. R. (1985). Relational contract: what do we do and do not know. *Wisconsin Law Review:* 483–525.

March, J. A. (1991). Exploration and exploitation: organizational learning. *Organization Science,* 2: 71–87.

Martell, K. D. (1989). Aligning executive human resource management with business unit strategy: an empirical study of the Fortune 500. Unpublished doctoral dissertation, University of Maryland, College Park.

Maslow, A. H. (1954). *Motivation and Personality.* New York: Harper and Row

Mathieu, J. E. and Zajac, D. M. (1990). A review and meta-analysis of the antecedents, correlates, and consequences of organizational commitment. *Psychological Bulletin,* 108: 171–94.

McClelland, D. (1961). *The Achieving Society.* Princeton, NJ: Van Nostrand.

McClelland, D. and Burnham, D. H. (1976). Power is the great motivator. *Harvard Business Review,* March–April: 100–10.

McEvoy, G. M. and Cascio, W. F. (1985). Strategies for reducing employee turnover: a meta-analysis. *Journal of Applied Psychology,* 70: 342–53.

Miles, R. H. and Snow, C. C. (1978). *Organizational Strategy, Structure, and Processes.* New York: McGraw-Hill.

Miles, R. H. and Snow, C. C. (1984). Designing strategic human resource systems.

Organizational Dynamics: 36–52.

Milgrom, P. and Roberts, J. (1995). Complementarities and fit: strategy, structure, and organizational change in manufacturing. *Journal of Accounting and Economics* 19: 179–208.

Mowday, R., Porter, L. and Steers, R. (1982). *Organizational Linkages: The psychology of commitment, absenteeism, and turnover.* New York: Academic Press.

Organ, D. W. (1990). The motivational basis of organizational citizenship behavior. In B. M. Staw and L. L. Cummings (eds), *Research in Organizational Behavior,* 12: 43–72.

Osterman, P. (1987). Choice of employment systems in internal labor market systems. *Industrial Relations,* 26 (1): 46–67.

Osterman, P. (1994). How common is workplace transformation and who adopts it? *Industrial and Labor Relations Review,* 47 (2): 173–88.

Osterman, P. (1997). The shifting structure of the American labor market. Paper presented at the conference "Job creation: the role of labor market institutions," IESE, Barcelona, June 19 and 20.

Pascale, R. T. (1991). *Managing on the Edge.* New York: Simon and Schuster.

Peck, S. R. (1994). Exploring the link between organizational strategy and the employment relationship: the role of human resources policies. *Journal of Management Studies,* 31 (5): 715–36.

Pérez-López, J. A. (1993). *Fundamentos de la Dirección de Empresas.* (Foundations of Management). Madrid: Rialp.

Peters, T. J. and Waterman, R. H. (1982). *In Search of Excellence: Lessons from America's best-run companies.* New York: Harper and Row.

Pfeffer, J. (1994). *Competitive Advantage Through People.* Boston, MA: Harvard Business School Press.

Pfeffer, J. (1996). When it comes to "best practices", why do smart organizations occasionally do dumb things? *Organizational Dynamics,* 25 (1): 33–44.

Pfeffer, J. (1998). *The Human Equation.* Boston, MA: Harvard University Press.

Porter, M. E. (1980). *Competitive Strategy: Techniques for analyzing industries and competitors.* New York: Free Press.

Porter, M. E. (1985). *Competitive Advantage: Creating and sustaining superior performance.* New York: Free Press.

Purcell, J. (1989). The impact of corporate strategy on human resources management. In J. Storey (ed.), *New Perspectives in Human Resource Management.* London: Routledge.

Rousseau, D. M. (1989). Psychological and implied contracts in organizations. *Employee Responsibilities and Rights Journal,* 2 (2): 121–39.

Rousseau, D. M. (1995). *Psychological Contracts in Organizations.* Thousand Oaks, CA: Sage Publications.

Rousseau, D. M. and McLean Parks, J. (1993). The contracts of individuals and organizations. In L. L. Cummings and B. M. Staw (eds), *Research in Organizational Behavior,* 15: 1–43. Greenwich, CT: JAI Press.

Rousseau, D. M. and Wade-Benzoni, K. A. (1995). Changing individual-organization attachment: A two-way street. In A. Howard (ed.), *The Changing Nature of Work.*

San Francisco: Jossey-Bass, 290–322.

Saxenian, A. (1994). *Regional Advantage: Culture and competition in Silicon Valley and Route 128.* Cambridge, MA.: Harvard University Press.

Schein, E. H. (1975). How "career anchors" hold executives to their career paths. *Personnel,* 52 (3): 11–24.

Schein, E. H. (1978). *Career Dynamics.* Reading, MA: Addison-Wesley.

Schein, E. H. (1988). *Organizational Psychology,* 3rd edn. Englewood Cliffs, NJ: Prentice-Hall.

Schuler, R. S. (1987). Personnel and human resource management choices and organizational strategy. In R. S. Schuler, S. A. Youngblood, and V. Huber (eds), *Readings in Personnel and Human Resource Management,* 3rd edn. St. Paul: West Publishing Co.

Schuler, R. S. (1992). Strategic human resource management: Linking the people with the strategic needs of the business. *Organizational Dynamics*: 18–32.

Schuler, R. and Jackson, S. (1987a). Linking competitive strategies and human resource management management practices. *Academy of Management Executive,* 1 (3): 207–19.

Schuler, R. and Jackson, S. (1987b). Organizational strategy and organizational level as determinants of human resource management practices. *Human Resource Planning,* 10 (3): 125–41.

Schumpeter, J. A. (1934). *The Theory of Economic Development.* Cambridge, MA: Harvard University Press

Schwartz, S. H. (1977). Normative influences on altruism. In L. Berkowitz (ed.), *Advances in Experimental Social Psychology,* Vol. 10. New York: Academic Press.

Shortell, S. M. and Zajac, E. J. (1990). Perceptual and archival measures of Miles and Snow's strategic types: A comprehensive assessment of reliability and validity. *Academy of Managemnt Journal,* 33: 817–32.

Sivasubramaniam, N. (1993). Matching human resources and corporate strategy. Unpublished doctoral dissertation, Florida International University, Miami.

Snell, S. A. and Dean, J. W., Jr. (1992). Integrated manufacturing and human resource management: A human capital perspective. *Academy of Management Journal,* 35: 467–504.

Snell, S. A., and Dean, J. W., Jr (1994). Strategic compensation for integrated manufacturing: The moderating effects of jobs and organizational inertia. *Academy of Management Journal,* 37: 1109–40.

Sonnenfeld, J. A. and Piperl, M. A. (1988). Staffing policy as a strategic response: A typology of career systems. *Academy of Management Review,* 13: 558–600.

Stalk, G. (1988). Time: the next source of competitive advantage. *Harvard Business Review,* July/August.

Tichy, N. M. and Sherman, S. (1995). *Control Your Destiny or Someone Else Will: How Jack Welch is making General Electric the world's most competitive corporation.* New York: Harper Collins.

Tushman, M. L. and O'Reilly, C. A. (1997). *Winning Through Innovation.* Boston, MA: Harvard University Press.

Van Dyne, L., Cummings, L. L. and McLean Parks, J. (1995). Extra-role behaviors: In pursuit of construct and definitional clarity (a bridge over muddied waters). In B. M. Staw and L. L. Cummings (eds), *Research in Organization Behavior*, 17: 215–85. Greenwich, CT: JAI Press.

Walker, J. (1980). *Human Resource Planning.* New York: McGraw-Hill

Walton, R. E. (1985). From control to commitment in the workplace. *Harvard Business Review,* 64 (2): 77–84.

Whyte, W. F. (1948). *Human Relations in the Restaurant Industry.* New York: McGraw-Hill.

Winter, S. G. (1971). Satisficing, selection, and the innovating remnant. *Quarterly Journal of Economics,* 85: 237–61.

Wittington, R., Pettigrew, A., Peck, S., Fenton, E. and Conyon, M. (1998). New forms of organization in europe: complementaries and performance. Paper submitted to the special issue on "New Forms of Organizing". *Organization Science,* September.

Wright, P. M. and McMahan, G. C. (1992). Theoretical perspectives for strategic human resource management. *Journal of Management,* 18 (2): 295–320.

Wright, P. M. and Snell, S. A. (1991). Toward an integrative view of strategic human resource management, *Human Resource Management Review,* 1: 203–25.

3. Strategic Human Resource Management and the New Employment Relationships: A Research Review and Agenda

Carlos Sánchez-Runde

3.1 INTRODUCTION

New forms of competition, national and international, threaten firm survival in virtually all industries. Well-established management tools do not seem responsive to changing business needs. Firms learn the hard way that interacting with more turbulent environments demands pulling together all their resources, their human resources being no exception. As a consequence, firms are changing the way they manage people. Human resource management (HRM) scholars propose some suggestions to address today's challenges. Briefly summarized, these suggestions can be stated in three points:

1. Traditionally isolated personnel policies and practices are to be integrated within coherent systems, so that HRM practices reinforce, rather than neutralize one another.
2. Operationalization of the HRM system is to have a greater role in the strategy formulation and implementation processes, so that it may help establish and accomplish firm objectives.
3. Systemic and strategic approaches to HRM need to leverage on and account for new forms of the employment relationship that are becoming increasingly salient in recent times.

We proceed as follows. In section 3.2, we briefly state the argument favoring a systemic HRM stance to our understanding of the relationship between firm strategy and HRM practices. Section 3.3 trace the evolution towards understanding the relationship between HRM practices and strategy. Section 3.4 introduces the consideration of the new forms of employment relationships that moderate the linkage between strategy and HRM practices. At the same time, we also review empirical work substantiating the issues in these sections. We then propose an agenda for future research in section 3.5.

3.2 THE SYSTEMS APPROACH TO HUMAN RESOURCE MANAGEMENT PRACTICES

Most empirical work on the relationship between strategy and HRM has focused on single, separate personnel practices. Reacting against this trend, scholars have recently begun to criticize traditional views of HRM for being piecemeal in their treatment of personnel practices (Wright and McMahan, 1992) and not looking at them as an integrated system (Wright and Snell, 1991).

Studies of HRM systems at the organizational level have been scarce and fragmentary (Ashmos and Huber, 1987; Fisher, 1989; Kerr and Jackofsky, 1989). There are two reasons, however, why theorists are beginning to look for models that consider personnel practices as highly integrated within HRM systems. First, it has been noted that the traditional isolation of HRM practices leads to organizational waste since different practices may be neutralizing, rather than reinforcing one another (Wright and McMahan, 1992; Wright and Snell, 1991). Second, a piecemeal approach to HRM is considered to have impeded full understanding of the main and interactive effects of HRM on organizational life (Beer *et al.,* 1984; Butler *et al.,* 1991).

Applying systems concepts (Boulding, 1956; Von Bertalanffy, 1972) to HRM is important for three reasons. First, the interaction of different practices may add explanatory power to that already achieved by merely considering the main effect of separate practices. Second, a systems view radically challenges the dynamism of HRM: thinking in terms of the individual design and efficiency of each practice makes little sense if what really matters is whether the system itself is well designed and efficient. Finally, while the operation of isolated HRM practices may be too unstable in periods of rapidly changing environments, a systems approach may help sustain more robust configurations of practices.

Systemic approaches are very demanding. They require consistent time horizons across practices, homogeneous criteria of explicitness among practices, and congruent risk propensities among employees toward different practices (Cummings, 1984). That is why it is worth investigating whether organizations with high strategic HRM integration are more or less likely to develop a systems approach and, vice versa, whether a systems approach to HRM helps develop closer ties between strategy and HRM.

The systems approach, while quite recent in its adoption by HRM researchers, has led to some strong findings. First, it has been shown that while many innovative HRM practices appear in bundles – that is, conforming to a coherent system – (Huselid, 1995; Ichniowski, 1990; Ichniowski *et al.*, 1997), most companies adopt just one or two innovative practices at a time, rather than the whole system (Katz *et al.*, 1987; Lawler and Mohrman, 1987; Lawler *et al*, 1995). Second, it has also been found that the introduction of new systems of HRM practices as a whole is more likely in greenfield sites (Lawler *et al.*, 1989; McCormick, 1990) with still a minority of firms adopting them (Dunlop and Weil, 1996; Lawler *et al.*, 1995; MacDuffie, 1995; Osterman, 1994). Finally, research also suggests that while innovative HRM systems tend to outperform traditional ones (Arthur, 1994; Ichniowski *et al.*, 1997; Macy and Izumi, 1993), they still need to be fitted to other compatible organizational systems – such as the production system – to reap the benefits of superior performance (Dunlop and Weil, 1996; Helper, 1995; MacDuffie, 1995).

3.3 THE STRATEGIC APPROACH TO HUMAN RESOURCE MANAGEMENT PRACTICES

Traditional personnel management was dominated by universalistic approaches prescribing exemplary practices of unlimited validity, regardless of circumstance. Neo-contingency perspectives (Miles and Snow, 1978) based on the concept of strategic choice (Child, 1972) presented a radically different view, that people management should be fitted to the changing circumstances of organizations and environments. This evolution, from universalistic to contingent HRM views, parallels changes in the field of industrial relations, where strategic choice currently guides research (Kochan *et al.*, 1984; Lawler, 1990; Weil, 1994) that used to favor universalistic models (Dunlop, 1958; Kerr *et al.*, 1960).

3.3.1 Universalistic approaches to the strategy–HRM relationship

Universalistic approaches to linking strategy and HRM practices come in two related forms. The strictest one, proposed by Pfeffer (1994, 1998), Lake and Ulrich (1992), and Ulrich (1997), defines a set of HRM practices that should be used by all firms on the grounds of their superior performance. These practices include employment security, selective hiring of personnel, self-managed teams and decentralization of decision making, comparatively high performance-based compensation, extensive training, reduced status barriers, and sharing of financial and performance information (Pfeffer, 1998: 64–5). These practices are meant to provide competitive success regardless of the specific strategy of the company, although recognizing that "how one would implement these practices will vary significantly, based on a given organization's strategy and its particular technology and market environment" (Pfeffer, 1994: 64–5).

The second, lighter approach has been championed by Osterman (1994; Kochan and Osterman, 1994), and posits a set of principles, rather than practices, that allow companies to outperform their competitors. These principles work as "idealized organizational practices" (Kochan and Osterman, 1994: 58) and include supportive business strategies, top management commitment, employee voice, staffing through employment stabilization, investment in training and development, contingent compensation, high standards for employee selection, broad task design and teamwork, employee involvement, and a climate of cooperation and trust (*ibid.*: 46). While acknowledging that "there is no single set of practices for implementing these broad principles" (*ibid.*: 75), many of them actually coincide with Pfeffer's practices.

There certainly is some empirical support for the universalistic view (MacDuffie, 1995; Dunlop and Weil, 1996), but the literature has also pointed at the possibility of confounding factors affecting the analyses, such as whether these models are picking up other attributes different than the HRM practices themselves to which they are indirectly related – like general philosophies of HRM which have positive performance effects irrespective of the practices (Kochan and Osterman, 1994: 75–6) – or whether these models "represent even more fundamental and basic underlying variables, such as trust" (Dyer and Reeves, 1995: 665). Also, studies of the universalistic approach show considerable variation as to the practices included and even as to whether a specific practice is positively or negatively related to performance (for details, see Becker and Gerhart, 1996; and Dyer and Reeves, 1995).

In either of their forms – stricter and lighter – the universalistic approaches are quite simple in that "they imply that the relationship between a given independent variable and a dependent variable is universal across the population of organizations" (Delery and Doty, 1996: 805). This simple categorization of the relationship between criterion and predictors masks the moderating effects of firm strategy, thus overestimating the validity of the universalistic approach (Wright and Sherman, 1999: 68–9).

Therefore, it may not be that surprising, as supporters of universalistic views otherwise recognize, that many companies "occasionally do dumb things" (Pfeffer, 1996) by "stubbornly refusing to adopt those practices" (Cappelli and Crocker-Hefter, 1996: 7).

Another possibility calls for reconciling the universalistic and contingency approaches so that they might supplement, rather than supplant each other. We will come back to this point after reviewing the contingency approaches.

3.3.2 Contingency approaches to the strategy–HRM relationship

Theory on the links between strategy and HRM has evolved along two levels of analysis, the individual manager and the system of HRM practices. Individual-based models propose that organizations secure people whose capabilities match the strategy. System-based models focus on matching HRM systems with strategic choices, thus eliciting employee behaviors that support those choices.

While it could seem that both individual and system-based approaches might complement each other, substantial differences between them explain why they are not usually recommended together. First, supporters of matching individual talent and strategy center their analyses on managers, while proponents of system-wide models think in terms of the whole workforce. Second, individual-based models emphasize passive compliance dynamisms by securing individuals who will naturally act in ways that fit the strategy, while system-based models try actively to elicit specific strategic behaviors out of the broader set of behaviors that employees can display. Finally, individual-based models focus on managerial selection and/or development, while system-wide models call for the whole set of HRM policies to select, appraise, train, develop, and reward employes.

Individual-based models

Individual-based models try to match leaders and firm strategy by taking the strategy as a given and HRM as an implementation device (Lengnick-Hall and Lengnick-Hall, 1988). Very few individual-based matching models allow for selecting managers who will in turn formulate the strategy (Rothschild, 1993), arguably because of lacking a strategy which has "matching" managers selects in the first place.

Matching people and strategy emphasizes four points:

1. that "there is no leader for all seasons" (Rothschild, 1993: 37) and general managers are not truly generalists (Kotter, 1982);
2. that different jobs and strategies require different implementation knowledge, skills, and abilities (Gupta, 1986; Jones, interviewed by Fombrun, 1982; Kotter, 1982; Smith, 1982);
3. that manager–strategy mismatch may cause the strategy to be reformulated according to the manager's preferences (Herbert and Deresky, 1987);
4. that matching managers and strategy increases performance (Gupta, 1986; Thomas *et al.*, 1991).

Most manager–strategy matching models propose a view of strategy strongly determined by the organization life cycle (Crandall, 1987; Gerstein and Reisman, 1983; Rothschild, 1993). Different authors select different organizational life stages to anchor the knowledge, skills, and abilities required from matching managers. The description of those personal capabilities tends to be sketchy and simplistic, often using single-word metaphors. A few models follow business unit strategy classifications to which managerial capabilities should then be matched (Herbert and Deresky, 1987; Thomas *et al.,* 1991). Again, little effort is put in describing those capabilities. See Table 3.1 for a summary of models.

Implementing manager–strategy matching models requires two things: first, either selecting outside managers, or developing currently available personnel, or both; second, establishing criteria for operationalizing those selection and development processes. Regarding the first point, selection, on the one hand, may allow for bigger pools of candidates and less political decision making, and it can be used to promote innovation and change when tapping capabilities not available in the organization. Managerial development, on the other hand, sends a message of normality in individual learning and change, improves manager socialization, and increases networking and communication. All considered, Kerr and Jackofsky (1989) suggest a contingent approach based on firm strategy, structure, and culture. In regard to the second point, on what criteria should be used for manager selection and development, Szilagyi and Schweiger (1984) propose a contingent view around two sets of "matching criteria" (knowledge, integration and administration) and "matching contingencies" (technical, political and cultural systems).

Support for individual-based models was found by Gupta and Govindarajan (1984), Herbert and Deresky (1987), and Thomas *et al.,* (1991).

Manager–strategy matching models (Gupta, 1986) have raised three criticisms:

1. that flexibility may be lost by closely fitting managers and strategy;
2. that managers who have not been selected and/or developed may feel demotivated;
3. that managers are given very limited autonomy in influencing strategy. More specifically, models based on life cycle considerations have been criticized because of their unrealistic assumptions (Kerr, 1982): organizational life cycle stages are difficult to measure and foresee; managerial characteristics allegedly best suited to each organizational life stage have not been validated; managerial style and capabilities are difficult to assess; and little consideration has been given to internal political and cultural dynamics that may prevent the matching process. Further, even if life cycle stages could be clearly defined, most firms would likely be at different stages simultaneously (Cummings, 1984; Smith, 1982).

Table 3.1   Summary of inividual-based models

Author(s)	Strategy model	Manager traits	Manager style/capabilities
Gerstein & Reisman (1983)	Life cycle: Start up Turnaround Extract Growth Redeploy Liquidation Acquisition	Hands on, charisma Negotiator, high risk Problem finder Vision, planner Politician, low risk Callous, tough minded Communicator	Team building Strong leadership Relationship building Organization building Interpersonal skills Autocratic, low participation Establish interdependencies
Crandall (1987)	Life cycle: Start up Growth Maturity	Flexible-action focus Vision-people focus Planner-efficacy focus	Autocratic, no participation More participative Persuader
Herbert & Deresky (1987)	Gupta & Govindarajan: Develop Stabilize Turnaround	Creative, flexible Conservative Autonomous, tough	Entrepreneurship Maintenance Autocratic, low participation
Thomas, Litschert, & Ramaswamy (1991)	Miles & Snow: Defender Prospector	Cautious, risk averse Younger, risk lover	Efficiency oriented Innovation oriented
Rothschild (1993)	Life cycle: Start up Growth Maturity Decline	Risk taker Caretaker Surgeon Undertaker	

System-based models

System-based models of strategy and HRM can be divided into formal and substantive. Formal models emphasize the nature of the relationship between HRM and strategy without discussing the content of either one. Substantive elaborations delineate the content of specific firm strategies and the corresponding personnel systems.

Formal elaborations

Surveys show that practitioners believe in the benefits of linking strategy and HRM (Burack, 1986; Devanna *et al.*, 1982; Mills, 1985). These surveys, however, note little progress in integrating strategy and HRM.

Failure to account for varying degrees of integration may explain the contradiction if linking strategy and HRM is understood as an evolutionary task in several phases (Baird and Meshoulam, 1988).

Golden and Ramanujam (1985) distinguish four integration stages. A mere administrative linkage between strategy and HRM characterizes personnel departments exclusively engaged in day-to-day administrative concerns, where employees are not seen as a key factor for business success and can be readily found in abundant supply in the labor market. One-way linkages characterize HRM systems aimed at implementing strategy, still in a rather reactive role. Two-way linkages respond to reciprocal and interdependent, though highly formalized, relationships between strategy and HRM, with employees being seen as key elements for the competitiveness of the firm. Finally, integrative linkages denote the richest formal and informal interplay between strategy and HRM, with HRM concerns impacting the organization over the long run and expanding the expertise of the firm to new areas, like managing change and developing people. In a word, different phases pave the way towards a fully strategic HRM.

The evolution of strategic HRM is also presented in four phases – development, initial link, developed link, maximization – by Butler and colleagues (1991). Similarly, the relationship between strategy and HRM has been explained (Smith *et al.,* 1992) in terms of a continuum between the isolation of an HRM function that becomes "strategic" on its own, and the consideration of HRM as an afterthought to business strategy, with a midpoint equivalent to Golden and Ramanujam's integrative stage. Another evolutionary model by Baird and Meshoulam (1988) is based on linking HRM systems to strategy on a stage-by-stage basis, closely following the organizational life cycle. An initiation stage focuses on recruitment and compensation. Functional growth triggers a strategic approach to training. Controlled growth adds strategic HRM considerations on productivity and cost effectiveness. As the organization matures, a complete strategic integration within HRM practices and with the strategy can be achieved.

Snow and Snell (1993) talk about three formal strategic HRM models. In the first one, organizations seek policies aimed at matching jobs and employees (Chatman, 1989; O'Reilly *et al.,* 1991). The second model, matching individuals and the organization as a whole (Wanous, 1992), focuses on strategy implementation. The third model emphasizes obtaining a diverse pool of individual capabilities to reduce present and future constraints in strategic formulation and implementation processes.

Examination of the models in Table 3.2 reveals a fundamental difference involving Snow and Snell's, since these authors do not think of strategic HRM in terms of stages in a continuum, but of more stable configurations specially suited for different environments: unpredictable environments would suggest a high level of integration between strategy and HRM, whereas environmental stability would only require matching jobs and individuals.

Table 3.2   System-based models: summary of formal elaborations

Author(s)	Nature of model	Strategy–HRM stages/states
Golden & Ramanujam (1985)	Continuous stages	Administrative linkage One-way linkage Two-way linkage Integrative linkage
Baird & Meshoulam (1988)	Continuous stages	Initiation Functional growth Controlled growth Functional integration Strategic integration
Butler, Ferris, & Napier (1991)	Continuous stages	Development phase Initial link phase Developed link phase Maximization phase
Smith, Borwoski, & Davis (1992)	Continuous stages	HRM afterthought Integration HRM isolation
Snow & Snell (1993)	Discrete states	Job–individual match Strategy implementation Strategy formulation

The effect of environmental uncertainty on HRM strategy is also noted by those who recognize the need to be prepared for capabilities, styles, and managerial ideologies that the organization will require in the future (Baird, 1992; Miles and Creed, 1995).

Formal models of strategic HRM also need to consider the causes behind different degrees of integration. This is important for practical purposes, since it may help improve the integration process. Relating his experience at General Electric, retired chairman and chief executive officer (CEO) Jones signaled the lack of training in strategic planning by human resource (HR) managers as a fundamental barrier to linking strategy and HRM (Fombrun, 1982). Some other related tendencies in the evolution of personnel departments may explain the lack of progress that, we have seen, surveys report: line managers have tended to overdelegate their human resource responsibilities to personnel staffers (Angle *et al.*, 1985), HR managers have lacked knowledge and awareness of the strategic process, its meaning and requirements (Walker, 1982), personnel managers have been "all too happy to relieve the general manager from the burden of people management" (Angle *et al.*, 1985: 52), and even when HR specialists do not lack planning skills they still may have isolated the strategic design of the human resource practices from the overall strategy process (Smith *et al.*, 1992).

Substantive elaborations

Formal elaborations of the relationship between strategy and HRM need to be complemented with considerations of the meaning of strategy and HRM as they relate to each other (see Table 3.3 for a summary of substantive models). In this way, we may further advance our knowledge of factors accounting for different stages or states of strategic integration, while illuminating zones where formulation and implementation overlap.

A few life-cycle models have been used to define the relationship between stages through which organizations go and corresponding HRM practices (Smith, 1982). However, most substantive models begin by either defining business (or corporate) level typologies of firm strategy and end up delineating the content of HRM systems that correspond to the strategy, or using already defined clusters of HRM practices to which business strategies are then matched. The difference between these alternatives is that the "first strategy, then HRM" mode usually reflects the typical "strategy formulation–HRM implementation" sequence, whereas the "first HRM clusters, then strategy" mode is simply benefiting from already developed theoretical elaborations of how HRM practices should and/or do cluster, without taking a stance on whether strategy or HRM takes precedence.

Miles and Snow (1978) and Porter (1980, 1985) have presented two of the most widely used typologies of business strategy. Miles and Snow's focus on both the internal and external organizational contexts gave their model a natural extension to the design of the HRM systems deemed more adequate for each strategic type (Miles and Snow, 1984).

In that way, a defender trying "to seal off a portion of the total market in order to create a stable domain" (Miles *et al.,* 1978: 550) develops "building" human resource strategies based on recruitment and selection at low entry levels, development and promotion from within, process-centered appraisal, and compensation determined by internal equity and hierarchical standards. A prospector concentrates on "finding and exploiting new product and market development ... maintaining a reputation as an innovator" (Miles *et al.,* 1978: 551) by "acquiring" human resources through recruitment and selection at all levels, limited and highly specialized training and development programs, results-oriented appraisal, and compensation inspired by standards of external competitiveness. Between defenders and prospectors, analyzers "allocate" human resources, emphasizing both "make" and "buy" approaches. A related model is used by Sonnenfeld and Peiperl (1988), who develop a typology of career systems along "supply flow" and "assignment flow" criteria which combine in four metaphorical organizational forms fortress, baseball team, club, academy – explicitly linked to the Miles and Snow typology – reactors, prospectors, defenders, and analyzers, respectively.

Table 3.3   System-based models: summary of substantive elaborations

Author(s)	Strategy model	Staffing	Appraisal	Rewards
Fisher (1989)	Life cycle & (Miles & Snow 1978, & Porter 1980):			
	Growth	External	Results	Highly variable
	Mature	Internal	Process	Highly fixed
Lengnick-Hall & Lengnick-Hall (1988, 1990)	Corporate growth & organizational readiness:			
	Development	High growth & low readiness		
	Expansion	High growth & high readiness		
	Productivity	Low growth & high readiness		
	Redirection	Low growth & low readiness		
Miles & Snow (1984)	Miles & Snow (1978):			
	Defender	Internal	Process focus	Internal equity
	Prospector	External	Results focus	Competitiveness
	Analyzer	Mixed	Mixed	Mixed
Ostrow (1992)	Porter (1980, 1985):			
	Low cost	Internal	Results	Below market
	Differentiation	External	Process	Above market
Purcell (1989)	BCG matrix:			
	Star	Mixed	Mixed	Competitiveness
	Cash cow	Internal	Minimal	Above market
	Dog	Minimal	Intensive	Below market
	Wild cat	Multi-level	Intensive	Competitiveness
Schuler (1988)	Gerstein & Reisman (1983):			
	Entrepreneurial	External	Results	Competitiveness
	Dynamic growth	External	Mixed	Mixed
	Extract profit	Internal	Results	Internal equity
	Liquidation	Minimal	Process	Below market
	Turnaround	Mixed	Results	Mixed
Schuler & Jackson (1987a)	Porter (1980, 1985):			
	Low cost	Efficiency	Short-term	Minimal
	Differentiation	Multi-level	Long-term	Competitiveness
	Focus	Mixed	Mixed	Mixed
Sivasubramaniam Inducement	Dyer & Holder (1988) & Miles & Snow (1978):			
	Internal	Process focus	Internal equity	
	Involvement	External	Results focus	Competitiveness
	Investment	Mixed	Mixed	Mixed
Smith (1982)	Life cycle:			
	Embryonic	Extensive		Highly variable
	High growth	Mixed		Highly variable
	Mature	Internal		Mostly variable
	Aging	Minimal		Highly fixed
Sonnenfeld & Peiperl (1988)	Sonnenfeld & Peiperl (Miles & Snow, 1978):			
	Fortress-reactor	Misfit	Misfit	Misfit
	Baseball-prospector	External	Results focus	Competitiveness
	Club-defender	Internal	Process focus	Internal equity
	Academy-analyzer	Mixed	Mixed	Mixed
Wright & Snell (1991)	Miles & Snow (1978):			
	Defender	Behavior control-coordin.; competence use		
	Prospector	Behav. coordinat.; compet. acquisit-displac.		
	Analyzer	Mixed behavior & competence		

Porter's model (1980, 1985), basically centered around the external competitive analysis of the firm, has also been used for linking strategy and HRM (Ostrow, 1992; Schuler and Jackson, 1987b). Cost leaders, achieving advantage through low cost, tend to use fixed job descriptions within narrowly defined career paths, encouraging efficiency, short-term and results-oriented appraisal, minimal training and development, and reduced wages. Differentiators who create unique products in their industries recruit and select at different levels, appraise employees by using quality and behavioral criteria, provide extensive training and development, and high levels of compensation. Operating within narrower market niches, firms following a focus strategy finally rely on either cost leadership or differentiation.

Fisher (1989) argued that strategy-based HRM contingency approaches – like those advanced by life cycle views, Miles and Snow, and Porter – converge along two poles: growth, prospector, high technology and entrepreneurial strategies on the one hand, and mature, defender, cost minimizing strategies on the other. Wright and Snell (1991) also pointed at integrating personnel practices with different typologies of strategy–HRM linkages by using the concepts of competence acquisition, utilization, retention, and displacement along with those of behavior modification and control.

Dyer and Holder (1988) delineated basic HRM systems which could then be matched to the Miles and Snow – or, arguably, Porter – typology (Sivasubramaniam, 1993), resulting in a parallel between strategies of human resource inducement and defenders, human resource involvement and prospectors, and human resource investment and analyzers. Walton's (1985) strategies of employee control and commitment relate to, respectively, inducement and involvement HRM strategies. Similarly, Ricart and Portales (Chapter 2 in this volume) develop the rationale for a co-variation of employment contracts and a business strategy typology that accounts for new organizational forms and innovation.

Linking corporate strategy and HRM has also received some attention. Lengnick-Hall and Lengnick-Hall (1988, 1990) synthesize corporate and HRM strategies in four types – development, expansion, productivity, redirection – along growth expectation criteria related to organizational goals and organizational readiness in terms of human resources availability. Schuler (1988) followed Gerstein and Reisman's (1983) corporate strategy typology – entrepreneurial, dynamic growth, extract profit, liquidation-divestiture, turnaround – in suggesting employee behaviors and personnel practices best suited to those strategies. Similarly, Purcell (1989) based his elaboration of strategic HRM practices on the corporate strategy matrix developed by the Boston Consulting Group. Finally, Caligiuri and Stroh (1995) hypothesized – and found – the link between a subset of HRM practices (recruitment, selection, and socialization) and global business strategies.

Quantitative studies testing substantive models have found results in the expected direction in six instances (Arthur, 1992; Caligiuri and Stroh 1995; Martell, 1989; Portales, Chapter 6 in this book; Schuler and Jackson, 1987b; Sivasubramanian, 1993) and mixed results in still another one (Buller and Napier, 1993). Qualitative research also supports substantive models (Beattie and Tampoe, 1991; Cappelli and Crocker-Hefter, 1996; Friedmanm *et al.*, 1984; Galbraith, 1984; Hendry *et al.*, 1995; Lundberg, 1985; Mirvis, 1985).

Nevertheless, substantive elaborations of the relationship between strategy and HRM are not without problems. Those based on organizational life cycle models – either at the corporate or business unit level – are subject to the same criticisms we saw when dealing with individual-based models using life cycle approaches. Models relying on business unit generic strategy typologies have been criticized on several grounds:

1. Generic strategies may become traps that, while initially leading to success, will later cause managerial, cultural, structural, and process factors to introduce too much simplicity and rigidity (Miller, 1992, 1993).
2. Second and similarly, it seems that organizations cannot keep relying on single sources of advantage: globalization increasingly demands being simultaneously excellent at apparently contradictory competencies like flexibility, efficiency, innovation, quality and cost (Hill, 1988; Miles and Snow, 1994; Snell *et al.*, 1996; Snow *et al.*, 1992; Snow and Ottensmeyer, 1990) or, as Dean and Susman put it, "pursuing more than one generic strategy without getting 'stuck in the middle'" (1989: 312).
3. While a case can be made on the commensurability of different generic strategies operating at the same organizational unit level (Fisher, 1989; Segev, 1989; Snow and Ottensmeyer, 1990), the fact remains that similar types across typologies have been linked to different and even contradictory HRM practices: performance appraisal by prospector organizations, for instance, is based on outcome or result standards (Miles and Snow, 1984), while differentiators look at the long-run behavior of their employees (Schuler and Jackson, 1987a); similarly, while mature business units mostly reward with variable packages (Smith, 1982), defenders and low cost producers emphasize fixed salaries (Fisher, 1989). For models centered on corporate level strategy, the linkages between strategy and HRM can also appear rather intractable, on the one hand, if they do not allow for specific HRM practices required by business units at different life stages or following different generic strategies. On the other hand, however, the unifying approach to HRM practices usually followed by corporate strategy models allows for easier solutions of internal equity and employee rotation and transfers across units (Fisher, 1989; Schuler and Jackson, 1989).

Another problem for most substantive elaborations is their reliance on the idea of "fit" (Cappelli and Singh, 1992). It has been shown in both organizational theory (Drazin and Van de Ven, 1985) and strategic HRM (Wright and Sherman, 1999) that fit is rarely defined in specific and consistent terms. Also, the concept of fit is generally used in a static mode that does not apply to the dynamic, flexible, changing, and ambiguous nature of the relationship between strategy and HRM (Evans, 1986; Fisher, 1989; Lengnick-Hall and Lengnick-Hall, 1988; Milkovich, 1988), which leads to the alternative of either relying on the concepts of "coherence" and "appropriateness" (Hendry and Pettigrew, 1990: 26), or "sustainable fit": complementing fit and flexibility through the incorporation of mediating variables like human capital and skills and adaptable employee behaviors (Wright and Snell, 1998: 758).

Finally, most substantive elaborations fail to point out the role of other variables mediating the relationship between strategy and HRM, particularly, the introduction of newer forms of the employment relationship. Before we go in depth with this, we will analyze the potential for reconciling the universalistic and contingency views.

3.3.3 Reconciling universalistic and contingency approaches

Despite their apparent opposition, the case can be made for the conciliation of universalistic and contingency approaches. First, both approaches could be operating at different levels. Becker and Gerhart (1996), for instance, differentiate between the "architecture" of the HRM system – at the level of which universalistic principles would apply – and the "practices" within the system wherein separate practices, contingent on firm strategy, would operate: "There may be a best HR system architecture, but whatever the bundles or configurations of policies implemented in a particular firm, the individual practices must be aligned with one another and be consistent with the HR architecture. In this sense the best practice and contingency hypotheses are not necessarily in conflict – they simply operate at different levels of an HR system" (*ibid.*: 786). As a matter of fact, Stroh and Caliguiri (1998), reflecting on their previous research, explicitly recognize the applicability of Becker and Gerhart's argument.

Second, universalistic and contingency approaches could be stressing alternative, although not incompatible, theories of firm performance. Gerhart *et al.*, for instance, make the point that "in some senses, the high potential for resource-based approaches begins where the benefits of institutional approaches end. For instance, after best practices add value to the firm . . . firms may extract additional benefits by adding complexity to the program and integrating it with other firm functions" (1996: 153, cited by Becker and Gerhart, 1996: 787).

Finally, given the reliance of most strategy–HRM matching models on a specific product market strategy or a given stage in the firm life cycle, implementation problems will loom large in corporations with multiple units, each with different strategies and going through different life cycle stages. Then, structural simplicity may be gained by introducing the same HRM system across units. Of course, when deciding on the specifics of that common system, universalistic views provide sensible packages that can be implemented across units. In some cases, firm size may thus constitute a good proxy for deciding whether to design an HRM system specifically tailored to each unit – the contingency way – or to go for a generalized, universalistic approach.

Having noted the viability of theoretical integration of universalistic and contingent approaches, it is worth restating the need for more comprehensive modeling of the strategy–HRM relationship. To do so, researchers can take advantage of elaborations that take into account the specific content of the HRM systems required by a given strategy. Also, research should further account for the behaviors, attitudes, and capabilities that organizations ask from their employees, both managerial (like individual-based models recognize) and rank-and-file (Olian and Rynes, 1984). Personnel departments also help formalize the design and implementation of strategic HRM systems, thus advancing through the integration stages and states noted by the formal elaborations of substantive models already reviewed.

Once all these streams of inquiry are integrated (which still are not), researchers need to attend to the newer, emerging forms of the employment relationship. To this we turn in the following section.

3.4 NEW EMPLOYMENT RELATIONSHIPS AND THEIR EFFECT ON THE STRATEGIC HRM SYSTEM

The concept of the employment relationship and the nature of work in the models of the strategy–HRM linkages just reviewed have changed dramatically in the late 1980s and 1990s. Because of this, the strategy–HRM relationship is becoming more complex.

We will first review the major changes affecting the employment relationship, from both the organization's and the employee's perspective. Then, we will delineate the effects of the changed employment relationship on the relationship between strategy and the system of human resource management practices, emphasizing the need for reformulating existing models. A concluding section will point at new research avenues that incorporate the new changes in the relationship between firm strategy and personnel practices:

1.   There is agreement on the increasing pace of change in what has been

variously referred to as today's "hyper-turbulent" (Meyer *et al.*, 1993), "high-velocity" (Eisenhardt, 1989), and "hyper-competitive" (D'Aveni, 1994) environments. Organizations adapting to these environments have tended to focus on the set of activities in which they can clearly outperform competitors. This tendency has led to concentration on each firm's core competencies (Hamel and Prahalad, 1994), externalizing non-core activities through outsourcing (Quinn, 1992), and downscoping (Hoskisson and Hitt, 1994). More generally, changes are taking place at the level of the organizational structure (decentralizing, delayering and project organization), processes (investment in information technologies, horizontal and vertical communication, and new employment arrangements), and boundaries (downscoping, outsourcing, and strategic alliances) towards new forms of organizing that supplement – rather than supplant – traditional arrangements based on hierarchical structures organized along vertical lines of communication through command-and-control mechanisms (Pettigrew and Massini, Chapter 7 in this volume; Wittington *et al.*, 1999). These changes in the strategy of the firm have had their counterpart in the structuring of the employment relationship along the lines of "core" versus "periphery" employees (Belous, 1989; Davis-Blake and Uzzi, 1993; Standing, 1997). At the same time, employees who can be alternatively defined as "core" or "periphery" represent evolving roles and functions, much more varied than the types usually found in the 1970s and 1980s. Davis (1995: 124–5), for instance, has talked about the presence of "virtual employees" like temporary and contract workers in lieu of full-time employees, full-time organization employees working on temporary teams, and full-time employees from multiple organizations working on joint projects. This phenomenon parallels the development of what has recently been named "virtual strategic HRM" (Lepak and Snell, 1998). However, despite the introduction of some pioneer work on the HRM implications of the new forms of organizing (Quintanilla and Sánchez-Runde, in press), we are far away from fully understanding these trends.

2.   Current personnel practices include changes in the employment relationship, which have been formulated along the concept of "new employment contracts" (Mirvis and Hall, 1996; Rousseau, 1995; Sparrow and Cooper, 1998; Sparrow, Chapter 9 in this volume). Several authors (Altman and Post, 1996; Kissler, 1994; Mills, 1996) describe the new employment patterns in the following terms: rejection of employment security, introduction of riskier labor market arrangements leading to "employment exchanges" rather than "employment relationships", shorter-term perspectives of the attachment between employers and employees, increased "job hopping" across employers, and new concepts of employee and

employer loyalty encompassing transitory relationships (Heckscher, 1995). The new approach to the employment relationship reflects firms' attempts at having it both ways: commitment from the "core", and flexibility through the "periphery" (Handy, 1994: 69–73)

3. Changes are also taking place in terms of the organization and nature of work. Firms are blurring the boundaries between jobs (Bridges, 1994) and introducing group forms of work organization (Davis, 1995). In parallel, decisions that used to be made from individual positions become the responsibility of teams working across distant locations and functions (Manz and Sims, 1995; Sánchez-Runde and Quintanilla, in press).

4. Some of the structural innovations of the 1990s, like the move towards outsourcing non-core capabilities, have had tremendous implications in terms of the design and implementation of HRM practices. This, of course, has the potential for affecting the relationship between outsourced practices and firm strategy. In those circumstances, developing systemic HRM approaches will require the consideration of relationships across practices involving different organizations. The inclusion of additional actors to the relationship between firm strategy and HRM practices makes the process much more complex and prone to mismatch. The involvement of other organizations is also necessary whenever different firms participate in joint ventures and alliances (also a characteristic trend of the 1990s), with the added challenges of reconciling separate organizational strategies and personnel practices.

How do these changes affect our understanding of the relationship between strategy and HRM practices? How do they relate to the existing models of that relationship?

First, the differentiation of core and periphery employees has strong implications for current models of the strategy–HRM relationship. Universalistic approaches have kept in mind a unified set of employees: those who would be included under the "core" label. It is clear that the typical set of best practices applies only to core employees, specially with regard to practices like employment security or high investment in training and development. Therefore, effort needs to be put into designing an equivalent set of practices for periphery employees. Also, it is not clear that all groupings of core employees may require the same set of best practices. Dunlop (1994), for instance, protested against the fiction of considering all internal labor market (ILM) systems as equivalent, and he distinguished at least eight different sets of employees within organizations (small companies, participants in worker pools, owner-operators, civil service, multitier ILM, short-tier ILM, clerical-oriented organizations, technical and professional amalgams). Similarly, we have seen that individual-based models emphasize finding the personnel who better match the current firm's strategy, which may not work in times of high rates of organizational change and environmental unstability. Further, content-based models need to address the issue of defining sets of practices that match not only the strategy of the company, but the characteristics of different groups of employees as well be they core or periphery. In this line, some authors (Hakim, 1990) caution that most segmentations of periphery employees follow generic flexibility logics that remain unrelated to specific firm strategies. This issue is further complicated by the possibility of different firms, with different strategies, collaborating in joint ventures and alliances (Evans and Doz, 1992; Lorange, 1986).

Second, recent developments in the relationship between the organization and the employees also affect traditional views of the strategy–HRM linkages. Universalistic models were premised on long-term employment relationships that often are not within the content of current psychological contracts (Kochan, 1999). Therefore, models suggesting best practices need to take account of new concepts of loyalty and commitment (Heckscher, 1995) and substitute shorter-term relationships for traditional forms of attachment based on lifelong organizational careers and employment security. At the same time, individual-based models need to adapt to the changed employment relationship. This means that these models will need to de-emphasize employment development as a mechanism for matching managers and firm strategy due to the shorter-term employee–organization attachments, and introduce more sophisticated forms of succession planning (an area virtually ignored by current individual-based models). Finally, substantive models of strategy and HRM will need to encompass within their configurations of HRM practices new ways of attracting and retaining employees, along the lines suggested by the latest literature as exemplified by Cappelli (1999, and Chapter 5 in this volume).

Third, regarding the new forms of work organization and the changing nature of work, it is true that universalistic models are extremely well prepared to confront the new challenges in that they have pioneered innovative work practices like self-directed work teams, job rotation, problem-solving groups and quality circles, and job re-design (Arthur, 1994; Huselid, 1995; Kochan and Osterman, 1994; MacDuffie, 1995). Of course, those new ways of arranging work demand new personal knowledge, skills, and abilities that need to be taken into account by individual-based models anchored in traditional forms of work organization based on clear job demarcations and individual, rather than team approaches. Similarly, substantive models of the relationship between strategy and HRM need to redefine the contingencies and contexts within which those new forms of work organization will provide close matches to the firms' strategies, a task that is still to be accomplished.

Finally, the new ways of organizing the design and implementation of HRM practices (outsourcing, joint ventures and alliances) have major effects on the evolution of HRM departments that need to provide systemic sets of practices, while responsibility over some of them will have been transferred to other organizations (Sánchez-Runde, 1998).

3.6 WHERE SHOULD WE GO FROM HERE? A RESEARCH AGENDA

Since its begining in the early 1980s, strategic HRM has become the major paradigm in the HRM field (Dyer and Reeves, 1995). Even when both universalistic and contingent approaches have mapped the basic elements of the strategy–HRM relationship, virtually all models have so far left out critical variables that are likely to impact that relationship. Factors internal to the organization, like its culture or political processes, as well as external ones, like the institutional and ecological environments of the firm, have been left out of the picture. We present them in turn.

Ecological perspectives stress the effect of population and community level dynamics on organizational life. For our purposes, labor market characteristics – such as the availability of people with the required skills – have been signaled as the major ecological factor affecting the relationship between strategy and HRM (Buller, 1988; Golden and Ramanujam, 1985; Mirvis, 1985) and, therefore, need to be included in further elaborations of that relationship.

Organization theory emphasizes strategy as an adaptive response to changing environmental circumstances to the point of virtually ignoring "the societal forces which create pressures and opportunities for change" (Miles and Creed, 1995: 342). The effect of strategic choice, however, is also moderated by the institutional environment of the firm. Institutional theories explain isomorphic tendencies among organizations by noting that organizations in the same environment tend to resemble one another in the way they compete for political power and social legitimacy (Meyer and Scott, 1983). Therefore, as Boxall (1999) explains, researchers in the strategic HRM paradigm need to extend their agendas so as to include industry, institutions, and regulatory variables.

Meyer and Rowan (1977) noted that institutional pressures often crystallize in organizational myths that, ceremonially adopted, may conflict with rational-efficient processes. Since, Meyer and Rowan argue, solving that conflict may ask for decoupling subunits and activities, a close fit between strategy and HRM, or among HRM practices, may not be the best way for organizations "to maintain standardized, legitimating, formal structures while their activities vary in response to practical considerations" (1977: 357).

DiMaggio and Powell (1983) distinguish three types of isomorphic processes: coercive, mimetic and normative. Relevant to strategy and HRM, legal and quasi-legal mandates from the state and agencies constitute a clear source of coercive pressure (Dobbin *et al.*, 1993; Sutton *et al.*, 1994). Mimetic processes specially relevant to the study of strategic HRM include rotation of employees among organizations, benchmarking of "best HRM practices" (Lake and Ulrich, 1992; Pfeffer, 1994), and diffusion of employment practices through consulting firms and HRM and industrial relations professional associations (Scott and Meyer, 1991). Normative isomorphic factors can be traced to the recruitment and selection of personnel from a few, homogeneous recruitment pools, the use of industry generic – not firm specific – socialization processes, and the professionalization of HRM departments (Baron *et al.*, 1986; Jacoby, 1984).

Organizational culture also needs to enter the strategy–HRM equation. Martin (1992) has shown that alternative metatheoretical perspectives on culture – integration, differentiation, fragmentation – require previous harmonization to fully understand the concept of culture, and she adds that organizational culture or cultures respond to issues posed by three dimensions: manifestations of meaning (consistency, inconsistency, or complexity), degree and level of consensus (organization-wide, subcultural, multiplicity of views), and orientation towards ambiguity (excluding it, channeling it, focusing on it). Therefore, how strategy and HRM practices relate to one another will be affected by, and will affect, how organizations respond to those three dimensions by, respectively, managing three things: the degree of consistency and complexity between and within strategy and HRM practices, the interaction of diverse units and people in charge of formulating and implementing a strategic approach to HRM, and the tighter or looser fit between strategy and HRM. Indeed, authors agree on the importance of organizational culture to understand the relationship between strategy and HRM practices (Buller, 1988; Cummings, 1984; Lundberg, 1985; Mirvis, 1985). Looking at the fundamental issues around the dimensions of culture, it is then clear why changing the organizational response to the linkages between strategy and HRM is not an easy task: culture becomes a powerful source of inertia both preventing and sustaining functional and dysfunctional strategic HRM change (Sánchez-Runde and Quintanilla, in press).

Virtually nobody disagrees that strategy formulation and implementation need to consider organizational politics and power. It is then amazing that most studies of strategic HRM do not isolate how organizational politics shape and constrain strategy and HRM (Purcell, 1999), since political activity is specially important when decisions are made at top organizational levels under conditions of interdependence among units with scarce resources (Pfeffer and Salancik, 1978; Pfeffer, 1992). Further, political dynamics are specially influential when decision processes deal with alternatives close to the goals of different constituencies and coalitions (Cyert and March, 1963; Pettigrew, 1973), which is clearly the case with strategic HRM issues over which employees, managers, and owners may hold different, if not contradictory, views. In this line, Kochan (1999) reminds strategic HRM researchers of defining dependent variables beside firm performance to address business and social challenges presented by different stakeholders.

Since higher integration between strategy and HRM also reflects the influence of personnel staff on the management of the firm, assessing the amount and use of political power in HRM departments will help explain the relationship between strategy and HRM.

Given that power does not only rest on formal structures and relationships (Barnard, 1938), we also need to look at how informal sources of power, materialized in symbolic action, rituals and ceremonies, language, and reputation, are used to achieve the objectives of those in charge of modeling the linkages between strategy and HRM (Jacoby, 1985).

In sum, by embedding the strategy–HRM relationship in ecological, institutional, political, and cultural variables, we can expect both to gain a better understanding of that relationship, thus making it more relevant for managerial practice (Snell *et al.*, 1996: 82). This kind of research, which will have to encompass the new forms of employment relationship reviewed in the previous section, is more complex but it will provide a more accurate portrait of the challenges that current organizations confront.

We have seen that research has already begun to demonstrate the effects of closely aligning strategy and HRM practices. However, very little is yet known on the specific mechanisms linking strategic HRM and performance (Dyer and Reeves, 1995; Paauwe and Richardson, 1997). To fill this gap, construct definition and measurement of performance needs to be improved along the lines of capturing its multifaceted dimensionality, divergent stakeholder criteria, and temporal dynamics (Rogers and Wright, 1998). Similarly, measurement improvements are needed to address random and systematic error in HRM and covariate measures (Gerhart, 1999), within a framework that connects metrics theory and strategic HRM theory (Boudreau and Ramstad, 1999). Only after those improvements have been accomplished – and with the use of longitudinal designs and/or time series studies (Huselid and Becker, 1996) – will researchers be able to analyze the "direction of causality" issue, solving the dilemma of whether it is only high performing companies that can afford the resources necessary for designing and implementing strategic HRM systems in the first place, or whether it is by first closely aligning strategy and HRM that firms actually improve performance, or both (Arthur, 1994: 684; Delery and Doty, 1996: 830).

Finally, future research will also have to be carried out in different national environments to make sure that findings are robust across countries and cultures. In this sense, it is not enough merely to introduce in our models the new international strategic HRM research issues – like the management of expatriates (Aycan, 1997) or the mutual influence of country of origin and country of operations in the design and implementation of strategic HRM within multinationals (Ferner and Quintanilla, 1998). Valuable as this is, we also need to test the transferability of strategic HRM models and practices across environments embedded with contrasting sets of norms and values (Dowling *et al.,* 1994). Multidiscipline and multicultural collaboration is stressed by De Cieri and Dowling (1999) in order to integrate contemporary organization theory into more elaborate models of international strategic HRM. Without that collaboration, for instance, we will not be able to understand phenomena like the effects of the internationalization and globalization of the economy on the changing relationship between strategy and HRM practices in Japan (Morishima, 1999), or the recent developments in the co-evolution of HRM systems and organizational strategy in Chinese state enterprises (Wang and Mobley, 1999).

At the end of the day, improvements in theory and research will be of little use if strategic HRM does not break from its strongly parochial, US centric heritage (Brewster, 1999), towards encompassing the challenges and promises of increasingly international and globalized environments.

REFERENCES

Altman, B. W. and Post, J. E. (1996). Beyond the "social contract": An analysis of the executive view at twenty-five large companies. In D. T. Hall (ed.), *The Career is Dead – Long Live the Career: A relational approach to careers,* pp. 46–71. San Francisco: Jossey-Bass.

Angle, H. L., Manz, C. C. and Van de Ven, A. H. (1985). Integrating human resource management and corporate strategy: A preview of the 3M story. *Human Resource Management,* 24: 51–68.

Arthur, J. B. (1992). The link between business strategy and industrial relations systems in American steel minimills. *Industrial and Labor Relations Review,* 45: 488–506.

Arthur, J. B. (1994). Effects of human resource systems on manufacturing performance and turnover. *Academy of Management Journal,* 37: 67–87.

Ashmos, D. P. and Huber, G. P. (1987). The systems paradigm in organization theory: correcting the record and suggesting the future. *Academy of Management Review,* 12: 607–21.

Aycan, Z. (ed.) (1997). *Expatriate Management: Theory and research.* Greenwich, CT: JAI Press.

Baird, L. S. (1992). *Managing Human Resources: Integrating people and business strategy.* Homewood, IL: Irwin.

Baird, L. S. and Meshoulam, I. (1988). Managing the two fits of strategic human resource management. *Academy of Management Review,* 13: 116–28.

Barnard, C. I. (1938). *The Functions of the Executive.* Cambridge, MA: Harvard University Press.

Baron, J. N., Dobbin, F. R. and Jennings, P. D. (1986). War and peace: the evolution of modern personnel administration in U.S. industry. *American Journal of Sociology,* 92: 350–83.

Beattie, D. F. and Tampoe, F. M. K. (1991). Human resource planning for ICL. In S. Rothwell (ed.), *Strategic Planning for Human Resources,* pp. 37–48. Oxford: Pergamon.

Becker, B. and Gerhart, B. (1996). The impact of human resource management on organizational performance: progress and prospects. *Academy of Management Journal,* 39: 779–801.

Beer, M., Spector, B., Lawrence, P. R., Mills, D. Q. and Walton, R. E. (1984). *Managing Human Assets.* New York: Free Press.

Belous, R. S. (1989). How human resource systems adjusts to the shift toward contingent workers. *Monthly Labor Review,* 112 (3): 7–12.

Boudreau, J. W. and Ramstad, P. M. (1999). Human resource metrics: can measures be strategic? In P. M. Wright, L. D. Dyer, J. W. Boudreau and G. T. Milkovich (eds), *Research in Personnel and Human Resource Management,* Supplement 4: 75–98. Stanford, CT: JAI Press.

Boulding, K. E. (1956). General systems theory: the skeleton of science. *Management Science,* 2: 197–208.

Boxall, P. F. (1999). Human resource strategy and industry-based competition: a conceptual framework and agenda for theoretical development. In P. M. Wright, L. D. Dyer, J. W. Boudreau and G. T. Milkovich (eds), *Research in Personnel and Human Resource Management,* Supplement 4: 259–81. Stanford, CT: JAI Press.

Brewster, C. (1999). Different paradigms in strategic HRM: questions raised by comparative research. In P. M. Wright, L. D. Dyer, J. W. Boudreau and G. T. Milkovich (eds), *Research in Personnel and Human Resource Management,* Supplement 4: 213–38. Stanford, CT: JAI Press.

Bridges, W. (1994). *Job-shift: How to prosper in a workplace without jobs.* Reading, MA: Addison-Wesley.

Buller, P. F. (1988). Successful partnerships: HR and strategic planning at eight top firms. *Organizational Dynamics,* 17: 27–43.

Buller, P. F. and Napier, N. K. (1993). Strategy and human resource management integration in fast growth vs. other mid-sized firms. *British Journal of Management,* 4: 77–90.

Burack, E. H. (1986). Corporate business and human resources planning practices: strategic issues and concerns. *Organizational Dynamics,* 15: 73–87.

Butler, J. E., Ferris, G. R. and Napier, N. K. (1991). *Strategic Human Resources Management.* Cincinnati, OH: South-Western.

Caligiuri, P. M. and Stroh, L. K. (1995). Multinational corporation management strategies and international human resource practices: bringing international HR to the bottom line. *International Journal of Human Resource Management,* 6: 494–507.

Cappelli, P. (1999). *The New Deal at Work.* Boston, MA: Harvard Business School Press.

Cappelli, P. and Crocker-Hefter, A. (1996). Distinctive human resources are firm's core competencies. *Organizational Dynamics,* 24: 7–22.

Cappelli, P. and Singh, H. (1992). Integrating strategic human resources and strategic management. In D. Lewin, O. S. Mitchell and P. D. Sherer (eds), *Research Frontiers in Industrial Relations and Human Resources* pp. 165–92. Madison, WI: Industrial Relations Research Association.

Chatman, J. A. (1989). Improving interactional organizational research: a model of person–organization fit. *Academy of Management Review,* 14: 333–49.

Child, J. (1972). Organizational structure, environment and performance. *Sociology,* 6: 1–22.

Crandall, R. E. (1987). Company life cycles: the effects of growth on structure and personnel. *Personnel,* 64: 28–36.

Cummings, L. L. (1984). Compensation, culture, and motivation: a systems perspective. *Organizational Dynamics,* 12: 33–44.

Cyert, R. M. and March, J. G. (1963). *A Behavioral Theory of the Firm.* Englewood Cliffs, NJ: Prentice-Hall.

D'Aveni, R. A. (1994). *Hypercompetition: Managing the dynamics of strategic maneuvering.* New York: Free Press.

Davis, D. D. (1995). Form, function, and strategy in boundaryless organizations. In A. Howard (ed.), *The Changing Nature of Work,* pp. 112–38. San Francisco: Jossey–Bass.

Davis-Blake, A. and Uzzi, B. (1993). Employment externalization: the case of temporary workers and independent contractors. *Administrative Science Quarterly,* 38: 195–223.

Dean, J. W. and Susman, G. I. (1989). Strategic responses to global competition: advanced technology, organization design, and human resource practices. In C. C. Snow (ed.), *Strategy, Organization, and Human Resource Management,* pp. 297–331. Greenwich, CT: JAI Press.

De Cieri, H. and Dowling, P. J. (1999). Strategic human resource management in multinational entreprises: theoretical and empirical developments. In P. M. Wright, L. D. Dyer, J. W. Boudreau and G. T. Milkovich (eds), *Research in Personnel and Human Resource Management,* Supplement 4: 305–27. Stanford, CT: JAI Press.

Delery, J. E. and Doty, D. H. (1996). Modes of theorizing in strategic human resource management: tests of universalistic, contingency, and configurational performance predictions. *Academy of Management Journal,* 39: 802–35.

Devanna, M. A., Fombrun, C., Tichy, N. and Warren, L. (1982). Strategic planning and human resource management. *Human Resource Management,* 2: 11–17.

DiMaggio, P. J. and Powell, W. W. (1983). The iron cage revisited: institutional isomorphism and collective rationality in organizational fields. *American Sociological Review,* 48: 147–60.

Dobbin, F., Sutton, J. R., Meyer, J. W. and Scott, W. R. (1993). Equal opportunity law and the construction of internal labor markets. *American Journal of Sociology,* 99: 396–427.

Dowling, P. J., Schuler, R. S. and Welch, D. E. (1994). *International Dimensions of Human Resource Management.* Belmont, CA: Wadsworth.

Drazin, R. and Van de Ven, A. H. (1985). Alternative forms of fit in contingency theory. *Administrative Science Quarterly,* 30: 514–39.

Dunlop, J. T. (1958). *Industrial Relations Systems.* New York: Holt, Rinehart and Winston.

Dunlop, J. T. (1994). Organizations and human resources: internal and external markets. In C. Kerr and P. D. Staudohar (eds), *Labor Economics and Industrial Relations,* pp. 375–400. Cambridge, MA: Harvard University Press.

Dunlop, J. T. and Weil, D. (1996). Diffusion and performance of modular production in the U.S. apparel industry. *Industrial Relations,* 35: 334–55.

Dyer, L. and Holder, G. W. (1988). A strategic perspective of human resource management. In L. Dyer (ed.), *Human Resource Management: Evolving roles and responsibilities,* pp. 1–46. Washington, D.C.: ASPA-BNA.

Dyer, L., and Reeves, T. (1995). Human resource strategies and firm performance: what do we know and where do we need to go? *International Journal of Human Resource Management,* 36: 656–70.

Eisenhardt, K. M. (1989). Making fast strategic decisions in high-velocity environments. *Academy of Management Journal,* 32: 543–76.

Evans, P. A. L. (1986). The strategic outcomes of human resource management. *Human Resource Management,* 25: 149–67.

Evans, P. A. L. and Doz, Y. (1992). Dualities: a paradigm for human resource and organizational development in complex multinationals. In V. Pucik, N. M. Tichy and C. K. Barnett (eds), *Globalizing Management: Creating and Leading the Competitive Organization,* pp. 85–106. New York: John Wiley.

Ferner, A. and Quintanilla, J. (1998). Multinationals, national business systems, and HRM: the enduring influence of national identity or a process of "Anglo-Saxonization". *International Journal of Human Resource Management,* 9: 710–31.

Fisher, C. D. (1989). Current and recurrent challenges in HRM. *Journal of Management,* 15: 157–80.

Fombrun, C. J. (1982). Conversation with Reginald H. Jones and Frank Doyle. *Organizational Dynamics,* 10: 42–63.

Friedman, S. D., Tichy, N. M. and Ulrich, D. O. (1984). *Strategic Human Resource Management at Honeywell.* In C. J. Fombrun, N. M. Tichy and M. A. Devanna (eds), *Strategic Human Resource Management* pp. 249–70. New York: John Wiley.

Galbraith, J. R. (1984). Human resource policies for the innovating organization. In C. J. Fombrun, N. M. Tichy and M. A. Devanna (eds), *Strategic Human Resource Management,* pp. 319–41. New York: John Wiley.

Gerhart, B. (1999). Human resource management and firm performance: measurement issues and their effect on causal and policy inferences. In P. M. Wright, L. D. Dyer, J. W. Boudreau and G. T. Milkovich (eds), *Research in Personnel and Human Resource Management,* Supplement 4: 31–51. Stanford, CT: JAI Press.

Gerstein, M. and Reisman, H. (1983). Strategic selection: matching executives to business conditions. *Sloan Management Review,* 24: 33–49.

Golden, K. A. and Ramanujam, V. (1985). Between a dream and a nightmare: on the integration of the human resource management and strategic business planning processes. *Human Resource Management,* 24: 429–52.

Gupta, A. K. (1986). Matching managers to strategies: point and counterpoint. *Human Resource Management,* 25: 215–34.

Gupta, A. K. and Govindarajan, V. (1984). Business unit strategy, managerial characteristics, and business unit effectiveness at strategy implementation. *Academy of Management Journal,* 27: 25–41.

Hakim, C. (1990). Core and periphery workers in employers' workforce strategies: evidence from the 1987 ELUS survey. *Work, Employment, and Society,* 5: 101–17.

Hamel, G. and Prahalad, C. K. (1994). *Competing for the Future.* Boston, MA: Harvard Business School Press.

Handy, C. (1994). *The Age of Paradox.* Boston, MA: Harvard Business School Press.

Hannan, M. T. and Freeman, J. (1989). *Organizational Ecology.* Cambridge, MA: Harvard University Press.

Heckscher, C. C. (1995). White-collar blues: management loyalties in an age of corporate restructuring. New York: Basic Books.

Helper, S. (1995). Human resource management practices in automobile supplier firms. Unpublished presentation to the Annual Meeting of the International Motor Vehicle Research Program, Toronto, Canada.

Hendry, C. and Pettigrew, A. (1990). Human resource management: an agenda for the 1990s. *International Journal of Human Resource Management,* 1: 17–43.

Hendry, C., Arthur, M. H. and Jones, A. M. (1995). *Strategy Through People: Adaptation and learning in the small-medium enterprise.* London: Routledge.

Herbert, T. T. and Deresky, H. (1987). Should general managers match their business strategies? *Organizational Dynamics,* 15: 40–51.

Hill, C. W. L. (1988). Differentiation versus low cost or differentiation and low cost: a contingency framework. *Academy of Management Review,* 13: 401–12.

Hoskisson, R. E. and Hitt, M. A. (1994). *Downscoping: How to tame the diversified firm.* Oxford: Oxford University Press.

Huselid, M. (1995). The impact of human resource management practices on turnover, productivity and corporate financial performance. *Academy of Management Journal,* 38: 635–72.

Huselid, M. and Becker, B. (1996). Methodological issues in cross-sectional and panel estimates of the human resource-firm performance link. *Industrial Relations,* 35: 400–22.

Ichniowsky, C. (1990). *Human Resource Management Systems and the Performance of U.S. Manufacturing Businesses.* National Bureau of Economic Research Working Paper No. 3449. Cambridge, MA: National Bureau of Economic Research.

Ichniowsky, C., Shaw, K. and Prennushi, G. (1997). The impact of human resource management practices on productivity: a study of steel finishing lines. *American Economic Review,* 87 (3): 291–313.

Jacoby, S. M. (1984). An historical perspective on internal labor markets. In W. Fogel (ed.), *Current Research in Labor Economics,* pp. 1–20. Los Angeles: University of California Press.

Jacoby, S. M. (1985). *Employing Bureaucracy: Managers, unions and the transformation of work in American industry, 1900–1945.* New York: Columbia University Press.

Katz, H. C., Kochan, T. A. and Keefe, J. H. (1987). Industrial relations and productivity in the U.S. automobile industry. *Brookings Papers on Economic Activity,* 3: 688–715.

Kerr, C., Dunlop, J. T., Harbison F. and Myers, C. A. (1960). *Industrialism and Industrial Man.* New York: Oxford University Press.

Kerr, J. L. (1982). Assigning managers on the basis of the life cycle. *Journal of Business Strategy,* 2: 58–65.

Kerr, J. L. and Jackofsky, E. F. (1989). Aligning managers with strategies: management development versus selection. *Strategic Management Journal,* 10: 157–170.

Kissler, G. D. (1994). The new employment contract. *Human Resource Management,* 33: 335–52.

Kochan, T. A. (1999). Beyond myopia: human resources and the changing social contract. In P. M. Wright, L. D. Dyer, J. W. Boudreau and G. T. Milkovich (eds), *Research in Personnel and Human Resource Management,* Supplement 4: 199–212. Stanford, CT: JAI Press.

Kochan, T. A. and Osterman, P. (1994). *The Mutual Gains Enterprise.* Boston, MA: Harvard Business School Press.

Kochan, T. A., McKersie, R. B. and Capelli, P. (1984). Strategic choice and industrial relations theory. *Industrial Relations,* 23: 16–39.

Kotter, J. P. (1982). General managers are not generalists. *Organizational Dynamics,* 10: 5–19.

Lake, D. G., and Ulrich, D. (1992). Introduction to exemplary practices, *Human Resource Management,* 31: 1–7.

Lawler, E. E. and Morhman, S. A. (1987). Quality circles: After the honeymoon. *Organizational Dynamics,* 15 (4): 42–55.

Lawler, E. E., Ledford, G. E. and Mohrman, S. A. (1989). *Employee Involvement in America.* Houston, TX: American Productivity and Quality Center Press.

Lawler, E. E., Mohrman, S. A. and Ledford, G. E. (1995). *Creating High-performance Organizations.* San Francisco: Jossey-Bass.

Lawler, J. J. (1990). *Unionization and Deunionization: Strategy, tactics, and outcomes.* Columbia, SC: University of South Carolina Press.

Lengnick-Hall, C. A. and Lengnick-Hall, M. L. (1988). Strategic human resources management: a review of the literature and a proposed typology. *Academy of Management Review,* 13: 454–70.

Lengnick-Hall, C. A. and Lengnick-Hall, M. L. (1990). *Interactive Human Resource Management and Strategic Planning.* New York: Quorum Books.

Lepak, D. P. and Snell, S. A. (1998). Virtual HR: strategic human resource management in the 21st century. *Human Resource Management Review,* 8: 215–34.

Lorange, P. (1986). Human resource management in multinational cooperative ventures. *Human Resource Management,* 25: 133–48.

Lundberg, C. C. (1985). Toward a contextual model of human resource strategy: lessons from the Reynolds Corporation. *Human Resource Management,* 24: 91–112.

MacDuffie, J. P. (1995). Human resource bundles and manufacturing performance: organizational logic and flexible production systems in the world auto industry. *Industrial and Labor Relations Review,* 48: 197–221.

Macy, B. A. and Izumi, H. (1993). Organizational change, design, and work innovation: a meta-analysis of 131 North American field studies (1961–1991). In W. A. Passmore and R. W. Woodman (eds), *Research in Organizational Change and Development,* Volume 7: 235–313. Greenwich, CT: JAI Press.

Manz, C. C. and Sims, H. P. (1995). *Business Without Bosses: How self-managing teams are building high-performing companies.* New York: John Wiley.

Martell, K. D. (1989). Aligning executive human resource management with business unit strategy: an empirical study of the Fortune 500. Unpublished doctoral dissertation, University of Maryland, College Park.

Martin, J. (1992). *Cultures in Organizations: Three perspectives.* New York: Oxford University Press.

McCormick, J. (1990). *Toshiba Consumer Products UK.* Teaching note, Ref. 5.491.069. Boston, MA: Harvard Business School.

Meyer, A. D., Goes, J. B. and Brooks, G. R. (1993). Organizations reacting to hyperturbulence. In G. Huber and W. Glick (eds), *Organizational Change and Redesign* pp. 66–111. New York: Oxford University Press.

Meyer, J. W. and Rowan, B. (1977). Institutionalized organizations: formal structure as myth and ceremony, *American Journal of Sociology,* 83: 340–63.

Meyer, J. W. and Scott, W. R. (with the assistance of B. Rowan and T. Deal) (1983). *Organizational Environments: Ritual and rationality.* Beverly Hills, CA: Sage.

Miles, R. E. and Creed, W. E. D. (1995). Organizational forms and managerial philosophies: a descriptive and analytical view. In L. L. Cummings and B. M. Staw (eds), *Research in Organizational Behavior,* Volume 17: 333–72. Greenwich, CT: JAI Press.

Miles, R. E. and Snow, C. C. (1978). *Organizational Strategy, Structure and Process.* New York: McGraw-Hill.

Miles, R. E. and Snow, C. C. (1984). Designing strategic human resource management systems. *Organizational Dynamics,* 13: 36–52.

Miles, R. E. and Snow, C. C. (1994). *Fit, Failure, and the Hall of Fame: How companies succeed or fail.* New York: Free Press.

Miles, R. E., Snow, C. C., Meyer, A. D. and Coleman, H. J. (1978). Organizational strategy, structure, and process. *Academy of Management Review,* 3: 546–62.

Milkovich, G. T. (1988). A strategic perspective on compensation management. In G. R. Ferris, and K. M. Rowland (eds), *Research in Personnel and Human Resource Management,* Volume 6: 263–88. Greenwich, CT: JAI Press.

Miller, D. (1992). The generic strategy trap. *Journal of Business Strategy,* 13: 37–41.

Miller, D. (1993). The architecture of simplicity. *Academy of Management Review,* 18: 116–38.

Mills, D. Q. (1985). Planning with people in mind. *Harvard Business Review,* 63: 97–105.

Mills, D. Q. (1996). The changing social contract in American business. *European Management Journal,* 14: 451–56.

Mirvis, P. H. (1985). Formulating and implementing human resource strategy: a model of how to do it, two examples of how it's done. *Human Resource Management,* 24: 385–412.

Mirvis, P. H. and Hall, Douglas T. (1996). New organizational forms and the new career. In D. T. Hall (ed.), *The Career is Dead – Long Live the Career: A relational approach to careers,* pp. 72–101. San Francisco: Jossey-Bass.

Morishima, M. (1999). Strategic diversification of HRM in Japan. In P. M. Wright, L. D. Dyer, J. W. Boudreau and G. T. Milkovich (eds), *Research in Personnel and Human Resource Management,* Supplement 4: 329–52. Stanford, CT: JAI Press.

Olian, J. D. and Rynes, S. L. (1984). Organizational staffing: integrating practice with strategy. *Industrial Relations,* 23: 170–83.

O'Reilly, C. A., Chatman, J. A. and Caldwell, D. F. (1991). People and organizational culture: a profile comparison approach to assessing person-organization fit. *Academy of Management Journal,* 34: 487–516.

Osterman, P. (1994). How common is workplace transformation and who adopts it?. *Industrial and Labor Relations Review,* 47: 173–87.

Ostrow, M. H. (1992). The relationship among competitive strategy, human resource management practices, and financial performance. Unpublished doctoral dissertation, University of Maryland, College Park.

Paauwe, J. and Richardson, R. (1997). Introduction to the special issue on strategic human resource management and performance. *International Journal of Human Resource Management,* 8: 257–262.

Pettigrew, A. M. (1973). *The Politics of Organizational Decision-making.* London: Tavistock.

Pfeffer. J. (1992). *Managing with Power: Politics and influence in organizations.* Boston, MA: Harvard Business School Press.

Pfeffer, J. (1994). *Competitive Advantage Through People: Unleashing the power of the work force.* Boston, MA: Harvard Business School Press.

Pfeffer, J. (1996). Why do smart organizations occasionally do dumb things? *Organizational Dynamics,* 25 (1): 33–44.

Pfeffer, J. (1998). *The Human Equation.* Boston, MA: Harvard Business School Press.

Pfeffer, J. and Salancik, G. R. (1978). *The External Control of Organizations. A resource dependence perspective.* New York: Harper and Row.

Porter, M. E. (1980). *Competitive Strategy: Techniques for analyzing industries and competitors.* New York: Free Press.

Porter, M. E. (1985). *Competitive Advantage: Creating and sustaining superior performance.* New York: Free Press.

Purcell, J. (1989). The impact of corporate strategy on human resource management. In J. Storey (ed.), *New Perspectives on Human Resource Management,* pp. 67–91. London: Routledge.

Purcell, J. (1999). Best practice and best fit: chimera or cul-de-sac? *Human Resource Management Journal,* 9 (3): 26–41.

Quinn, J. B. (1992). *Intelligent Enterprise.* New York: Free Press.

Quintanilla, J. and Sánchez-Runde, C. In press. Network governance, company culture and human resource management practices: the case of Fremap. In A. Pettigrew and

E. Fenton (eds), *Innovating Organizations*. London: Sage.

Rogers, E. W. and Wright, P. M. (1998). Measuring organizational performance in strategic human resource management: problems, prospects, and performance information markets. *Human Resource Management Review,* 8: 311–31.

Rothschild, W. E. (1993). Avoid the mismatch between strategy and strategic leaders. *Journal of Business Strategy,* 14: 37–42.

Rousseau, D. M. (1995). *Psychological Contracts in Organizations: Understanding written and unwritten agreements.* Thousand Oaks, CA: Sage.

Sánchez-Runde, C. (1998). A conceptual approach to the creation and early development of human resource management departments. Paper presented at the Annual Meeting of the Academy of Management. San Diego, CA, August 8–12.

Sánchez-Runde, C. and Quintanilla, J. In press. Initial steps in the path toward new forms of organizing: two experiences within the Group Aguas de Barcelona. In A. Pettigrew and E. Fenton (eds), *Innovating Organizations.* London: Sage.

Schuler, R. S. (1988). Human resource management choices and organizational strategy. In R. S. Schuler, S. A. Youngblood and V. L. Huber (eds), *Readings in Human Resource Management,* pp. 24–39. St. Paul, MN: West.

Schuler, R. S. and Jackson, S. E. (1987a). Linking competitive strategies with human resource management practices, *Academy of Management Executive,* 1: 207–19.

Schuler, R. S. and Jackson, S. E. (1987b). Organizational strategy and organization level as determinants of human resource management practices. *Human Resource Planning,* 10: 125–41.

Schuler, R. S. and Jackson, S. E. (1989). Determinants of human resource management priorities and industrial relations, *Industrial Relations,* 42: 157–84.

Scott, W. R. and Meyer, J. W. (1991). The rise of training programs in firms and agencies. In L. L. Cummings and B. M. Staw (eds), *Research in Organizational Behavior,* Volume 13: 297–326, Greenwich, CT: JAI Press.

Segev, E. (1989). A systematic comparative analysis and synthesis of two business-level strategic typologies. *Strategic Management Journal,* 10: 487–505.

Sivasubramaniam, N. (1993). Matching human resources and corporate strategy. Unpublished doctoral dissertation, Florida International University, Miami.

Smith, B. J., Borowski, J. W. and Davis, G. E. (1992). Human resource planning. *Human Resource Management,* 31: 81–93.

Smith, E. C. (1982). Strategic business planning and human resources: Parts I and II. *Personnel Journal,* 61: 606–10, 680–82.

Snell, S. A., Youndt, M. A. and Wright, P. M. (1996). Establishing a framework for research in strategic human resource management: merging resource theory and organizational learning. In G. R. Ferris (ed.), *Research in Personnel and Human Resources Management,* Volume 14: 61–90. Greenwich, CT: JAI Press.

Snow, C. C. and Ottensmeyer, E. J. (1990). Managing strategies and technologies. In M. W. Lawless and L. R. Gomez-Mejia (eds), *Strategic Management in High Technology Firms*, pp. 181–93. Greenwich, CT: JAI Press.

Snow, C. C. and Snell, S. A. (1993). Staffing as strategy. In N. Schmitt and W. C. Borman (eds), *Personnel Selection in Organizations,* pp. 448–78. San Francisco: Jossey-Bass.

Snow, C. C., Miles, R. E. and Coleman, H. J. (1992). Managing 21st century network organizations, *Organizational Dynamics,* 20: 5–20.

Sonnenfeld, J. A. and Peiperl, M. A. (1988). Staffing policy as a strategic response: a typology of career systems. *Academy of Management Review,* 13: 588–600.

Sparrow, P. and Cooper, C. L. (1998). New organizational forms: the strategic relevance of future psychological contract scenarios. *Canadian Journal of Administrative Sciences,* 15 (4): 356–71.

Standing, G. (1997). Globalization, labour flexibility, and insecurity: the era of market regulation. *European Journal of Industrial Relations,* 3 (1): 7–37.

Stroh, L. K. and Caligiuri, P. M. (1998). Strategic HR: A new source for competitive advantage in the global arena. *International Journal of Human Resource Management,* 9: 1–17

Sutton, J. R., Dobbin, F., Meyer, J. W. and Scott, W. R. (1994). The legalization of the workplace, *American Journal of Sociology,* 99: 944–71.

Szilagyi, A. D. and Schweiger, D. M. (1984). Matching managers to strategies: a review and suggested framework. *Academy of Management Review,* 9: 626–37.

Thomas, A. S., Litschert, R. J. and Ramaswamy, K. (1991). The performance impact of strategy-manager coalignment: an empirical examination. *Strategic Management Journal,* 12: 509–22.

Ulrich, D. (1997). *Human Resource Champions: The next agenda for adding value and delivering results.* Cambridge, MA: Harvard Business School Press.

Von Bertalanffy, L. (1972). The history and status of general systems theory. *Academy of Management Journal,* 15: 407–26.

Walker, J. W. (1982). Linking human resource planning and strategic planning. *Human Resource Planning,* 1: 1–18.

Walton, R. E. (1985). From control to commitment in the workplace. *Harvard Business Review,* 63: 77–84.

Wang, Z. M. and Mobley, W. H. (1999). Strategic human resource management for twenty-first-century China. In P. M. Wright, L. D. Dyer, J. W. Boudreau and G. T. Milkovich (eds), *Research in Personnel and Human Resource Management,* Supplement 4: 353–66. Stanford, CT: JAI Press.

Wanous, J. P. (1992). *Organizational Entry, Recruitment, Selection, Orientation, and Socialization of Newcomers.* Reading, MA: Addison-Wesley.

Weil, D. (1994). *Turning the Tide: Strategic planning for labor unions.* New York: Lexington.

Wittington, R., Pettigrew, A. M., Peck, S. I., Fenton, E. M.and Conyon, M. (1999). Change and complementarities in the new competitive landscape: a European pannel study, 1992–1996. *Organization Science,* 10 (4): forthcoming.

Wright, P. M. and McMahan, G. C. (1992). Theoretical perspectives for strategic human resource management. *Journal of Management,* 18: 295–320.

Wright, P. M. and Sherman, W. C. (1999). Failing to find fit in strategic human resource management: theoretical and empirical problems. In P. M. Wright, L. D. Dyer, J. W. Boudreau and G. T. Milkovich (eds), *Research in Personnel and Human Resource Management,* Supplement 4: 53–74. Stanford, CT: JAI Press.

Wright, P. M. and Snell, S. A. (1991). Toward an integrative view of strategic human

resource management. *Human Resource Management Review,* 1: 203–25.
Wright, P. M. and Snell, S. A. (1998). Toward a unifying theory for exploring fit and flexibility in strategic human resource management. *Academy of Management Review,* 23: 756–72.

4 Employment Security, Employability and Sustainable Competitive Advantage

Sumantra Ghoshal, Peter Moran and Christopher A. Bartlett*

4.1 INTRODUCTION

The employment relationship is undergoing fundamental change and promises of employment security, long a central feature of the modern employment relationship, are increasingly losing credibility (Cappelli, 1995). Many see this change as an inevitable response to a dilemma brought about by the increasingly dynamic competitive environments that many employers must reckon with: "dynamic environments require flexible workers, flexible workers require a stable employment relationship, but stable employment relationships may not be possible in dynamic environments" (Heath *et al.*, 1993: 89). Whatever the reason for its demise, however, companies worldwide are abandoning long-held promises and policies of employment security, with no clear alternative to replace it. In this chapter, we present a model of sustainable competitive advantage in dynamic environments that points to one way of overcoming this dilemma and provides a theoretical basis for addressing the observed changes in employment practices. In our model, rent creation replaces rent appropriation as the key source of competitive advantage and employability substitutes for employment security as the defining characteristic of the employment relationship. Such a relationship, we show, can provide for stable and adaptable employment relationships and may, therefore, be of advantage for the firm as well as for the employee.

4.2 EMPLOYMENT SECURITY, EMPLOYABILITY AND SUSTAINABLE COMPETITIVE ADVANTAGE

The rational reconstruction of society ... is now upon us in full force ... It is the task of sociologists to aid in that construction (in the design of organizations,

> institutions and social environments), to bring to it the understanding of social processes, to ensure that this reconstruction of society is not naive, but sophisticated, to ensure, one might say that it is indeed a rational reconstruction of society. (Coleman, 1992: 14)

The importance of social organization to our lives and to our sense of self has long been a driving force that has motivated the study of sociology and of organizations. Moreover, the ubiquity of "constructed" organizations and their growing influence on the economic activity of modern society is widely acknowledged (e.g., see Simon, 1991). Indeed, Coleman (1992) has argued that "the very basis of organization" in modern societies is itself in the midst of a two-century-long transformation away from what he labelled "primordial social organization" (namely, organizations developed through birth and the social relations of blood ties and related "primordial" institutions, such as religious bodies) toward social organizations that are "purposively constructed."

While, as individuals, our interaction and likely relationship with constructed organizations may have become nearly inescapable, the stability of that relationship is now being called into question as never before. At the same time that constructed organizations and, among them, business firms in particular, are becoming more important to our economic and social lives (even if only by default), they are also finding it increasingly difficult to fulfill the roles of the institutions they are replacing. This is, at least in part, because the nature of the employment relationship – a fundamental basis of many of these organizations– is currently being shaken at its very roots by the increasing uncertainty associated with employment security.

Over more than a decade now, facing an increasingly competitive and dynamic environment, firm after firm – in the US and abroad – has abandoned its policy of providing secure employment to "downsize" its organization.

Used initially as a stop-gap measure to stem the flow of red ink to the bottom line of ailing firms, downsizing has since been almost institutionalized as a standard operating procedure, to be employed repeatedly by even the healthiest of firms (see Cappelli, 1995).

The lingering threat that survivors of one downsizing will emerge only to be caught in the undertow of future waves of downsizing has effectively destabilized the employment relationship, causing profound dismay and anger among employees – at least in large corporations – who see it as a violation of their psychological contract (Rousseau, 1989).

This uncertainty in the employment relationship and its profound implications for individuals, firms and societies provide both the background and the motivation for this chapter. Our purpose here is twofold, in that we have both positive and normative objectives. Our first objective is to redirect positive theory of the employment relationship. While it is generally recognized that the employment relationship can assume many different forms (Pfeffer and Baron, 1988), the theories we have to explain it tend to focus categorically on employment security as its core defining characteristic (Pfeffer and Cohen, 1984).

There is little by way of theory development to guide us in understanding what it means to have an employment relationship that is more or less marketlike, or a job that is more or less secure. Yet these are the types of relationships that probably have always been present in the employment landscape but that have now become much more common and far too visible to ignore. By focusing on the concept of "employability" – an alternative to employment security now being considered in practice (see Waterman *et al.*, 1994; Bartlett and Ghoshal, 1995) and defined by Kanter (1989: 92) as an employee's "increased value in internal and external labor markets" – we seek to exhume a more solid foundation on which a more general theory of the employment relationship can ultimately be built.

Our second objective is more normative. The uncertain terms of the emerging employment relationships represent the greatest challenge now confronting large companies and their people and, through them, the social fabrics of most developed as well as developing societies. By examining the theoretical implications of the employment relationship in a more dynamic framework than is currently employed in related theories, we seek to suggest a direction that can and (we believe) needs to be taken by at least some categories of employers to cope with this challenge in the interests of their firms and the people they employ, as well as the societies that support and are supported by them.

In this normative goal, we see ourselves as responding to Coleman's clarion call, quoted at the beginning of this chapter, for theorists to direct their efforts not just to chronicling and conceptualizing the changes of the past but also to influencing the design of the institutional arrangements needed for a rational (i.e., better) reconstruction of society. As he said, "The ultimate justification of all these [theory development] endeavours will be their contribution to the optimal design of the constructed social organizations of the future" (1992: 14). The proposals we present here, both with regard to the role of the firm in society that they imply and the nature of the employee–employer relationship that they are premised upon, we hope and believe, represent a move in this direction.

4.2.1 The employment relationship in a dynamic context

Our argument, in essence, is as follows. We wish to link the employment relationship of a firm with its viability, and hence its strategy. Historically, this link has not been a major theme within either the literature on firm strategy, which has focused on the external environment (e.g., Porter, 1979) or internal resources (conceptualized somewhat abstractly, see Conner, 1991) as the starting point of analysis, or the literature on the employment relationship, which has tended to ignore or underemphasize the inescapable fact that the viability, and hence much of the value, of the employment relationship is inexorably tied to the viability of the employer itself. In the recent past, several scholars have argued for the need to bridge this gap.

For example, within the fields of organization theory and human resource management, Baron and Pfeffer (1994), Cappelli and Sherer (1991), Lado and Wilson (1994), and Jackson and Schuler (1995) have been among those who have argued for and contributed to the small but growing literature on "human resource management in context", a literature that aims to incorporate the internal and external contextual factors such as business strategy, firm performance, and industry and labor market conditions that affect and are affected by the organizational "system that attracts, develops, motivates and retains employees" (Jackson and Schuler, 1995: 238). Similarly, within the strategy field, the rising popularity of the resource based view has shifted the focus of analysis from factors external to the firm (such as industry structure) to factors internal to the firm and there is now a growing recognition that many of the "dynamic capabilities" that underlie a firm's competitive advantage are grounded in its people and their relationships both among themselves and with the organization (Teece *et al.*, 1994). It is to these evolving streams of literature that this chapter aims to contribute by proposing a theory that relates the expected outcomes of a given employment relationship with the conditions necessary to support it.

However, in doing so, we depart from much of this literature in one important way. With a few notable exceptions (e.g., Teece *et al.*, 1994), most of these authors have grounded their work in an explicit or implicit assumption of a relatively stable environment. In the strategy field, for example, while the historically dominant IO-based theories (e.g. Bain, 1956; Caves and Porter, 1977; Porter, 1979) were explicitly grounded in a static equilibrium framework, even much of the emerging literature on the resource based view is based on equilibrium definition of a firm's competitive advantage, that can neither provide a compelling explanation of how such advantage is initially developed (except by luck or foresight) nor relate it to any notion of the length of time it can be expected to be sustainable (see Barney, 1991: 103, 119). As a result, HR scholars aiming to develop a theory of "human resource management in context" and drawing their characterization of context from this strategy literature (among others) have similarly grounded their conceptualization of context in relatively static terms (e.g., Lado and Wilson, 1994; Wright *et al.*, 1994). In contrast, we seek to link the employment relationship of a firm with its strategy and viability in the context of a dynamic environment.

This shift from a static to a dynamic perspective matters a great deal because it explicitly acknowledges the possibility – indeed, the likelihood – that a sustainable competitive advantage in one evolutionary period will become a persistent (i.e., costly to eliminate) source of competitive disadvantage at some later time. As Peteraf (1993: 184) has noted, in a dynamic environment specialization becomes a double-edged sword. While the mutual dependency it engenders can be a source of competitive advantage, it can also reduce the firm's flexibility to respond to environmental and technical changes. Heath *et al.* (1993: 89) have highlighted one possible implication of this stability–flexibility dilemma in the context of a firm's human resource practices, in general, and its employment relationship, in particular: "Dynamic environments require flexible workers, flexible workers require a stable employment relationship, but stable employment relationships may not be possible in dynamic environments."

In the context of our analysis, the change from a relatively static to a dynamic perspective has two specific implications. First, in a dynamic environment, quasi-rents are not sustainable. Therefore, in such an environment, a strategy based on sustained appropriation of quasi-rents – the underlying premise of much (but not all) of the strategy literature – is inappropriate. As argued by Winter (1995), D'Aveni (1994), Moran and Ghoshal (1996b) and others (see, for example, the collection of essays in Montgomery, 1995), in a dynamic environment, a firm's competitive advantage flows from its ability to continuously create and appropriate transient Schumpeterian rents. Therefore, in our analysis of competitive advantage, we focus on a firm's ability to create new rent sources, rather than to protect existing ones.

Second, in a dynamic environment, firm-specific human skills can quickly become obsolete, because of the risks of substitution, in the short-term, and of innovation, in the long-term. Therefore, in such an environment, a theory of the employment relationship that focuses primarily on the benefits of firm-specific human skills and capabilities – one of the key arguments offered in support of employment security (Doeringer and Piore, 1971; Pfeffer and Cohen, 1984) – is also inappropriate. In such an environment, competence destroying discontinuities (Tushman and Anderson, 1986) can break the reinforcing cycle of employee specialization leading to the need for employment security and, hence, to greater specialization by making the specialization of a firm's employees a primary contributor to the ultimate likelihood of the simultaneous erosion of a firm's competitive advantage and the employee's job security. Therefore, in our analysis of the employment relationship, we substitute the current theoretical focus on employment security with one on employability, which, we argue, reduces the potential cost of skill obsolescence and enhances both the firm's and the employee's flexibility to cope with the possibility of discontinuous environmental change.

Table 4.1 provides an overall summary of our arguments as well as a roadmap for the remaining part of the chapter. The column titled "dominant model" identifies the key concepts that theoretically link employment security to a firm's competitive advantage in a relatively stable environment, as can be inferred from the mainstream literatures on the employment relationship and on firm-level strategy. In essence, therefore, it identifies the concepts and arguments that define our point of departure. These concepts and arguments are briefly explicated in the following chapter.

The column titled "alternative model" summarizes the key concepts in our theory relating employability with a firm's competitive advantage in the context of a dynamic environment. While some elements of our argument linking the different concepts may be relatively new, it will be manifest from the table that most of the concepts we use are drawn from the work of others, much of it in the domain of a nascent but rapidly growing literature at the intersection of the resource based view of strategy and the evolutionary theory of the firm. These concepts and arguments are presented in the section 4.3.

We must emphasize at this stage that we are not presenting the alternative model as an inherently superior one, from either a theoretical or a practical perspective. The value of employability as the basis of the employment relationship depends on its viability and its usefulness to both employees and employers. Such viability and usefulness, in turn, are likely to be influenced by other characteristics of the external and occupational labor markets within which the firm must operate and by the characteristics of the firm's own internal labor market and its business environment. The last section of the chapter identifies these boundary conditions of our theory, and concludes with a discussion of its implications for research and practice.

4.3 EMPLOYMENT SECURITY AND COMPETITIVE ADVANTAGE: THE POINT OF DEPARTURE

The employment relationship is a principal defining element of most formal organizations (Simon, 1951). Pfeffer and Baron (1988: 257) have characterized this relationship as a "continuum ... " ranging from long-term attachments between workers and organizations under a system of bureaucratic control, to arrangements in which workers are only weakly connected to the organization either in terms of physical location, administrative control, or duration of employment. Until the early 1980s, however, the historical evolution of the employment relationship, not only in the US but also worldwide, has been marked by a shift from the latter to the former – that is, from simple, market or

Table 4.1   Alternative integrated models of firm strategy and the employment relationship

Theoretical attributes	Dominant model	Alternative model
Strategic approach	Value appropriation: sustaining current (i.e., specifiable) rents and enhancing appropriability (Porter, 1979; Barney, 1991)	Value creation: facilitating the creation of new rents and new sources of rents (Moran & Ghoshal, 1996b; D'Aveni, 1994)
Type of rents	Specifiable appropriable quasi-rents (Barney, 1991; Klein *et al.*, 1978; Williamson, 1975)	Non-specifiable transient Schumpeterian rents (Rumelt, 1987; Winter, 1995)
Performance sustaining processes/mechanisms	Isolating mechanisms (Rumelt, 1984); entry and mobility barriers (Porter, 1979)	• Accumulating mechanisms (Dierickx & Cool, 1989) • Linking mechanisms (Cohen & Levinthal, 1990; Kogut & Zander, 1992) • Bonding mechanisms (Kim & Mauborgne, 1996; Organ, 1990)
Resource structure of the firm	Firm specific knowledge & skills (Becker, 1962; Doeringer & Piore, 1971; Williamson, 1975)	Advanced general knowledge and skills
Nature of employment relationship	Employment security (Jacoby, 1985; Pfeffer & Baron, 1988; Baron *et al.*, 1986 Pfeffer & Cohen, 1984)	Employability (Bartlett & Ghoshal, 1995; Kanter, 1989; Waterman *et al.*, 1994)

craft-based control (i.e., employer–employee exchanges mediated by either open labor markets or craft-based trade unions or guilds) to bureaucratic control that relies on long-term employment relations and a hierarchy of formal rules and internal advancement policies as the primary means of securing and controlling workers (Jacoby, 1985; Pfeffer and Baron, 1988). This trend has been most pronounced in the case of large corporations: contrary to popular caricatures, employment security has been as central to the management practices of Western companies like IBM in the United States and Philips in Europe as it has for Eastern companies like Toyota in Japan and Samsung in Korea, at least in the four decades following the Second World War (see Hall, 1982).

It is not surprising, then, from its pervasiveness in practice, particularly among the world's largest and most successful organizations, that employment security and the internal labor markets (ILMs) that are commonly associated with long-term employment relations feature prominently in most theories of the employment relationship. The emergence and institutionalization of such relationships have been attributed to many factors. These include:

1. firm-specific explanations, including those concerning the impact of technology and technological change (Doeringer and Piore, 1971; Pfeffer and Cohen, 1984) on the need to develop and/or preserve idiosyncratic human capital that is of relatively greater value to a single firm (see also Becker, 1962);
2. transaction-specific explanations, where idiosyncratic capital is of relatively greater value to a specific transaction or job with a single firm (Baron *et al.*, 1986; Williamson, 1975); and
3. institutional and structural explanations, where political and institutional forces inside and outside the organization, e.g., the presence of and the focal organization's relationship with other internal units, unions or professional groups (Pfeffer and Cohen, 1984), or of gender differentiation (Baron *et al.*, 1986) create some dependency for or in the focal organization (Pfeffer and Salancik, 1978).

As is readily apparent from the diversity of these explanations, there are not only multiple determinants of the structure of employment but there also exist considerable differences among theories over the particular reasons for ILMs, the nature of the long-term employment relationships they enable and the mechanisms through which ILMs emerge and influence these relationships. There is, however, a common theme that extends throughout much of the received view that it is employment security and the ILMs supporting it that most distinguish the employment relationship from the types of transactions (of labor for service) that are commonly observed in external labor markets. However employment is structured, when it involves employment security (however determined) and that security is threatened, firm specific human capital comes to the fore as a pivotal issue. For this reason and because firm specific human capital is, perhaps, the single attribute that most readily connects the nature of the employment relationship with the sources of a firm's competitive advantage, we focus this chapter on firm specific explanations.

Such firm-specific explanations of the benefits of employment security emphasize three factors which also help establish the link between employment security and the competitive advantage of a firm (see Table 4.1)

First, employment security provides both the firm and the employee with an incentive for investing in the development of firm-specific, idiosyncratic knowledge, skills and competencies (Doeringer and Piore, 1971; Becker, 1962; Williamson, 1975). It is the idiosyncratic or heterogeneous characteristics of these firm-specific resources that, in turn, provide the source of rents for the firm. As the strategy literature emphasizes, heterogeneity is "the sine-qua-non of competitive advantage" (Peteraf, 1993: 185); it is the inherent cause of scarcity necessary for rent generation and is the key defining characteristic which separates industries, strategic groups and individual firms from the forces of competitive markets and, consequently, allows them to earn quasi-rents (Rumelt, 1984; Barney, 1991).

Second, employment security also reduces turnover by, among other things, reducing employee mobility. Firm-specific knowledge and skills are imperfectly mobile outside the focal firm.

Hence, they are difficult for employees to market to the external labor market (Williamson, 1985). There is perhaps a positive aspect too to this lack of mobility in as much as employment security can provide an opportunity for employees to safely combine their local knowledge and skills with other investments (e.g., time and effort) in their organizations but, in both economics and organization theory, this idea has been overshadowed by the notion that employers benefit from such investments in firm-specific skills only when it is more difficult (i.e., costly) for their employees to leave their organizations (see, for example, Pfeffer and Baron, 1988: 261, and Wachter and Williamson, 1978: 556).

Without this reduced mobility, firm-specific knowledge and skills generated through employment security would not contribute to the firm's competitive advantage. While resource heterogeneity is necessary for sustainable advantage, it is not sufficient; for the advantage to be sustainable, heterogeneity must be preserved. This is accomplished through what Rumelt (1984) described as "isolating mechanisms" which operate at the firm level – just as entry and mobility barriers operate at the industry and strategic group levels (Porter, 1979) – to impede the mobility and imitability of resources between firms and, thereby, retard any tendency by them to become more homogeneous and to dissipate rents to actual or potential competitors or to buyers or suppliers or even to the ultimate consumer. In other words, while employment security contributes to the creation of firm-specific knowledge and skills, it also contributes to the development of isolating mechanisms by impeding the mobility of employees and thereby creates the condition for sustainability of the competitive advantage arising from those firm-specific resources.

Third, employment security also contributes to the efficiency advantages of the firm by depressing employees' wage demands. As argued in internal labor market theories, individual workers often tend to be more risk-averse than the employer which creates an opportunity for arbitrage: in return for the protection that ILMs offer from external labor market competition, employees accept lower wages and remain with the organization. This yields quasi-rents, together with considerable discretion for the employer to appropriate these rents (Milgrom and Roberts, 1992: 350).

Collectively, these arguments provide a consistent explanation of how employment security can lead to a firm's competitive advantage (see Figure

4.1). To summarize, employment security increases investments made by the firm and by its employees in building firm-specific knowledge and skills. This has the twin effect of enhancing the firm's efficiency in executing its existing activities and of reducing the employees' mobility and wage demands. These effects collectively create quasi-rents which the firm appropriates to its competitive advantage. The advantage, in turn, provides the resources and the incentives for building firm-specific skills.

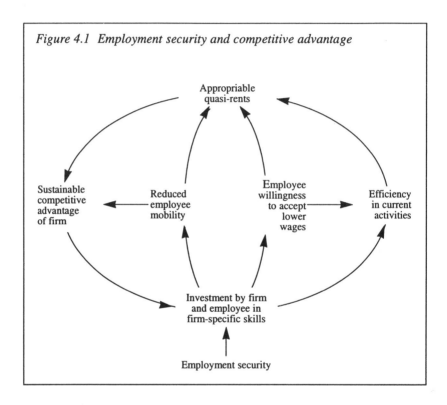

Figure 4.1 Employment security and competitive advantage

4.4 COMPETITIVE ADVANTAGE IN DYNAMIC ENVIRONMENTS: A THEORY OF EMPLOYABILITY

While this model of the association between employment security and competitive advantage is simple, clear and logical, in the introductory section of this chapter we have already identified some of its key limitations. As we have suggested, the theoretical premises of this model are drawn from an equilibrium framework, and the model, therefore, relates to the context of a relatively stable environment. In the context of a dynamic environment some of the main links in its internal logic break down.

More specifically, at the present time, for many firms and their employees, neither the starting point of the model, namely an employment relationship based on employment security, nor the key outcome, namely achievement of competitive advantage through sustained exploitation of specifiable, appropriable quasi-rents, is viable. As Pfeffer and Baron (1988: 257) have documented, from the mid 1980s, there has been a general reversal in the historic trend toward long-term stable employment relationships, and as Cappelli (1995: 563) has argued, this reversal is not a limited (i.e., applicable only to the periphery of the organization, to protect its core of permanent employees, as argued by Pfeffer and Baron) or temporary phenomenon but represents a breakdown across many aspects of internal labor markets, even of permanent employees.

Similarly, in dynamic environments, a strategy based on sustained appropriation of quasi-rents does not work because of obsolescence. Worse still, given that the resources generating such quasi-rents in a particular evolutionary period need to be valuable, rare, non-tradable and non-substitutable (Dierickx and Cool, 1989), they are likely to become distinct liabilities in future periods (Leonard-Barton, 1992). As they are slow and costly to accumulate, they are also likely to be slow and costly to dispose of.

Therefore, for such dynamic environments, one needs a different theory of competitive advantage and, to the extent that there is a link between the nature of the employment relationship and the competitive advantage of the firm, one also needs a different theory of the employment relationship.

The arguments of Schumpeter (1934) and Penrose (1959) provide the starting point for such a theory. According to both of them, the competitive advantage (and growth) of a firm depends not on its ability to appropriate quasi-rents built through monopoly positions in product or factor markets but on its ability to continually create Schumpeterian rents through innovation and entrepreneurship. More recently, Winter has re-emphasised this argument by suggesting that "the emphasis the strategy literature gives to sustainable advantage may have the unintended consequence of diverting attention from the effective pursuit of transient rents" (1995: 159).

Further, in making the distinction between resources and resource conversion activities, Rumelt (1987) has already provided the basic intuition necessary for building such a theory of competitive advantage based on a firm's ability to create Schumpeterian or entrepreneurial rents – i.e., temporary excess returns to innovation and uncertainty (Peteraf, 1994; Winter, 1995).

Resource conversion, according to Rumelt, is the ability of a firm to flexibly exchange resources within the firm and with the market, and to use and combine those resources with other readily available resources in ways that are not available to other firms. This is Schumpeter's classic definition of entrepreneurship, which Penrose proposed as the key driver of firm growth.

Employability, we suggest, may be an appropriate basis of the employment relationship if the creation of Schumpeterian rents through dynamic efficiency and entrepreneurial growth is the goal, just as employment security may be the more suitable mechanism for the appropriation of quasi-rents accrued through achieving higher static efficiency in existing activities (see Figure 4.2).

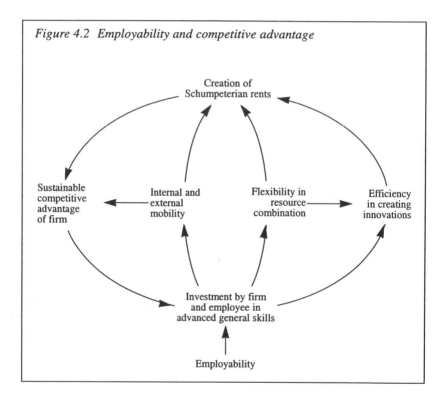

Figure 4.2 Employability and competitive advantage

4.4.1 Advanced general skills

The key difference between the models represented in Figures 4.1 and 4.2 (and contrasted in Table. 4.1) lies in the distinction between firm-specific skills and what we have labeled "advanced general skills" as the source of the firm's competitive advantage. In the first model, firm-specificity of individuals' skills is the source of appropriable quasi-rents; in the second model, it is the firm's organizational capability of creating particular skill combinations internally and of linking those skill combinations to appropriate external opportunities that is the primary source of Schumpeterian rents for the firm. The firm's advantage in the second model is based on its ability to induce innovative behavior rather than on its ability to exercise monopoly power over the capabilities of its people.

In this second, more dynamically sensitive model, both the rent creation potential of the firm and the employability of the firm's employees are enhanced by skills that are general but advanced, i.e., superior to those widely available in the market. General skills may be of many types. For example, they may be content skills, such as those associated with specific disciplines (e.g., from basic reading, language or farming skills to more advanced facilities with certain nuances of these disciplines, like higher-order mathematics), technologies (e.g., opto-electronics) or tasks (e.g., brand management) that, by themselves, are quite general in the sense that they are relevant in a wide variety of business contexts and organizations. They may also be process skills, such as in coordinating specific horizontal chains of activities like project management or new product creation, which also are more general than firm-specific.

While general, none of these skills is undifferentiated. Just as there are better and worse economists, there are better and worse molecular biologists as well as more or less competent managers of the new product creation process or of large and complex projects. In the model of competitive advantage we have presented in Figure 4.2, firms aim to enhance the quality and level of the knowledge and skills of their employees so that, while general, their skills are also advanced.

The most important distinction between firm-specific skills and advanced general skills is that the latter cannot be a source of appropriable quasi-rents for the firm. At one extreme, completely specific skills have no opportunity cost. All returns to them are economic rents, i.e., "excess returns to a factor over its opportunity cost" (Peteraf, 1994: 154). Similarly, at the other extreme, none of the returns from completely general skills are rents. By further delineating general skills as advanced, we introduce the notion of differential quality and, hence, scarcity (at least temporary scarcity) into consideration. To the extent that general skills are advanced, at least a portion of their returns can be appropriately classified as scarcity rents, i.e., monopoly rents but with no incentive to restrict output (Winter, 1995: 21–2). But because they are general, these skills are mobile. Hence, they are free to move to similar or even higher value applications in a variety of settings, both inside and outside the firm in which they were developed. Consequently, any rents derived solely from such skills are appropriable by the owner of the skills, i.e., the employee, and not the employer.

Such advanced general skills are clearly attractive to the employee. In an environment of frequent exogenous shocks which can reverse the fortunes of even the healthiest companies almost overnight, job security with a single company cannot fulfill the role of employment security that is implied in the literature we referred to in the preceding section. Advanced general skills, by being fungible across many firms, offer the promise of employability as a much more credible, general and secure form of employment security (Kanter, 1989). Further, because they enhance employability, advanced general skills "level the playing field" by relaxing the binding hold that specific skills can, and often do, have on employees. By eliminating the employee as a source of appropriable quasi-rents, the firm can no longer gain at its employees' expense and must look elsewhere (namely, new rent creation) for appropriable rents. As a result, the employee gains not only through reduced vulnerability to rent expropriation hazards but also in the potential opportunities associated with the alternative sources of rents that the firm must now create to remain viable.

For the firm too, there are some obvious advantages in having its human capital in the form of a pool of differentiated, advanced and general skills. Of all its assets, the risk of substitution in firm-specific human assets may be the most costly substitution risk for the firm to bear. Most other assets often can be abandoned for little additional cost. However, human assets, like physical sites which pose significant environmental liabilities, are increasingly costly to dispose of. By reducing the "half life" of investments in firm-specific resources, dynamic environments increase both the risk and the cost of such substitution. Advanced general skills of employees reduce this risk and the cost of substitution. Employability not only raises the employees' qualifications for jobs with other firms but also for other jobs within the firm, enhancing the firm's flexibility to reassign people to new opportunities as they emerge. Therefore, in uncertain environments where the risk of skill obsolescence is high, enhanced employability can actually enhance a firm's ability to maintain employment stability and also allow employees to extend their value and tenure with the same firm, if they wish.

Advanced general skills also contribute to individual and, thereby, the expansion of organizational absorptive capacity. "The premise of the notion of absorptive capacity is that the organization needs prior related knowledge to assimilate and use new knowledge" (Cohen and Levinthal, 1990: 129). By implication, then, some, if not all, of this "prior related knowledge" is non-specific and, therefore, general. Advanced general skills provide individuals with the "breadth of categories into which prior knowledge is organized, the differentiation of those categories, and the linkages across them" which "permits individuals to make sense of and, in turn, acquire new knowledge" (*ibid.*). Appropriate contextual knowledge is needed to make knowledge fully intelligible. Since prior related knowledge is necessary to assimilate new knowledge, the nature and content of the newly created or assimilated knowledge is influenced by that of the old. Advanced general skills enable the individual to develop a finer grained resolution of the knowledge structures in which newly encountered information is embedded and interpreted.

However, as has been noted earlier, because advanced general skills are mobile and relatively scarce, the "service flows" (Winter, 1995) from these resources applied as generic inputs are likely to be fairly priced and, therefore, unlikely to yield the firm any particular advantage. Nor is any particular firm likely to be or to remain the optimal developer or user of such skills for any specifiable length of time. Over time, other firms are likely not only to compete away any expected advantage from such skills, but also to compete away the resource itself, leaving the initial firm the liability of having incurred the cost of developing such skills essentially as a public good. Advanced general skills, therefore, are a necessary but insufficient condition for building a theory of sustained competitive advantage that is consistent with employability as the basis of the employment relationship. A number of questions must be addressed before such a model can be made useful:

1. How can individual advanced general skills be accumulated and deployed in a cost effective manner?
2. How can individual advanced general skills be transformed into a firm capability to create and to appropriate Schumpeterian rents?
3. How can a firm's potential for creating such transient rents through on-going innovations be exploited and protected to ensure a sustainable competitive advantage? We consider each of these questions in turn.

4.4.2 Developing advanced general skills through accumulating mechanisms

Scarcity is the essence of advanced general skills. Firms can acquire and develop such skills through what we will call accumulating mechanisms, which include mechanisms for recruiting from among the highest levels of such general skills available in the external labor market (e.g., McKinsey hires the top graduates from the most reputable business schools and AT&T's Bell Laboratories goes to great lengths to attract the most respected graduate students from the best technical institutions around the world), and for investing large amounts of resources in continually enhancing those skills internally through both training and work assignments (Andersen Consulting, for example, allocates 10 percent of its revenues to training).

The role of accumulating mechanisms is twofold. First, they influence the context in which individual advanced general skills are acquired, and thereby, influence the nature of the fields in which these skills are most likely to be applied and further developed by the employee. Second, accumulating mechanisms ensure and promote the development of organizational level advanced general skills and, thereby, define the context in which organizational level absorptive capacity is ultimately created and developed.

While the need for effective selection, training and development mechanisms, so as to develop a pool of people with advanced knowledge and skills in different fields, is fairly straightforward, these mechanisms also have certain consequences for the development of advanced general skills that need to be highlighted. To develop advanced general skills (as with the creation of rents in general), a firm must deploy its existing stock of advanced general skills to this task, which may not represent the most efficient use of those skills in a static equilibrium sense. This raises the need to address the issue of sacrifice, i.e., why innovation (that is, achieving dynamic efficiency) often requires the sacrifice of valuable current resource deployment opportunities.

Sacrifice

It has recently been argued by Winter (1995: 155) that "the value of idiosyncratic resources to the firm – i.e., the present value of their future rent streams – is affected by the fact that their possible uses include development of more idiosyncratic resources". He has further suggested that in many cases "when resources are creatively applied to extend the capabilities of the firm ... this source of value may greatly outweigh the present value of directly productive service flows" from such resources (*ibid*: 155–6). A similar argument has also been made by Itami (1987: 17) in his suggestion that "Too much emphasis on effective utilization" of those assets that are both inputs and outputs "prevents efficient accumulation" of such assets.

Herein lies both the theoretical and the practical crux of accumulating mechanisms. They imply a sacrifice on the part of the firm. While recruitment and selection are essential components of a firm's accumulating mechanisms, internal training and development are relatively the more important source of the scarcity inherent in advanced general skills. Such training and development, in turn, require the investment of the firm's existing stock of advanced general skills (partners of Andersen Consulting, for example, are given quotas for the time they must spend as instructors in the firm's formal in-house training programs, as well as for the time they must allocate to mentoring individual consultants in their ward). Such use in developing further advanced general skills may not be the most efficient deployment of the firm's existing stock of such skills, in a static equilibrium sense (nor is it likely to be the best use of such skills in terms of their owners' individual interests), but it is essential for creating the self-reinforcing cycle that allows a firm to continually stay ahead of the ongoing enhancement of such skills in the external labor market.

Such sacrifice of static efficiency on the part of the firm, in turn, engenders similar sacrifice on the part of employees that is essential for the sustainability of the firm's advantage from such advanced general skills; we shall revert to this later in this chapter.

As we have noted earlier, while the ability to create advanced general skills is a necessary condition for achieving competitive advantage through employability, it is not sufficient. Although the acquisition and enhancement of advanced general skills, through accumulating mechanisms, constitute both necessary and sufficient conditions for building an individual's employability, for the firm they pose a significant liability that must be offset by additional rent producing and sustaining mechanisms to ensure the creation of sustainable competitive advantage. The firm must be capable of deploying its advanced general skills in ways which allow it to create and realize more value than can be realized by those same skills optimally deployed in other firms. This is accomplished largely by expanding the firm's organizational absorptive capacity beyond the sum of the independent absorptive capacities of its individual employees, i.e., through linking mechanisms.

4.4.3 Building rent-creating potential through linking mechanisms

The shift from firm-specific skills to advanced general skills removes human capital as a source of appropriable quasi-rents for the firm. Now the only way the firm can build a sustainable competitive advantage from its employment relationship is if it finds a way to create Schumpeterian rents. As Conner (1991) has suggested, it is the way in which a firm's resources are linked together that is key to such a rent creation process: "it is the linkage of an input to the firm's existing asset base – and especially, the relative strength of that linkage as compared to that which competitors would achieve" that is central to rent creation (*ibid.*: 136). Linking mechanisms enhance the firm's potential for creating rents from a given set of resources (including resource conversion activities) by doing precisely this, i.e., by enhancing the underlying "linkedness" of these resources.

Whereas accumulating mechanisms build the firm's stock of human (and physical) capital, from which its employees are the principal beneficiary, linking mechanisms build social capital that benefits both employer and employee. Linking mechanisms permit resources to be accumulated, combined and deployed in ways that facilitate the creation and appropriation of rents. That is, they promote the building of organizational "appropriative capabilities" (Szulanski, 1993). The rents we focus on here are similar to those which Rumelt (1987) refers to as "entrepreneurial rents" but their source of value resides not in a single entrepreneur but in the firm's collective stock of knowledge and skills embedded in its people and in the mechanisms which link them together. Linking mechanisms are those that bundle and deploy a firm's human and other resources in ways that enable a firm to assimilate new information and facilitate the exploitation of new rent opportunities. Like Kogut and Zander's (1992) organizing principles, linking mechanisms link people to one another internally and to market opportunities externally.

Linking mechanisms are distinguished best, perhaps, by their role in facilitating the provision of more or less open access to multiple sources of information and knowledge without unnecessarily binding linked parties to each other and, thereby, isolating them from others. They include those organizational policies, practices, values and norms which: shape networks of formal and informal relationships and communication flows; influence personnel assignments, rotations and training; encourage the seeking and provision of information, advice and support; and minimize the potential for information or power asymmetries. But while the list of potential linking mechanisms continues almost indefinitely, it is important to note that by distinguishing "open access" from "binding dependencies" this definition of linking mechanism excludes many links that serve to channel or impede access.

Indeed, linking mechanisms are, perhaps, more usefully characterized by the types of links they seek to avoid than by those they support. High on the list of what could be considered as mechanisms which impede linking, by their tendency to isolate information sources and to influence (typically by regulating or controlling) the content and flow of information, would be hierarchical or power relationships, which can use the power of authority, status or political influence to narrowly specify (either explicitly or implicitly) and attempt to direct the relevancy, access, transmission, and use of all types of information. Besides common hierarchical (i.e., superior–subordinate) reporting relationships, other examples of structural impediments to linking include "gatekeeping" or "boundary-spanning" roles in organizations (Tushman, 1977). Structural impediments, while useful (e.g., in economically focusing attention) and sometimes necessary, become dysfunctional for those types of problems and requirements for action which Burns and Stalker (1961: 6) argue "cannot be broken down and distributed among specialist roles within a clearly defined hierarchy".

By enhancing firm-specific social capital, linking mechanisms serve a number of critical functions. First, they create the potential for enhanced innovativeness, which increases the rent creating capacity of the firm by increasing the absorptive capacity of the organization as a whole as well as that of its individual members. Second, they enable the firm to appropriate the rents they help make possible.

Rent creation potential

While no systematic formula for rent creation or innovation can exist (Barney, 1986; Dierickx and Cool, 1989: 1506n; Rumelt, 1984) and specific opportunities for rent creation are largely triggered by unexpected events (Rumelt, 1984), firms, like individuals, can improve their chances of benefiting from knowledge that is diffused in the public domain. The process of doing something different with current knowledge also inevitably leads to new knowledge creation. Whether or not firms are capable of exploiting their share of opportunities depends on their capacity to absorb relevant information and on their ability to appropriate knowledge from it. By increasing their knowledge appropriation capacity, firms can enhance their capabilities to generate innovations and quickly and/or creatively to imitate or adapt the innovations of others and, consequently, enhance their rent creation potential. Just as advanced general skills enhance individual absorptive capacity, linking mechanisms allow individuals to access firm specific organizational routines (Nelson and Winter, 1982) to expand the absorptive capacity of the organization as a whole. Linking mechanisms comprise the communication network which is influenced by those efforts to deploy resources to directed activities (Teece *et al.,* 1994) and which, in turn, influences those more autonomous initiatives which are likely to emerge and give rise to new knowledge creation and innovation.

Opportunities for the creation of Schumpeterian rents increase with increasing absorptive capacity (Cohen and Levinthal, 1990: 131): "An organization's absorptive capacity will depend on the absorptive capacities of its individual members. To this extent, the development of an organization's absorptive capacity will build on prior investment in the development of its constituent, individual absorptive capacities, and, like individuals' absorptive capacities, organizational absorptive capacity will tend to develop cumulatively. A firm's absorptive capacity is not, however, simply the sum of the absorptive capacities of its employees ... ".

Linking mechanisms helps the organization and its members build absorptive capacity at both the individual and the organizational level. Greater absorptive capacity, in turn, increases the potential for identifying, assimilating and exploiting innovation enhancing knowledge as it is created inside and outside the firm.

Rent appropriation

As indicated in the discussion above, linking mechanisms are not hardwired linkages among the firm's human and other resources; they are the intangible resources of an organization that allow both directed and spontaneous linkages among these resources to emerge as and when new innovation-creating opportunities become available. As such, they are organizational assets that are nearly impossible to trade, imitate or substitute for. Because the mechanisms for forming and disbanding such linkages are embedded in the firm's organizing principles (Kogut and Zander, 1992) and exist only incompletely in the minds of its employees, no individual or group of individuals can walk away with this intangible resource in an easily reproducible form. As a result, such linking mechanisms allow the firm to create and appropriate rents, despite the general nature of the component assets and skills.

Together, accumulating mechanisms and linking mechanisms comprise both the hardware and software (both tangible and intangible) for accumulating the resources and arranging the resource conversion activities necessary for building the organization's capacity or potential for creating rents. But ability alone, whether individual or organizational, is not enough to ensure the behavior that it enables. To convert the potential for rent creation into actual rents, the firm must elicit the appropriate behavior from its capable employees and organizational sub-units. Further, for the resulting competitive advantage to be sustainable, it must also ensure that most, if not all, of those employees choose to remain with the organization, even when they have the opportunity to leave. These are the functions of bonding mechanisms which are described and discussed next.

4.4.4 Achieving sustainability through bonding mechanisms

When applied to human capital, isolating mechanisms (which impede the mobility of this capital) permit the firm to appropriate rents that the individual generates within the firm but cannot realize himself or herself either in the firm or elsewhere. In enhancing employability of its employees by enhancing their general skills, firms consciously reject the idea of binding people through the constraint of immobility. But, to sustain the ability to create Schumpeterian rents through flexible combination of such skills, firm's must create bonding mechanisms that enhance the mutual attractiveness of both the firm and the employee to one another. These mechanisms include those that create a shared sense of purpose and a common set of values and, thereby, help shape a coherent and attractive institutional context within the firm (Moran and Ghoshal, 1996a). As Douglas North (1990: 26) has argued, "institutions alter the price paid for one's convictions". By creating an alignment between the convictions of its members and the overall purpose of the firm, bonding mechanisms achieve continuity in the employment relationship through mutual seduction and choice rather than through reciprocal dependence and the lack of alternatives.

In the context of an employment relationship based on employability, accumulating mechanisms also serve as perhaps the most important bonding mechanism. The continual development and renewal of advanced general skills provides an effective inducement to attract and retain a high quality workforce. Creating an environment where each individual has ample opportunity to realize his or her highest potential only reinforces this inducement. The sacrifice made by the firm in deploying its stock of advanced general skills to build further advanced general skills also induces a reverse sacrifice on the part of the employees who choose to stay with the firm.

In other words, while the first-order effect of employability may be to enhance employees' monitoring of alternative opportunities and the likelihood of their exploiting such opportunities, its second-order effect may be exactly the opposite and, over time, the second-order effect may prove to be the more powerful. In a dynamic and competitive environment where the risk of job obsolescence is high, employment security can be sustained only if the individual's employability is "current". Leaving an organization with enhanced employability to exploit other job opportunities exposes the individual to the next round of job obsolescence. Only by working for and remaining with a firm which continuously updates and enhances employability can one achieve employment security and offset the loss of long-term employment guarantees.

There are important differences, however, between employment stability as viewed in the traditional employment relationship and that which may result from an employment relationship based on the notion of employability. While the vulnerability of both employer and employee is greater in dynamic environments, the burden on the employee is more because of "one labor power and one job" (Horvat, 1982: 447) and because the capabilities and marketability of the employee increase in importance relative to the viability and reliability of the employer as determinants of long-term employment security. Enhanced employability adjusts for this asymmetric dependency by shifting the balance in the need for employment stability more toward the employer. As such, employability places more squarely on the employer the burden of earning (as opposed to merely "granting") greater stability in the employment relationship. Employment stability, then, is achieved, not by binding the employee to the firm (i.e., through reduced mobility) but through bonding, by enhancing the attractiveness of remaining with the organization.

But inducing individuals to join and remain in the firm is not enough. The firm must also ensure that its people and other resources are effectively deployed to earn enough money to support its commitments and to maintain its attractiveness to its employees. In other words, the firm must stimulate those behaviors among its employees that would ensure continuous engagement and adaptation of the processes through which it can maintain its competitive advantage. Bonding mechanisms promote such behavior by establishing and reinforcing a consistent pattern of affective and normative links through which employees identify with their organization. By what we have referred to earlier as "levelling the playing field," an employment relationship based on employability provides a foundation for building the kind of internal context that motivates employees' affinity for (i.e., affective commitment) or sense of obligation to (i.e., normative commitment) the organization's social community (Allen and Meyer, 1990), instead of a preoccupation with only the need to keep their jobs (i.e., continuance commitment).

Both affective and normative commitment are more likely to lead to extra-role behaviors (Bateman and Organ, 1983; Kim and Mauborgue, 1996) and to individual initiative and consummate cooperation, while continuance commitment is more likely to lead to only the minimum perfunctory compliance that is necessary to stay employed. Such extra initiative and cooperation engendered by employability can themselves be the sources of additional rents and, to the extent these rents may not be available in alternative jobs outside the firm, they represent increased quasi-rents which may offset both those that may be lost through the exercise of the mobility option by some, and by the enhanced wages that this option might create for others. However, unlike the quasi rents appropriated from isolated resources made immobile through employment security, the quasi-rents that are created through enhanced employability stem from the enhanced potential capabilities of the people within the firm.

Hence, it is the source of rents and not their existence that distinguishes the alternative models of competitive advantage that we have contrasted in this chapter (see Figures 4.1 and 4.2). Absent any substantive theory of rent creation (i.e., save luck or foresight), the static efficiency framework of the first model emphasizes the preservation of current period monopoly rents, primarily through restrictions in the mobility of a workforce with few employment alternatives and whatever increases in current period productivity that can be extracted from it. In contrast, the dynamic efficiency framework of the second model emphasizes future rent creation, through attracting and developing a cadre of individuals whose relatively scarce skills are in high demand, motivating them to make short-term sacrifices in the productivity of their scarce skills and enhancing their individual and collective potential to achieve a level of performance that is unobtainable elsewhere.

4.5 BOUNDARY CONDITIONS AND IMPLICATIONS

Historically, relatively stable environments have suppressed the demands for adaptability and have allowed firms to focus instead on building stable long-term employment relationships and on inducing those productivity gains that such relationships make possible. Indeed, employee and employer alike benefit from such stable employment relationships. As

Heath *et al.,* (1993: 89) have argued, "Employees who feel assured about their future with a firm do not have to be paid as much, are more willing to make sacrifices for the firm, and are willing to allow paternalistic managers to withhold information from them." But more important than the benefits in lower labor cost and greater employee tolerance that can be attributed to such attitudes, firms able to provide employment stability can also derive productivity gains from enhanced employee commitment and accumulation of firm-specific knowledge and skills. Moreover, there is little to suggest a priori that firms that are serious in their commitments to employment security cannot also achieve all the benefits we have posited to accrue in our alternative model (we would merely add that these firms also are likely to employ some combination of accumulating, linking and bonding mechanisms to maintain their competitive advantages in innovation). As environments become more dynamic and competitive, however, this mutually reinforcing attribute of the employment relationship begins to unravel and the potential benefits of the relationship, itself are called into question. Our purpose in this chapter has been to explore the implications of this situation, when the conditions necessary for the historical model are no longer satisfied. In other words, our arguments do not mean to suggest that an employment relationship based on employability is in general superior to one based on employment security, but only present an alternative when, for whatever reason, employment security is either not viable or not credible. Therefore, it is important at this stage to identify the boundary conditions of our model.

In moving from stable to dynamic environments, rents become more transient and their half-lives become shorter. For firms hoping to shift attention and resources from one rent stream to another, the transition becomes increasingly more problematic. As rents become shorter lived and their sources more varied and uncertain, it is less likely that the pursuit of one rent stream will provide the firm with the requisite set of knowledge and skills to pursue the next, and more likely that people whose knowledge and skills were once highly valued will ultimately become a liability. Also, the interests of employer and employee can easily become more incongruent as the gap between required and available resources widens. Consequently, the basis for and nature of an employee's commitment to the organization is likely to undergo a significant transformation if that employee is bound to the organization only through his or her lack of any alternative and the employer desperately needs new human capital that the employee does not have. The employment relationship, once the source of mutual dependency and benefit (based on a sense of mutual gain from mutual identification and obligation) becomes a major source of uncertainty and potential liability (based on an increasingly asymmetric dependency of the employee and burden for the employer). It is here that the effects of our model exhibit their full force.

Obviously, such dynamic environments require both employer and employee to be more flexible and adaptive (Heath *et al.,* 1993). As we have argued in this chapter, employability can provide greater flexibility to both employee and employer (i.e., in terms of both skills and opportunities to use those skills), enabling each to adapt more readily to changing circumstances and to exit the relationship without significant loss if there is no acceptable alternative. Employability offers a more credible route to career employment security (Kanter, 1989) for the employee in dynamic environments and reduces the firm's exposure to obsolescence in its human resources and its liability in caring for individuals with obsolete skills.

However, even in such environments, the viability of employability is influenced by other characteristics of the external and occupational labor markets within which the firm must operate and by the characteristics of the firm's own internal labor market (including job characteristics and career opportunities).

Where guarantees of employment security are perceived as credible (in the short run, whether they, in fact, are or are not, in the long run), and the firm's other commitments are secure, additional commitments to employability are less important to (some or even many) employees and are, therefore, less valuable to the employer but are just as costly (or even costlier) as when there is no employment security. Even where employment security is in decline but there still exists only rudimentary (i.e., imperfect or missing) external labor markets, like in Japan, the value of employability will be less because the infrastructure needed to match employees who have valuable knowledge and skills with job opportunities is likely to be inadequate at various stages in a worker's career. Moreover, the concept of employability has little relevance in labor markets that approximate the ideal of standard economic theory (i.e., many buyers and sellers of homogeneous labor units), like the market for migrant farm workers, where neither employment security nor employability is prevalent. This is so in these cases primarily because it would only serve to redistribute existing rents and cannot give rise to circumstances to create new value.

Indeed, as we have stressed throughout the chapter, the opportunity for employees to create value for their employer through some discretionary behavior is a necessary condition for employability to be of practical use. Hence, employability is likely to be most beneficial for individuals with careers that are likely to span job stints with multiple employers and that necessitate continuous updating of relevant knowledge and skills. Similarly, employability should most exhibit the effects we propose when it is found among employees whose jobs not only entail considerable discretionary behavior but where such behavior also affords the individual some potential to add value to the firm (e.g., by improving the job's productivity, the quality of its performance, or even by eliminating the job itself). On the other hand, if a job's tasks are highly routinized and difficult to change, the job holder has few degrees of freedom to improve its performance characteristics. In such a situation, employability would be less likely to benefit the firm.

In addition, it bears reiteration that employability alone is not a sufficient condition for building sustainable competitive advantage from the employment relationship. Indeed, firms that replace employment security with employability, without the requisite complement of accumulating, linking and bonding mechanisms, are likely to lose more human and social capital than they are able to accumulate. Further, we also believe that some degree of employment stability for both employer and employee is necessary and possible in dynamic, as well as in stable environments and, as we have argued earlier, such stability is partly achieved (at least in dynamic environments) as the seemingly paradoxical consequence of enhanced employability.

4.5.1 Implications for research

We began this chapter by noting the increasing uncertainty that surrounds the employment relationship and the overall decline in employment security that has gone on for over a decade. As jobs become more uncertain and more dear, employers' bargaining power to extract concessions from their employees increases. In such a situation, any need to replace losses in employment security with employability or any other costly alternative will perhaps be apparent to only a few firms. Fewer still of these employers will actually back up the costless rhetoric in their recruiting brochures that extols their commitment to employability with the more difficult to build accumulating mechanisms that are necessary to enhance the employability of their workers. Out of perhaps a handful of firms that might actually contribute to increasing the employability of their employees, many are likely to stumble in building the linking and bonding mechanisms that are needed to make it possible and desirable for their employees to add value to the firm and, hence, find reason to stay on.

Indeed, if none of these firms is able to make employability work, the concept is likely to wither away before any fair test of its power can be made. Firms would then have more justification (and pressure) than they will need to continue the current world-wide trend to turn the employment relationship into what Weber (1978: 40–41) referred to as an "associative social relationship" (i.e., a social relationship that is based on a "rationally motivated adjustment of interests" between the parties of the relationship, see also Cornfield, 1981) and away from a "communal social relationship" (i.e., based on a "subjective feeling of the parties, whether affectual or traditional, that they belong together"). Unfortunately, treating the employment relationship more like a market relationship will not allow exchanges to be conducted as if they were mediated by well functioning markets (to do this, significant transaction costs must be eliminated, which is likely to be impossible for implicit contracts). Consequently, a potentially significant opportunity for practitioners and researchers to experiment with a form of relationship that might encourage the creation of value will have slipped away.

Hopefully, however, at least a few of these firms will find the right mix of accumulating, linking and bonding mechanisms to find some way to make employability work. If this happens – if even a single firm manages to remain viable while enhancing the mobility of its employees to other employers – it could (if it has the effects proposed in this chapter) induce many other firms to do the same.

More than a handful of firms with employment relationships built around enhanced employability would have significant implications for the nature of work. Firms with employees who are becoming more employable will have to make their work environment more rewarding and stimulating to their employees in order to retain their best people. Obstacles currently standing in the way of efforts to provide such conditions (because of bad management or coercive organizational structures that persist with asymmetric power differences, for example) might then begin to fall.

Along the way, there is much to be done to test and improve our understanding of the concept of employability. For instance, the extent to which the model can be generalized within (and perhaps beyond) the boundary conditions we speculated on above needs to be established. A number of fundamental questions, implicit in the theory presented here, also need to be addressed. For example:

- Can firms significantly boost their workers' employability merely by augmenting their level of advanced general skills?
- What if anything else is required and how can this be accomplished?
- How can/should employability be measured?
- Can employers with highly employable workers keep them long enough to benefit from their enhanced mobility?
- How long is long enough?
- To what extent do accumulating, linking and bonding mechanisms contribute to employability?
- To employment security?
- Does it matter if employability is restricted to one's current industry or occupational group?
- Does it matter who provides for an individual's employability – i.e., are the hypothesized effects the same whether the employee or the firm contributed to employability or should we expect interactions?
- What affect, if any, will the stickiness in mobility that comes from factors other than employability (like immobile health care policies or pension benefits) have on the more mobile employee's behavior or on the firm's performance?

Clearly there is more to employability than skills and their half-life or generalizability. Otherwise, highly skilled professionals would not experience such steep non-monotonic declines in their success in re-entering labor markets in the months following a termination or layoff. The first priority would appear to be to establish that employability varies among workers in similar jobs for similar industries, and to identify the factors that cause this variance. Ideally, one could conduct longitudinal studies tracking the careers of similar individuals with similar backgrounds through a sample of firms to establish the impact of job assignments and of training (on the job and other, firm-specific and general) on each individual's ability to find progressively better jobs either within a single organization or in different organizations (time between jobs and compensation differentials would be two important indicators). At the same time, cross-sectional studies to establish a strong association among the variables as specified in the causal relationships proposed in the model (i.e., accumulating mechanisms and advanced general skills; advanced general skills and employability; linking mechanisms, advanced general skills and absorptive capacity; bonding mechanisms and organizational commitment; organizational commitment, absorptive capacity and firm performance) would also provide avenues for fruitful and rigorous empirical inquiry.

Further, given our objective of exploring the association between the employment relationship and competitive advantage of a firm, our analysis has focused on the implications of employability for the firm, rather than the employee. Clearly, a host of important research questions will arise from an analysis of the effects of employability on the individual employee, e.g., what would its implications be on the concept of a career that has historically been such an important element of the employment relationship? As Homans (1950) argued so long ago, a job has a social as well as an economic dimension: it provides a focal point for the structure of social groups that allow individuals to maintain their equilibrium under the ordinary shocks of life. How would a relationship based on employability affect an individual's ability to create and maintain his or her "small group life"? What individual characteristics may make an employee more or less open to an employment relationship based on the concept of employability? Similarly, a more complete analysis of our model would also require an understanding of how different social and institutional factors – from cultural norms to the role of trade unions – may influence the viability and efficacy of employability, as well as how those social, political, cultural and institutional forces may themselves be affected by the progressive institutionalization of such an employment relationship. While outside the scope of our present argument, these and a variety of other individual and societal implications of employability clearly provide important and exciting avenues for both theoretical and empirical research.

4.5.2 Implications for management practice

In much of the literature we have reviewed in this chapter, related both to theories of business strategy and theories of the employment relationship, there is no explicit attention given to the role, if any, of management. Within the resource based view of strategy, for example, the resources themselves are the primary focus of analysis, with their various ascribed characteristics such as heterogeneity, immobility and imperfect imitability being related to firm performance with little attention to the intervening management variables that often endow the resources with their desired characteristics. Some authors acknowledge the role of the manager in creating and maintaining resource-based competitive advantage, but usually in a limited analytic role. Wernerfelt (1984), for example, assumes that managers can balance the need to exploit existing resources against the need to develop new ones by employing a resource–product matrix. And Barney's (1986) manager is assumed to be focused on organizational analysis of existing resources to determine the future value of assets they can acquire in factor markets.

Some key contributors to the resource based view have, however, begun to question this invisible or highly constrained management role. Dierickx and Cool (1989) have argued that many inputs are not freely tradable, but can only be accumulated, and that the uniqueness of each firm is determined by the way in which management uses the resources to create the actual inputs into the production process. Rumelt (1987: 558) has reflected a similar view that "the task of general management is to adjust and renew these resources and relationships as time, competition and change erode their value".

In this chapter we have presented a view of sustained competitive advantage in dynamic environments that suggests the specific tasks involved in the role ascribed to management by Dierickx and Cool, Rumelt and others. It is management's responsibility to develop, sustain and continuously enhance a firm's accumulating, linking and bonding mechanisms. They must establish the priority for and the mechanisms of recruitment, training and development through which the firm can accumulate its stock of advanced general skills. Similarly, they must create the processes for linking people to one another and to external opportunities through what we have described as "open access". And, finally, they must shape the purpose, values and norms of the firm so as to create a coherent and exciting internal context that bonds the members of the organization to one another and to the firm.

As we have argued earlier, accumulating, linking and bonding mechanisms are firm-specific resources and it is the co-specialization of these resources with the advanced general knowledge and skills of employees that enables a firm to develop sustainable competitive advantage in dynamic environments. Therefore, in the model we have presented, while a vast majority of the firm's employees maintain their employability, it is the managers of the firm who sacrifice their own career flexibility by specializing their roles, tasks and skills to the unique requirements of the firm. This is a sharp departure from the existing view in which most employees are seen as contributing to the development of firm-specific resources by specializing their skills to the requirements of the company while managers are seen as the integrating "generalists" whose skills are fungible across firms. In other words, our model suggests a fundamental reversal of roles: those who are commonly seen as the "generalists" because of their broad knowledge of the firm's processes, practices, resources and norms are actually the specialists because their skills and knowledge are firm-specific, while those who are presently called the "specialists" because of their expertise in specific technical, functional or process disciplines are actually the generalists because of the fungibility of their skills across firms. Such a role reversal has some profound implications not only for the internal labor market within firms but also for the structure of the external labor market in societies.

NOTE

* The authors are grateful to Richard Pascale, Michael Goold, Marcus Alexander, Yrjö Koskinen, James Henderson, Jim Christiansen, Subi Rangan, Simon Rodan, Alice de Koning and Gerhard Holt for their helpful comments on earlier drafts of this paper and in discussions on its subject matter.

REFERENCES

Bain, J. S. (1956). *Barriers to New Competition*. Cambridge, MA: Harvard University Press.

Barney, J. B. (1986). Strategic factor markets: Expectations, luck, and business strategy. *Management Science,* 32 (10 October): 1231–41.

Barney, J. B. (1991). Firm resources and sustained competitive advantage. *Journal of Management,* 17(1): 99–120.

Baron, J. N. and Pfeffer, J. (1994). The social psychology of organizations and inequality. *Social Psychology Quarterly.*

Baron, J. N., Davis-Blake, A. and Bielby, W. T. (1986). The structure of opportunity: How promotion ladders vary within and among organizations. *Administrative Science Quarterly,* 31 (June): 248–73.

Bartlett, C. A. and Ghoshal, S. (1995). Changing the role of top management (part 3): Beyond systems to people. *Harvard Business Review,* 3 (May–June): 132–43.

Bateman, T. S. and Organ, D. W. (1983). Job satisfaction and the good solider: The relationship between affect and employee "citizenship". *Academy of Management Journal,* 26, 587–95.

Becker, G. S. (1962). Investment in human capital: A theoretical analysis. *Journal of Political Economy,* 70: 7–44.

Burgelman, R. A. (1991). Intraorganizational ecology of strategy making and organizational adaptation: Theory and field research. *Organization Science,* 2 (3): 239–62.

Burns, T. and Stalker, G. M. (1961). *The Management of Innovation.* London: Tavistock.

Cappelli, P. (1995). Rethinking employment. *British Journal of Industrial Relations,* 33 (4): 563–602.

Cappelli, P. and Sherer, P. D. (1991). The missing role of context in OB: The need for a meso-level approach. In B. M. Staw and L. L. Cummings (eds), 55–110. Greenwich, CT: JAI Press.

Caves, R. E. and Porter, M. E. (1977). From entry barriers to mobility barriers: Conjectural decisions and contrived deterrence to new competition. *Quarterly Journal of Economics,* 91 (May): 241–61.

Cohen, W. M. and Levinthal, D. A. (1990). Absorptive capacity: A new perspective on learning and innovation. *Administrative Science Quarterly,* 35 (1): 128–52.

Coleman, J. S. (1992). The rational reconstruction of society. *American Sociological Review,* 58 (February): 1–15.

Conner, K. R. (1991). A historical comparison of resource-based theory and five schools of thought within industrial organization economics: Do we have a new theory of the firm? *Journal of Management,* 17 (1): 121–54.

Cornfield, D. B. (1981). Industrial social organization and layoffs in American manufacturing industry. In I. Berg (ed.), *Sociological Perspectives on Labor Markets*: 219–48. New York: Academic Press.

D'Aveni, R. A. (1994). *Hyper Competition: Managing the dynamics of strategic maneuvering.* New York: Free Press.

Dierickx, I. and Cool, K. (1989). Asset stock accumulation and sustainability of competitive advantage. *Management Science,* 35 (12): 1504–11.

Doeringer, P. B. and Piore, M. J. (1971). *Internal Labor Markets and Manpower Analysis.* Lexington, MA: D. C. Heath.

Hall, R. E. (1982). The importance of lifetime jobs in the US economy. *American Economic Review,* 72 (4): 716–24.

Heath, C., Knez, M. and Camerer, C. (1993). The strategic management of the entitlement process in the employment relationship. *Strategic Management Journal,* 14: 75–93.

Homans, G. C. (1950). *The Human Group.* New York: Harcourt, Brace and World.

Horvat, B. (1982). *The Political Economy of Socialism.* New York: M. E. Sharpe.

Itami, H. (1987). *Mobilizing Invisible Assets.* Cambridge, MA: Harvard University Press.

Jackson, S. E. and Schuler, R. S. (1995). Understanding human resource management in the context of organizations and their environments. *Annual Review of Psychology,* 46: 237–64.

Jacoby, S. M. (1985). *Employing Bureaucracy: Managers, unions, and the transformation of work in American industry, 1900–1945.* New York: Columbia University Press.

Kanter, R. M. (1989). The new managerial work. *Harvard Business Review,* (November–December): 85–92.

Kim, W. C. and Mauborgne, R. A. (1996). Procedural justice and managers' in-role and extra-role behavior: The case of the multinational. *Management Science,* (April).

Kogut, B. and Zander, U. (1992). Knowledge of the firm combinative capabilities and the replication of technology. *Organization Science,* (August): 383–97.

Lado, A. A. and Wilson, M. C. (1994). Human resource systems and sustained competitive advantage: A competency-based perspective. *Academy of Management Review,* 19 (4): 669–727.

Leonard-Barton, D. (1992). Core capabilities and core rigidities: a paradox in managing new product development. *Strategic Management Journal,* 13: 111–25.

Milgrom, P. P. R. R. and Roberts, J. (1992). *Economics, Organization and Management.* Englewood Cliffs, NJ: Prentice-Hall.

Montgomery, C.A. (ed.) 1995. *Resource-based and Evolutionary Theories of the Firm.* Boston, MA: Kluwer Academic Publishers. .

Moran, P. and Ghoshal, S. (1996a). Theories of economic organization: The case for realism and balance. *Academy of Management Review,* 21 (1): 58–72.

Moran, P. and Ghoshal, S. (1996b). Value creation by firms. *Academy of Management Best Paper Proceedings,* 41–5.

Nelson, R. R. and Winter, S. G. (1982). *An Evolutionary Theory of Economic Change.* Cambridge, MA: Harvard University Press.

North, D. C. (1990). *Institutions, Institutional Change and Economic Performance,* Cambridge: Cambridge University Press.

Penrose, E. T. (1959). *The Theory of the Growth of the Firm.* New York: John Wiley.

Peteraf, M. A. (1993). The cornerstone of competitive advantage: A resource-based view. *Strategic Management Journal,* 14: 179–91.

Peteraf, M. A. (1994). Commentary. The two schools of thought in resource-based theory: Definitions and implications for research. In P. Shrivastava, A. S. Huff and J. E. Dutton (eds), *Advances in Strategic Management:* 153–8. Greenwich, CT: JAI Press.

Pfeffer, J. and Baron, J. N. (1988). Taking the workers back out: Recent trends in the structuring of employment. In B. M. Staw and L. L. Cummings (eds), 257–303. Greenwich, CT: JAI Press.

Pfeffer, J. and Cohen, Y. (1984). Determinants of internal labor markets in organizations. *Administrative Science Quarterly,* 29 (December): 550–72.

Pfeffer, J. and Salancik, G. R. (1978). *The External Control of Organizations: A resource dependence perspective.* New York: Harper.

Porter, M. E. (1979). The structure within industries and companies' performance. *Review of Economics and Statistics,* (May): 214–27.

Rousseau, D. M. (1989). Psychological an implied contracts in organizations. *Employee Responsibilities and Rights Journal,* 2 (2): 121–39.

110   *Strategy, Organization and the Changing Nature of Work*

Rumelt, R. P. (1984). Towards a strategic theory of the firm. In R. B. Lamb (ed.), 556–70. Engelwood Cliffs, NJ: Prentice-Hall.

Rumelt, R. P. (1987). Theory, strategy, and entrepreneurship. In D. J. Teece (ed.), *The Competitive Challenge*: 137–58. Cambridge, MA: Ballinger.

Schumpeter, J. A. (1934). *The Theory of Economic Development.* Cambridge, MA: Harvard University Press.

Simon, H. A. (1951). A formal theory of the employment relationship. *Economica,* 19: 293–305.

Simon, H. A. (1991). Organizations and markets. *Journal of Economic Perspectives*, 5 (2): 25–44.

Szulanski, G. (1993). Intra-firm transfer of best practice, appropriative capabilities, and organizational barriers to appropriation. (Working Paper).Fontainebleau: INSEAD.

Teece, D. J., Pisano, G. and Shuen, A. (1994). Dynamic capabilities and strategic management. *Strategic Management Journal,* Special Issue: forthcoming.

Tushman, M. L. (1977). Special boundary roles in the innovation process. *Administrative Science Quarterly,* 22: 587–605.

Tusmhman, M. L. and Anderson, P. (1986). Technological discontinuities and organizational environments. *Administrative Science Quarterly,* 31: 439–65.

Wachter, M. L. and Williamson, O. E. (1978). Obligational markets and the mechanics of inflation. *Bell Journal of Economics,* 9: 549–71.

Wallis, J. J. and North, D. C. (1986). Measuring the transaction sector in the American economy, 1870–1970. In S. L. Engerman and R. E. Gallman (eds), *Long-term Factors in American Economic Growth*: 95–161. Chicago: University of Chicago Press.

Waterman, R. H. Jr., Waterman, J. A. and Collard, B. A. (1994). Toward a career-resilient workforce. *Harvard Business Review,* 72 (4): 87–95.

Weber, M. (1978). Economy and society. In G. Roth and C. Wittich (eds), Berkeley: University of California Press.

Wernerfelt, B. (1984). A resource-based view of the firm. *Strategic Management Journal,* 14: 4–12.

Williamson, O. E. (1975). *Markets and Hierarchies: Analysis and antitrust implications.* New York: Free Press.

Williamson, O. E. (1985). *Economic Institutions of Capitalism.* New York: Free Press.

Winter, S. G. (1995). Four Rs of profitability: Rents, resources, routines, and replication. In C. A. Montgomery (eds), *Resources in an Evolutionary Perspective: A synthesis of evolutionary and resource-based approaches to strategy:* 147–78. Norwell, MA, and Dordrecht: Kluwer Academic.

Wright, P. M., McMahan, G. C. and McWilliams, A. (1994). Human resources and sustained competitive advantage: A resource-based perspective. *International Journal of Human Resource Management,* 5 (2): 301–26.

5. The New Deal with Employees and its Implications for Business Strategy

Peter Cappelli

5.1 INTRODUCTION

Most observers of the US business community believe that the traditional relationship in corporations between employer and employee, with its expectations of long-term commitments and an exchange of security for loyalty, is gone. What ended the traditional employment relationship is a variety of new management practices, driven by a changing environment, that essentially bring the market – both the market for a company's products and the labor market for its employees – directly inside the firm. And once inside, the logic of the market quickly becomes dominant, pushing out of its way administrative practices based on the behavioral principles of reciprocity and long-term commitment, internal promotion and development practices, and general concerns about equity inside the organization that underlie the more traditional employment contract. As a result, the policies and practices that buffered the relationship with employees from outside pressures are gone. The end of employee loyalty to an organization, replaced by greater attachment to careers in the market, is one important manifestation of this change.

In the context of the management community, these developments are associated with practical topics such as problems of retention or declining commitment. In the academic community, they fall under the heading of the decline of internal labor markets and the rising importance of external labor markets.

There is some debate in the US as to exactly how wide spread these developments are,[1] but no serious observers argue that there has been no change in the nature of the employment relationship. Similar developments are underway in most Anglo-Saxon countries where employment law offers relatively little opposition to the changes, especially Australia, New Zealand, and the United Kingdom.[2] Anecdotal reports suggest that the job hopping that has become the most noticeable characteristic of the new relationship was perhaps most pronounced not in the US but in former communist countries, especially for multinational companies, where the employees had no history of corporate loyalty. The extent to which these practices transfer to Europe will depend in large measure on whether the management practices that drove them, such as outsourcing, profit centers, and especially outside recruiting, become common enough to overcome the current regulatory and cultural opposition to them.[3]

It is tempting to think of the new relationship as something like free agency or a completely open market where legal contracts can be used to govern all aspects of the relationship, much as they do for professional sports or temporary help. For most positions, especially those in management, such contracts cannot define an employment relationship. At least some of the skills are unique to the employer and developed on-the-job, the tasks are interdependent with others or with systems in the organization, and performance is difficult to monitor accurately, all of which make contracts imperfect at best. Nor do managers have the equivalent of a professional labor market. Their work is governed by standards inside the organization, not professional codes, and their success is inextricably linked to that of their employer. The most important rewards for managers are still associated with success inside a company and achievement of company goals.

The contradiction inherent in the new relationship comes from the fact that the nature of the work that most managers perform does not lend itself to market-based relationships and contracts. It is much more suited to open-ended relationships where the obligations can be adjusted, performance can be observed, and rewards allocated accordingly as situations change. Some level of mutual commitment and trust to facilitate changing needs is inevitable, as is the need to develop some unique skills inside the organization and to retain them indefinitely. At the same time, the pressures from markets and the need to change organizations means that truly open-ended, long-term employment relationships are largely dead. The pressures to shed obsolete skills (compounded by the uncertainty of knowing which ones will be obsolete) and the problem of poaching skills from other employers makes it difficult to maintain commitment and trust, develop skills internally, and retain important skills. The defining problem of the new relationship, therefore, is how to graft the model of the market onto occupations for which it is poorly suited.

Observers sometimes refer to the traditional, lifetime employment relationship as something like a marriage. Using that analogy, the new employment relationship is a lifetime of divorces and remarriages. It is not simply dating.

That suggests relationships that are too casual and short-term to facilitate the functions that need to be performed in most organizations. It is more like serial monogamy, a series of close relationships governed by the expectation going in that they need to be made to work and yet will inevitably not last. And the adaptations to a life of serial monogamy – always keeping your options open with other partners, avoiding long-term investments in each other with prenuptial agreements, reducing the issues on which violations of trust matter (e.g., no big life insurance policies naming them as the beneficiaries) – are not unlike the career advice given to employees in the modern workplace.

It is not obvious that such relationships must fail or even that they necessarily destroy commitment. There are many successful relationships involving mutual commitments that we know going in will not last. The relationships between alumni and colleges is but one example. But the difference is that both parties go into those relationships not only knowing that the relationship will end but also, generally speaking, when it will end. What is different about the new employment relationship is that while both parties know that the relationship is unlikely to last forever, it has no finite ending point, and either side can end it unilaterally when they want.

So the new employment relationship is an uneasy dance between an open-ended relationship and the pull of the market. The parties are constantly negotiating their commitments in light of uncertain future needs and opportunities elsewhere.

Pressures from outside the relationship, from the labor market in particular, are now the important forces shaping the nature of the relationship. When labor markets are slack and jobs are difficult to find, employees become more loyal to their employer and bear most of the costs of restructuring; when labor markets tighten, employee commitment falls and employers become more willing to make investments in their employees.

As with any change, the new employment relationship where the labor market dominates employee behavior is creating a new set of winners and losers. For most the past two decades, employers won and employees lost because with this new, market-mediated relationship, slack labor markets allowed employers to push most of the costs of restructuring onto employees. Once labor markets begin to tighten, however, the problems for management are no longer simple. When bargaining power becomes a bit more equal, then the problem of negotiating this open-ended relationship in the context of a market becomes very tricky indeed.

There are solutions to the human resource challenges associated with the new deal. They include retaining key talent in the face of outside hiring, managing employees who no longer have lifetime commitments to the employer, and financing training investments for employees who may well leave before their improved performance can pay off the investments. The more complicated problem, which is the focus of this chapter, is to consider how the new constraints thrown up by this changing employment relationship challenge the traditional ways in which employers have been able to develop competencies and, in turn, business strategy.

5.2 THE FORCES BEHIND THESE CHANGES

What we think of as the "traditional" employment relationship of long-term duration and internal employee management is really a very recent phenomenon. At the turn of the century in the US, most industrial employees either worked for contractors within a company's facilities or turned over so quickly that they were essentially "temps," very much like the trends that we see now. Companies that kept accurate records of costs found that contractors working inside their facilities were very efficient, and the costs were often well below those incurred working with their own direct employees, just as many companies who are outsourcing discover today.

What ended the contracting system, bringing the workforce into long-term relationships inside the firm, was the need to coordinate more complex organizations and to ensure that the skills were there to make that happen.

The skill of manpower planning, forced upon industry by wartime controls beginning first in World War I, eventually led to what we now see as the traditional employment relationship as companies needed to ensure the supply of labor for their vast, integrated operations.[4]

Especially in the managerial ranks, long-term relationships and systems of internal development, including promotion, served three key purposes:

1. They facilitated investments in training which were recouped by the employer over time after the employee's performance rose. Particularly in large corporations, a crucial skill was understanding the organization's systems and procedures, a skill that could only be developed through long-term service to the corporation.
2. The security that employees found in these relationships helped produce loyalty and commitment. In large, complex organizations, loyalty was especially important because it was difficult to measure any individual's performance.
3. The possibility of moving up the ladder provided powerful motivation at relatively little cost, since few employees could ever make it to the top.

These long-term relationships were not without their downside, however. Even in their heyday beginning in the 1950s, they were rightly criticized in books such as *The Organizational Man* as creating something like an industrial feudalism where employees essentially could not leave (corporate managers could not move to similar jobs elsewhere unless other corporations would hire them from outside) and where inbreeding stifled new thinking.[5]

The developments that eroded the benefits of these long-term relationships became noticeable in the 1980s. They included the following:

- more competitive product markets that not only created pressure to cut costs but, more importantly, to reduce time to market and pursue differentiated market niches. These changes made long-term, fixed investments – in people as well as in capital – problematic as they became obsolete much more quickly;
- information technology that could take over the functions of coordinating and monitoring, tasks traditionally performed by middle management. With these technologies in place, an outside supplier could be easily monitored and integrated into one's operation. It was not necessary to own them and have them under one's corporate umbrella, managed by a corporate staff. As a result, a huge range of functions could now be outsourced. For those who remained within the company, the threat of being outsourced was always present;
- new arrangements have made it possible for the financial community to advance the interests of shareholders far ahead of other traditional stakeholders within publicly held companies. Pressures to increase shareholder value put the squeeze on costs, especially fixed costs;
- new techniques for managing companies – profit centers, outside bench marking, core competencies – brought the discipline of markets inside the firm and made every aspect of the business and every employee feel like they were exposed to market pressures.[6]

5.3 CHANGING THE RELATIONSHIP

These developments make it very difficult for firms to retain long-term relationships with employees and much easier to rely on the market to meet their needs. The behavior of employees has changed as a result, as has the way in which they are managed, altering fundamentally the relationship between employer and employee. And that process is far from over. Indeed, some of these developments now appear to be a permanent part of the business landscape. The downsizing trend, for example, continued non-stop since its beginnings around 1982, largely independent of the business cycle. The most recent estimates from the American Management Association data suggest that more than one-third of the firms that are downsizing are hiring at the same time, suggesting that the goal of downsizing is no longer simply to get down to a more efficient size. It is to rearrange the competencies of the organization. Companies continue to hire while they are downsizing because they are shedding workers with obsolete skills while taking in new ones with skills in demand.[7]

While the challenges facing employees under these new arrangements are clear, very little attention has been given to the substantial problems that they pose for employers. For example, turnover, especially of key employees, is almost always a crucial issue for employers, and it becomes much more difficult to manage in this new environment. Research on employee turnover finds that most people who quit generally do so in order to take jobs elsewhere. The more employees are focused on the labor market and the more information they have on other jobs, the more likely they are to leave. New workplace contracts that push workers to focus on their "employability" direct them toward an orientation outside the firm.

Voluntary turnover has been less of a problem for the corporate world until recently because virtually all corporations have been downsizing at the same time, creating a big surplus of talent on the market and also restricting those voluntary quits. But in tight labor markets, such as information systems, companies are already bemoaning the difficulty in retaining employees. And if labor markets tighten further, expect turnover even of traditionally loyal employees to skyrocket as they are pulled away to jobs elsewhere. Employers obviously lose their investments in employees who leave, so the ability to recoup those investments declines as the expectation that workers will remain with the firm erodes. Investments in training for new entrant workers, that is, investments to teach them their job, are declining. In some cases, this reduction in training creates a vicious circle of skill shortages which leads to even more outside hiring. Not only has this led to wages being bid up, it has also sharply reduced the interest of these companies in developing any of their own talent because they fear – rightly – that they will lose investments in new employees to a higher bidder who can pay more for a trained worker. As employee development declines, the shortage of skilled labor can worsen.

Virtually all organizations need their employees to make investments in company-specific capabilities, but this also becomes much more difficult as they understand the risk that those investments may not pay off for them. Will employees take an undesirable assignment that is crucial to the company on the chance that the promised payoff of a plum job at headquarters two years later may be wiped out by a downsizing or restructuring? Again, recent evidence suggests that they are much less likely to do so.[8]

The traditional reliance on mentoring that companies used to develop employees has eroded as both turnover and restructuring lead to frequent changes in bosses and reporting arrangements. Companies have turned to "centers of excellence" somewhere in the organization to deal with the concern that employees no longer can expect to turn to their boss to get help on technical issues. For career advice, managerial employees increasingly have to look for help outside the organization, again in the outside market. The exploding field of management coaches or mentors for hire exists because management employees want development so desperately that they leave the firm and buy it in the market.

Compensation is widely accepted as being the most important mechanism for managing and motivating employees, especially in the US. These changes in the employment relationship turn most existing compensation principles on their head. Traditional compensation policies, based on job evaluation, were designed to promote internal equity between employees in different jobs. Those concerns have gone out the window. Instead, wages are set based on prevailing levels in the labor market; if not, people holding jobs that are in demand walk for better offers, and it becomes impossible to bring in skills from the outside. But complaints about equity skyrocket, typically as junior people with "hot" skills end up making much more than their senior colleagues. The widespread use of contractors, consultants, and temps, each with different pay rates, sets up another group of invidious comparisons.

In fields like information systems where the demands are constantly changing, the wage structure within the firm may have little apparent order: older skills may suddenly have virtually no market value since new programming skills do not build on old ones. Young programmers find their wages may be highest when they first enter the labor market because their programming skills are on the cutting edge. From that point on, their value and market compensation erodes, and they may well find themselves unemployable unless their skills are updated.

Beyond simply securing a skilled workforce lies the much more complicated challenge of ensuring its performance, a task that focuses on issues like motivation and commitment. This task is made more difficult by the new employment relationship because work-related attitudes are also driven much more by outside circumstances that are beyond the control of the employer. Companies that work hard to maintain good morale find that the results of their climate surveys rise and fall with events outside, such as the state of the labor market. Some of the most interesting research on employee commitment finds that it is driven by one's labor market options: the more an employee searches and the more job options they have, the lower is their commitment to their current employer.[9] On the other hand, downturns in the economy and in opportunities elsewhere raise satisfaction and commitment to one's current job.

The possibility of promotion was perhaps the most important incentive for individuals to act in the interests of the employer. Flat organizations and reduced job security have cut the probability of promotion dramatically and reduced that incentive. Securing cooperation within the organization becomes much more of an issue as employees see their interests as less linked to the overall success of the corporation. Competition between individual employees to build their résumés for the outside market means greater competition for choice assignments, fighting for credit and to avoid blame when projects are finished. These situations are particularly intense in professional organizations like law firms or investment banks where employees on the same level must work together on discrete projects.

5.4 THE NEW DEAL AND ITS EFFECT ON STRATEGY

The traditional arrangements were useful to employers in three main ways:

- By retaining employees and developing them internally for more senior positions, they provided a predictable supply of workers at the requisite skill levels.
- They facilitated the acquisition and retention of company-specific skills.
- They made for employees who acted in the company's interests even when it was not always in their short-term interest to do so because the practices focused their incentives on the long run.

The traditional arrangements related to fundamental issues of business strategy in a straightforward way. An increasingly accepted perspective on strategy is the resource-based view of the firm where a firm's competitiveness is seen as not so much a function of market positioning but of competencies that originate within the organization.[10] It is difficult to think of situations where such competencies are not inextricably linked to employee skills. In many organizations, such as professional service firms, the intellectual capital of the employees is not only the basis of the competencies but is essentially the only real resource the organization has. To the extent that the factors behind the new deal are changing the relationship with employees, it would not be surprising to find that they are also changing the competencies of organizations as well and, in turn, their approach to business strategy.

The changes outlined above help explain why employers find it difficult to make long-term investments and commitments in their employees. But another factor is even more important in its effects on firm competencies, and that is the problem of "poaching" or hiring away talent from competitors. Poaching is driven by two factors. The first is the need for firms to restructure more quickly. One way to think of this problem is that product cycles, and the associated cycles of restructuring competencies, are not shorter than employee life cycles. Other changes in the boundary of the firm, such as mergers and acquisitions or decisions about outsourcing, lead to more or less instant changes in required competencies. When firms restructure or otherwise change their business strategies in ways that demand new competencies, it is difficult and in many cases impossible to meet those new demands in a timely fashion internally. When a pharmaceutical company sees its research needs shift from physical chemistry to biotechnology, for example, it cannot effectively retrain its physical chemists and make them biochemists in anything like a reasonable time frame. Instead, it goes into the market and hires biochemists.

If the above factors can be considered the demand side of the equation, then the second set of factors relates to the supply side. From the perspective of employees, their willingness to be hired away has greatly increased. In part this is because of the factors described earlier that make it difficult for firms to provide long-term relationships. The employees understand this and no longer see their long-term interests as necessarily tied to their current employer. The change in their expectations is also driven by flatter corporate hierarchies, which mean fewer promotion prospects, once the main reward for long service. This situation is exacerbated by the greater willingness of firms to fill the positions that remain with outsiders. So employees are increasingly willing to move as a way to circumvent being blocked in their current careers. The fact that pay scales are also more market-based, and less internally focused, means that there are fewer rewards to seniority and less incentive for staying put.

The rise of executive recruiting companies, whose world-wide revenues rose by a factor of three in the mid-1990s, has also facilitated poaching by providing much better information about applicants and available positions, about supply and demand. This information makes matches more possible.

Poaching affects the competencies of firms and their business strategies in straightforward ways. For firms that compete on the basis of speed, poaching can be a tremendous asset as it allows them to restructure and adapt to changing markets even more quickly. Businesses operating in Silicon Valley would seem to fit this model. For firms that do not rely on speed, however, and instead rely on long-term investments in employees and competencies and/or firm-specific skills, it is a tremendous hindrance. Such firms become net exporters of skill. Not only do their investments walk out the door, but their organizational competencies and strategies are eroded as well.[11]

Similar arguments apply to entrepreneurship. This modern poaching approach is a tremendous advantage for entrepreneurs who can now much more easily assemble the skills that are needed to develop new products and businesses, attracting risk-taking employees with the possibility of stock options and other compensation based on the eventual success of the new products. A well-known phenomenon, for example, is for entrepreneurs to come from other locations in order to base start-up operations in Silicon Valley despite its very high cost structure. They come simply because of the breadth of available skills and the willingness of employees in that community to be hired away for interesting opportunities.

The other side of the entrepreneurship argument is that poaching makes it much more difficult for firms to develop new products inside their existing structures. The reason is that the greater ability to start up new ventures gives their own employees who have the ideas and expertise a powerful alternative to staying within the firm. They can much more easily take their intellectual capital with them and expropriate a much larger share of the eventual gains from it.

These new pressures and alternatives may eventually lead to a redistribution of strategies or approaches to competitiveness across firms. We may well see, for example, a substantial decline in firms who try to compete through long-term investments and a rise of firms who compete through speed, even independent of changes in product markets that seem to reward faster adaptation.

Another alternative might be changes in the distribution of strategies according to the national characteristics of firms. Different national economic and legal systems provide obstacles and constraints to the new employment relationship. European countries, for example, increasingly regulate the labor market in ways that reduce the ability to shed employees and, in turn, the incentives to hire new employees. Firms in these countries, then, may find that strategies aimed at long-term investments may have greater appeal in part because they find alternative strategies too difficult to implement and because many of their competitors in other countries have already shifted away from that approach because of poaching in their own systems.

For multinational firms, we may see a related development, and that is to have them distribute their operations geographically to match the needs of certain projects to the labor market characteristics of regions. The international division of labor is already a well-known phenomenon, although it has typically been based on the cost and availability of distinctive skills. But it is easy to imagine the criteria changing to reflect differences in the employment relationship.

One might see, for example, the long-term projects that require stable project teams being based in France because "poaching" and other aspects of employment mobility are less there while the fast-moving projects are based in Ireland or the US where it is easier to assemble new teams – and also to disband them when the project finishes. The relative absence of regulations restricting layoffs in some countries may also be an attraction to locating short-term projects there. Examples of this phenomenon already occur within the US where employers base research and development operations in Silicon Valley, in order to have access to the changing mix of the latest skills, but then base production operations with stable skill demands elsewhere, typically in rural areas, where it is easier to retain employees.

The new deal employment relationships may also give greater importance to the role of infrastructure which is necessary to substitute for the cross-subsidies that were common under the old model. Specifically, large employers in particular made substantial investments in new employees, often in skills that were generally useful to employers elsewhere. One might think of these investments as public goods that contributed in important ways to the infrastructure of the economy because many employees eventually took those skills on to other employers and other roles in society. If employers are no longer providing the same investments in the skills of their employees, then the importance of alternative sources of skills increases. The most obvious of these are schools, both in the private and public sectors.

5.5 CONCLUSIONS

The arguments above suggest that human resource management is undergoing profound changes as the "traditional" employment relationship, based on internal development and long-term prospects, gives way to a very different relationship driven much more strongly by the outside labor market. The effect of this development on employees, particularly the increase in their insecurity, is well-known. The effects on their organizations, in contrast, is not so well understood. And, in particular, possible effects on the manner in which firms compete has not been considered.

The typical arguments relating business strategy and human resource issues, broadly defined, long suggested that firms picked their strategies and then created human resource practices to align with those strategies. To what extent this ever was the case is not clear, but if the arguments above that individual employers have lost much of their ability to dictate human resource practices to the greater power of the labor market are correct, then we might expect a very different situation in the future. One might expect the ability of firms to develop and impose certain business strategies to be substantially constrained. Specifically, strategies that rely on long-term investments in human capital become much more difficult to execute. Those that rely on poaching of skills from elsewhere, in contrast, become easier to pursue. The need to innovate and restructure more quickly was, of course, one of the factors that drove the trend toward hiring human capital from competitors that helped destroy internalized, long-term employment relationships. Once those relationships become difficult to sustain, then the business strategies that they support become difficult to sustain as well.

One of the more interesting consequences of the above situation is, as noted above, that firms might have to change their locations in order to find employment relationships that suit their business strategies. These location decisions might involve countries of operation given differences in the characteristics of national employment systems. Companies may move in order to find employees who are willing to stay in place (should they want to protect human capital) or to move (should they want to hire), but they also may move in order to take advantage of training and education systems that reduce their own need to train. Such developments further the importance of national employment systems and their associated infrastructure in understanding the business decisions of firms.

NOTES

1. For an example, see the debate between Sanford Jacoby, "Accounts of the decline of career jobs are premature" and Peter Cappelli, "Career jobs are dead", in *California Management Review*, forthcoming.
2. A brief summary of the evidence for these other countries is in Peter Cappelli, "Rethinking work." *British Journal of Industrial Relations*, 1995.
3. Space constraints make it difficult to review the considerable body of research offering evidence concerning the extent of these changes. Evidence from the perspective of the overall labor market is presented in Peter Cappelli *et al., Change at Work*, New York: Oxford University Press, 1997, while evidence focusing more on developments within firms is presented in Peter Cappelli. *The New Deal at Work*, Boston, MA: Harvard Business School Press, 1999.
4. A longer discussion of the historical precedents for the contemporary developments in the employment relationship is in Peter Cappelli, "We've been here before: historical examples of arm's-length employment relationships." In Margaret Blair and Thomas A. Kochan (eds), *Corporate Responsibility for Human Capital*. (Washington, DC: Brookings Institution, forthcoming).
5. See William H. Whyte, *The Organizational Man*. New York: Simon and Schuster, 1956.
6. This material is discussed more thoroughly in Chapter 3 of Cappelli 1999, op. cit.
7. American Management Association, *Annual Survey on Downsizing*. New York, AMA, 1996.
8. This evidence includes surveys from MBA students suggesting that their priority in selecting first jobs is the immediate experience they will secure to build their résumés and surveys of executives indicating their reluctance to move for better jobs if it takes them away from their networks, leaving them stranded if the new job does not work out. For example, a recent international survey of MBA

students finds only 7 percent anticipate staying with their employer 10 or more years. See PricewaterhouseCooper's *International Student Survey*. New York: PWC, May 1999. This evidence is reviewed in Chapters 5–7 of Cappelli 1999, op. cit.

9. See, e.g., Charles O'Reilly III and Jennifer Chatman, "Organizational commitment and psychological attachment: the effects of compliance identification and internalization on prosocial behavior." *Journal of Applied Psychology*, 1986, 429–99.

10. See Robert Grant, *Contemporary Strategy Analysis*. Oxford: Basil Blackwell, 1997, for a discussion of the resource-based view of the firm.

11. Descriptions of the competitive advantage of Silicon Valley firms suggest that poaching skilled employees drives their ability to innovate quickly and, in turn, to secure first-mover advantages. See Anna Lee Saxenian, *Regional Advantage: Culture and competition in Silicon Valley and Route 128*. Cambridge, MA: Harvard University Press.

6. Business Strategy and Employment Systems in Spain: an Empirical Analysis

Carlos Portales

6.1 INTRODUCTION

There is a growing consensus among business managers that traditional sources of advantage such as product and process technology, market regulations, access to financial resources, and economies of scale, among others, are becoming less relevant for competitive success. In turn, their people and how firms organize and manage them are increasingly more important elements as a basis of firms' success, especially because they constitute key components in the implementation of firms' business strategies.

The field of human resource management (HRM) has also acknowledged the growing strategic role of human resources (HR). A strategic perspective of HRM, which has been labeled strategic human resource management (SHRM), suggests that the behavior of employees within firms has important implications for organizational performance (Schuler and Jackson, 1987a; Bailey, 1993). SHRM authors argue that employment systems – the set of work organization practices, HR policies and other organizational characteristics that firms implement to support their business strategy – can affect individual employee performance. Through their influence over employees' skills and motivation and through organizational structures these systems may allow those employees to improve their job performance.

There is a strong consensus among SHRM researchers that work organization practices such as job rotation, empowerment, and teamwork, or HRM policies like employment guarantees, recruitment, selection, evaluation, compensation, promotion, training and development, plus other organizational arrangements such as employees' linking and bonding mechanisms, are key instruments for organizations to achieve their business objectives. In contrast, very little empirical work testing these ideas is available. Moreover, the small number of research pieces available show inconclusive results.

The main contribution of this chapter is precisely that it is one of the few that empirically test the relationship between different business strategies and particular employment systems that intend to support those strategies. Moreover, our study is the first piece of empirical research that tests SHRM hypotheses outside both the US and the UK. Using a sample of 218 Spanish firms across many different industries we show that specific employment systems are implemented to support particular business strategies. We found a strong tendency among Spanish firms to align their employment systems with their competitive strategies to compete successfully in the market place.

One problem with SHRM hypotheses, however, is that both business strategies and employment system types have been mostly developed in the United States and the United Kingdom. Our chapter contributes in filling a gap in the SHRM literature by being one of the first report on empirical research work conducted outside those two countries. We found that some of the business strategy dimensions and specific theoretically derived employment systems previously employed in empirical research for the Anglo-Saxon business context also apply in the Spanish economic setting. Therefore, previous results obtained in a particular business context might be comparable to and lessons might be drawn from similarities as well as from differences found in such diverse environments.

A second contribution of our study is a methodological one. In our view, inconsistent empirical results in the SHRM field are mainly due to poor definitions and measurements of both business strategies and employment systems. Typologies developed for these purposes in recent research works capture only a portion of such a complex phenomenon by compressing the multidimensionality of business strategies and employment systems in an excessively reduced number of archetypes. Moreover, these existing typologies have been developed in the Anglo-Saxon literature and doubts exist about their applicability in different business contexts.

This chapter, in contrast, goes beyond traditional definitions and measures coming from that Anglo-Saxon tradition and, instead, introduces more sophisticated definitions and operationalization of business strategy and employment system variables. We also found that these enriched definitions and operationalizations are actually consistent with the Spanish business reality. Strong evidence is presented showing that Spanish companies are actually adopting the proposed competitive strategy types and employment systems.

The rest of the chapter is organized as follows. We first present the dominant theoretical debate that has oriented most of the existing empirical work in the field of SHRM. Despite the broad agreement in the field of SHRM about the key role that work organization practices, HRM policies, and other organizational characteristics play in supporting competitive strategies, a theoretical debate exists, however, about the particular ways in which HR management can support those business strategies. Two conflicting theoretical paradigms dominate the field of SHRM: the contingency approach and the universalistic perspective. Moreover, the scarce empirical research available has not been able to strongly support either of them. This debate is treated in depth by Sánchez-Runde, in Chapter 2.

In section 6.2 we discuss the main ideas of each one of these approaches.

In section 6.3, as was mentioned earlier, we first develop a more comprehensive and enriched typology of business strategy. Five different competitive strategies result from our analysis. Each one of them is described in detail.

Then, in sub-section 6.4.1 we propose a typology of employment systems. Drawing extensively from previous theoretical work in the field six different employment systems are proposed. Each of them is defined as a function of 13 different work organization practices, HRM policies, and other organizational characteristics. Next, an underlying logic needs to be developed in order to establish a coherent linkage between particular business strategies and specific supporting employment systems. Based on both our own work (Ricart and Portales, Chapter 2 and on the analysis of employees' skills and behaviors required to implement each of the business strategies we propose a rationale for linking competitive strategies with employment systems.

In sub-section 6.4.3, we explore the universalistic arguments. Specific hypotheses proposing a relationship between business strategies and the best practices employment system are presented.

Later on, in section 6.5, we described in detail the sample of 218 Spanish firms utilized in this study. The characteristics of the instruments used and the procedures followed in order to conduct our empirical work are also explained here. In addition, this section discusses the research methodology utilized.

Section 6.6, discusses the research instruments being used in our study. An overview of the data analysis plan is also provided here. Methods used to establish the psychometric properties of the instruments are also discussed in this section.

Section 6.7, presents the empirical results of this study. Specific statistical procedures to test the hypotheses are also discussed in this section. Both contingency theory and universalistic hypotheses are contrasted with figures resulting from the analysis. Finally, some preliminary results regarding the impact of an alignment between business strategies and employment systems are presented. Conclusions and implications of the research findings for future research and practice are discussed in section 6.8.

6.2 THEORETICAL DEBATE WITHIN THE FIELD OF SHRM

Two modes of theorizing have been increasingly employed in the field of SHRM: the contingency approach and the universalistic view. In Chapter 3 of this book Sánchez-Runde elaborates extensively on both perspectives. Here, we briefly synthesize the main arguments of both views.

In the strategy literature, at least since the publication of Alfred Chandler's (1962) *Strategy and Structure*, many authors have followed a contingency approach, arguing that, in order to be effective, the employment systems should be consistent with firms' business strategy. Chandler argued that a firm's business strategy, its organizational structure and its managerial processes should be aligned in order to be mutually effective. Along the same lines, Miles and Snow (1978), Galbraith and Kazanjian (1986) argued, later on, that organizations' systems and processes need to be strongly linked to business strategy in effective organizations. Similarly, Mintzberg (1978) and Quinn (1978), who considered strategy formulation and implementation to be integrated processes, also described the close interdependence of internal practices and competitive strategy in successful companies.

More recently, SHRM authors have argued that employment systems are part of the systems and processes that need to be consistent with strategy (Miles and Snow, 1984; Wright and McMahan, 1992; Milgrom and Roberts, 1995; MacDuffie, 1995). Many authors suggested that since employment systems influence employee behavior and these behaviors in turn are required to implement different business strategies, employment systems should systematically vary with the type of business strategy a company is pursuing (Smith, 1982; Schuler and Jackson, 1987a, b; Lengnick-Hall and Lengnick-Hall, 1988; Schuler, 1988; Fisher, 1989; Wright and Snell, 1991; Arthur, 1992; Ostrow, 1992; Sivasubramaniam, 1993; Peck, 1994).

A second group of researchers has followed a different theoretical approach labeled the universalistic perspective (Dewar and Werbel, 1979) to explain how different work organization practices, HRM policies, and other organizational characteristics affect employees' behavior and, as a result, company performance. They have argued that there are certain "best practices" that, irrespective of the company's business strategy, are more effective in achieving competitive success through the way they manage people (Delaney *et al.*, 1989; Terpstra and Rozell, 1993; Osterman, 1994; Pfeffer, 1994, 1998; Huselid, 1995). Osterman (1994), for example, identified four work organization practices – teamwork, job rotation, quality circles, and total quality management – that resulted in higher levels of productivity across a wide variety of American industries and firms. Similarly, Pfeffer (1994, 1998) developed a list of 16 practices which he labeled "high performance work practices." He included practices such as self-managed teams and decentralization of decision making, people's cross-utilization and cross-training, high wages contingent on organizational performance, wage compression, employment security, promotion from within, profit sharing, employee ownership, great amounts of training, and information sharing.

To date, the contingency approach towards SHRM has received small empirical support. Sánchez-Runde 1995, and Chapter 3 of this book, argues that empirical studies so far are still scarce and inconclusive. He found that only a few studies have looked for linkages between strategy and employment systems (Arthur, 1992; Delery and Doty, 1996; Ostrow, 1992; Peck, 1994; Schuler and Jackson, 1987b; Sivasubramaniam, 1993; Huselid, 1995). Only Schuler and Jackson (1987b), Arthur (1992), and Sivasubramaniam (1993) found support for relationships between strategy and employment systems. The rest of the work either did not find significant relationships between business strategy and employment systems or, when significant relationships appeared, they contradicted the hypotheses they were intended to support. Quantitative studies, then, have shown poor results in confirming the presence of strategic HRM systems that support particular business strategy.

As in the case of empirical work testing contingency arguments, according to Sánchez-Runde, only a small number of studies have supported universalistic hypotheses. Ichniowski *et al.*, (1993), Arthur (1994), Huselid (1995), MacDuffie (1995), Delery and Doty (1996) and Dunlop and Weil (1996) are among the few studies that have found a positive correlation between the adoption of a set of HRM "best practices" and firms' performance.

6.3 TYPOLOGY OF BUSINESS STRATEGIES

To test their hypotheses empirical studies following the contingency theory have developed employment systems types and linked them to firm strategy, arguing that particular sets of practices are suited for specific firm strategies (Miles and Snow, 1984; Walton, 1985; Dyer and Holder, 1988; Lengnick-Hall and Lengnick-Hall, 1988; Schuler, 1988; Purcell, 1989; Kerr and Slocum, 1987; Osterman, 1987; Sonnenfeld and Pieperl, 1988; Arthur, 1992; Ichniowski *et al.*, 1994; MacDuffie, 1995).

We considered two dimensions in order to develop a more comprehensive business strategy typology than those employed in previous empirical research within the SHRM field. The first dimension captures the different manners in which firms establish a competitive position in the markets where they are established. The second dimension tries to capture different ways by which firms create and develop resources and capabilities and how they change their bases of competitiveness over time.

In order to determine what type of product and market positioning firms adopt we use Porter's (1980, 1985) strategy framework, since it is probably the best known, is well accepted and internally consistent (Dess and Davis, 1984; Hambrick, 1983). Porter (1980, 1985) identified two generic ways in which an organization can gain a sustainable competitive advantage over other firms in its industry: "cost leadership" and "differentiation". A cost leadership strategy emphasizes the need to be the lowest-cost producer of a given product or service in the industry. This strategic option is based on "aggressive construction of efficient-scale facilities, vigorous pursuit of cost reductions from experience, tight cost and overhead control, avoidance of marginal customer and cost minimization in areas like R&D, service, sales force, advertising, and so on" (Porter, 1980: 35).

A differentiation strategy means that the company seeks to be unique among its competitors on some basis other than low cost that is highly valued by buyers. A firm that follows this strategy "selects one or more attributes that many buyers in an industry perceived as important, and uniquely positions itself to meet those needs. It is rewarded for its uniqueness with a premium price" (Porter, 1985: 14). Through differentiation, then, firms try to position their products and services in a distinctive way and to increase customers' willingness to pay a premium price, compared with its competitors.

Differentiation may arise from many different sources. This chapter emphasizes two of them:

1. product variety and speed and
2. quality and brand image.

Some authors (Stalk, 1988) have argued that firms can compete through differentiation by increasing the variety of the products offered and the speed at which they are delivered to the market. They emphasized swiftness as an important organizational capability. Many companies compete with flexible manufacturing, rapid-response systems, and expanding variety of products and services. These types of strategies emphasize time-based competition with organizational structures and distributions systems enabling fast responses to serve customers. Companies following these strategies do not build their positions with just one innovation; they continue to innovate all the time and they tend to concentrate on reducing delays and using their response advantages to attract customers.

A second source of differentiation considered in this study is the pursuit of quality and brand image. Following a long-term focus companies pursuing this strategy try to build a brand image through the superior features and service they offer to customers in their products. Quality enhancement means, then, a high concern for process, that is, how the goods or services are made or delivered. At the same time, companies following this strategy understand that besides a good product they need to establish a superior reputation and a close relationship with customers supported by appropriate marketing and communication efforts. Both Mercedes and Honda are good examples of this type of company in the automobile industry. In other sectors, Canon, Xerox, and Andersen Consulting also exemplify this kind of strategy based on high quality and a strong brand image. Each of these organizations creates and markets new and superior products better than anyone else. In contrast, some companies choose to decrease quality and even degrade their products and services without selecting any other strategic alternative.

Porter's (1980, 1985) strategic typology represents only one aspect of a firm's strategic picture. Implicitly, underlying a company's market/product positioning, either through cost leadership or differentiation, there is a static view of strategy since once a firm has established its strategic positioning, nothing is said on how to improve or change that particular position in markets and products. Thus, we want to introduce dynamism in our typology of business strategies by drawing on some extension of the traditional resource-based view of the firm (Penrose, 1959; Wernerfelt, 1984). In particular, we introduce a second strategic dimension that has to do with the different ways firms develop their pool of resources and capabilities and how they change their resource basis over time.

At one extreme, we would expect some organizations at a certain point in time to show strategic continuity, that is, searching continuously for innovations and improvements within their current set of resources and capabilities. Ghemawat and Ricart (1993) have referred to this organizational mindset as the search for static efficiency. At the other extreme, we should expect firms to continuously reconsider their set of resources and capabilities and therefore to relentlessly introduce significant changes in the way they compete. Ghemawat and Ricart have called this organizational mindset the search for dynamic efficiency. This bidimensional and enriched approach toward business strategy types may provide five different strategies (Figure 6.1).

The first one is cost leadership. In our view, cost leadership should be more compatible with a static efficiency approach rather than a dynamic efficiency strategy. Cost leadership and dynamic efficiency seem to be incompatible given the nature of the two strategies. While a cost minimization strategy emphasizes, "doing more of the same" in order to achieve economies of scale and efficiency in processes, dynamic efficiency means risk taking and exploration of possibilities outside current products, markets and operations' domain. UPS in the package delivery business and Commodore in computers are examples of a cost leadership strategy. Southwest Airlines is also a firm following a cost leadership business strategy. Every activity in the company is directed towards cost reduction and productivity increases. For instance, no meals are served on board, only one type of airplane is used to reduce maintenance costs, and crews are paid per miles flown as a way to increase their productivity. At the same time, Southwest's strategy is driven by a static efficiency approach, since each of its activities represents incremental additions to the airline's existing operational procedures.

Figure 6.1 Strategy typology

	Product/market		
Product/market	Cost leadership	Variety–speed static efficiency	Quality–brand name static efficiency
		Variety–speed dynamic efficiency	Quality–brand name dynamic efficiency

A second business strategy is characterized by differentiation through product variety and the high velocity by which products are developed and delivered to the market. Concurrently, firms following this second type of strategy develop their capabilities and resources through static efficiency. Companies like PepsiCo in the beverage industry is a good example of a firm pursuing a strategy of differentiation through variety and velocity in launching new products. At the same time PepsiCo's new products represent, in most cases, incremental innovations of existing ones. Sony is another example of a firm within this category. It constantly develops a wide variety of products that are rapidly delivered to customers. Indeed, over just 10 years, Sony was able to develop four Walkman product families and more than 160 incremental versions of those four families. Its leading incremental product proliferation helped Sony control industry standards in its product class and outperform its Japanese, American, and European competitors.

The third type of competitive strategy in the typology developed here is based on differentiation through quality and brand image and the pursuit of a static efficiency approach toward capability development. Firms in this category seek competitive advantage through developing or exploiting superior product quality or relations with customers, achieved through a particular attention to product design, branding, or by using non-standard methods of sales and distribution or superior capabilities in marketing, sales, and customer service. At the same, these companies build on previous experience. Their products and services, technologies and operating procedures are generally incremental improvements of their existing products, standards and processes. Examples of firms following differentiation through quality and brand name and concurrently emphasizing a static efficiency approach are IBM in computers and Philips in electronics. Oticon, a Danish company in the hearing-aid business, is a firm where managers were good at incrementally improving their products' quality and performance, building on existing technologies. The company emphasized new product development focused on technical superiority and improvements consisted of minor modifications of their behind-the-ear hearing aid without ushering in breakthrough products and technologies.

Firms that differentiate through a wide product variety and a high velocity of product development and delivery follow the next business strategy type. At the same time, these firms adopt a dynamic efficiency approach towards the development of their resources and capabilities. Examples of companies adopting a dynamic efficiency strategy are HP in computers, Ciba-Geigy in agrochemicals, and Intel in semiconductors. All of them are constantly cannibalizing their old products and developing new technologies not incorporated in their previous versions.

Intel is a company of this kind since it is an extraordinarily time-paced corporation (Brown and Eisenhardt, 1998). Time pacing involves the need to change and to try to anticipate the future instead of merely reacting to external shocks. Central to Intel's time pacing is the so-called Moore's Law. In 1975, founder Gordon Moore prophesied that in order to maintain the lead Intel would need to double the power of microprocessor computer chips every 18 months. The company has consistently done that, moving and thinking at a tempo unknown in other companies. Over time, Intel managers have elaborated on Moore's Law to create a flow of new technology and product introductions that has outpaced competitors. In the late 1980s, for example, Intel won the 386-chip battle against AMD and NEC. The company repeated this feat again in the 1990s; it picked up the pace against Motorola's PowerPC microprocessor and again widened the gap. Moreover, all these innovations have been driven by a dynamic efficiency approach toward resource and capability development. Changes in products, technologies, and forms of operating have represented dramatic shifts from previous ones. Products, technologies, and processes are achieved, go through a short cycle, become obsolete, and are then replaced by new ones that have been gestating quietly in the meantime.

Finally, companies that choose differentiation through quality and brand image and at the same time follow a dynamic efficiency approach toward resource and capability development characterize a fifth type of competitive strategy. Andersen Consulting's strategy, for example, is characterized by the pursuit of uniformly high standards of quality, accuracy, and thoroughness to which Andersen's associates hold themselves (Ghoshal and Bartlett, 1997: 154). Andersen is an extremely customer-driven company where employees continuously pursue better ways to meet client needs and stay at the forefront of its rapidly evolving business. It is this firm commitment to client service which justifies the overtime that professionals at the company work, as well as the enormous investments the firm makes – often ahead of demand – to build the capabilities to meet emerging market opportunities. From its first investment in a new computer to its first steps in internationalization, every major step in the growth of the firm has come from this concept that the client always comes first, regardless of efforts of personal sacrifice. At the same time, Andersen Consulting's focus is on continuously creating new products and services that represent important departures from existing ones. Professionals at Andersen are always looking for services and developing processes that are radically different from their existing ones. This consulting firm has always been avoiding the constant commoditization of products and services in the industry. Its success is based upon its capacity to stay ahead of the commoditization, constantly developing radically new alternatives for its clients. Andersen Consulting has moved from developing accounting processes in the 1940s to the business integration market in the 1990s and throughout all these decades it has always stayed ahead of competition in terms of the quality, complexity and advancement of its services.

6.4 EMPLOYMENT SYSTEMS AND THEIR RELATIONSHIP WITH BUSINESS STRATEGIES

In this work we argue that a linkage might exist between competitive strategies and employment systems. It is assumed that employment systems are an essential part of the implementation process of those business strategies.

6.4.1 Typology of employment systems

Based on previous work, Ricart and Portales (Chapter 2 of this book) found that work organization practices, HRM policies and other organizational fctors can be bundled in five different types of employment systems. Three of them, transactional, relational, and balanced employment systems were considered more traditional types of employment systems.

In contrast, the remaining types were defined as two different forms of a new type of employment relationship that emphasizes the employability of the workforce. These two forms have been labeled market employability and organizational employability, due to their emphasis on the external versus internal labor market aspects of this employability relationship, respectively. Market employability systems are treated extensively in Chapter 5 by Peter Cappelli, whereas organizational employability systems are the type of employer–employee relationship that Ghoshal, Moran and Bartlett describe in Chapter 4.

Ricart and Portales (Chapter 2) also provide a rationale for the possible linkage between business strategies and employment systems. They argue that employment systems are intended to promote certain employees' behaviors and develop specific abilities and knowledge in them. At the same time, the policies, practices and other organizational characteristics conforming the different employment systems can shape employees' behavior and performance because they in turn respond to three particular categories of employees' desires: extrinsic, work, and social needs. In other words, employment systems may shape employees' behavior and skills since they are also a main source of satisfaction of employees' needs. Thus, according to the authors, a series of simultaneous exchange relationships are then established among companies and the people who work for them. The different type of exchanges can, according to Ricart and Portales, be present in various degrees and with different intensities in a specific labor relation.

This rich array of possible exchanges creates, in turn, five viable and distinctive potential employment contracts between the firm and its employees. These contracts define what the company obtains from its workers and what they give in return. Specifically, employer and employees might exchange certain levels of output, effort, accountability and loyalty for some salary, opportunities for professional development, and a sense of identity provided by the company.

Thus, according to Ricart and Portales, these employment contracts are mutually beneficial for both firms and employees. On the one hand, the particular HRM policies, work organization practices and other organizational arrangements bundled into different employment systems serve as an important source of satisfaction of employees' needs. At the same time, these employment systems may foster specific employees' decisions and actions and develop particular skills that are then required to successfully implement competitive strategies.

All these five employment systems defined above were perceived, as we argued before, to work well under specific conditions. According to many authors following the contingency perspective (Schuler and Jackson, 1987a, b; Baird and Meshoulam, 1988; Arthur, 1992; Wright and McMahan, 1992; Peck, 1994; Milgrom and Roberts, 1995), each of these systems is supposed to respond appropriately under certain competitive conditions and to work well only for certain type of organizations.

In section 6.2 we mentioned, however, that in recent years a group of researchers has selected specific practices from the previously defined employment systems and bundled them into what they have labeled the "best practices" employment system. In other words, besides the five employment systems resulting from our contingency analysis we should add a sixth one, called the best practices employment system arising from universalistic arguments. This best practices system is nothing more than a combination of the five previous ones. It selects the most distinctive elements of the transactional, balanced, relational, market employability, and organizational employability systems and tries to fit with every possible business strategy.

The universalistic perspective toward SHRM is clearly in contradiction with contingency arguments. Researchers following the best practices approach think that irrespective of the company's characteristics, a system of exemplary practices should work well under any kind of competitive conditions and for any type of company (Osterman, 1994; Pfeffer, 1994, 1998; Huselid, 1995). Osterman (1994), for example, identified four work organization practices – teamwork, job rotation, quality circles, and total quality management – that may result in higher levels of productivity across a wide variety of American industries and firms. Similarly, Pfeffer (1994, 1998) developed a list of best practices which he labeled "high performance work practices." The list includes policies such as self-managed teams and decentralization of decision making, people's cross-utilization and cross-training, high wages contingent on organizational performance, wage compression, employment security, promotion from within, profit sharing, employee ownership, great amounts of training, and information sharing.

In Table 6.1 we describe in detail each of the five employment systems previously defined by Ricart and Portales and, additionally, the best practices employment system described in this chapter. An ideal type for each of these systems is defined with respect to a total of thirteen policies and practices. Three of them are work organization practices:

1. level of job rotation;
2. empowerment; and
3. teamwork.

The next eight are HRM policies:

4. degree to which firm provides job security to employees;
5. percentage of variable pay with respect to total pay;
6. compensation criteria (market and individual performance-based versus tenure and aggregate corporate performance oriented);
7. source of recruitment – emphasis on internal versus external hiring;
8. level of experience/skills;
9. teamwork abilities required at recruiting;
10. breadth of training or the range of abilities and skills that are

emphasized in training programs; and
11. generality of the skills covered by those training programs, emphasis
on general versus specific skills.

Two additional organizational characteristics associated with ways by
which organizations establish bonding and linking mechanisms among
their employees are considered. We take into account:

12. the level of personalized training such as counseling and mentoring
widely considered a key form of socialization within organizations;
13. the number of communication channels existing in the firm.

These 13 work organization practices, HRM policies, and other
organizational characteristics compose the different ideal profiles of each
of the six employment systems. The level of intensity that, according to
the theory, each one of these practices, policies and characteristics should
have in each of the different employment systems is also shown in the
Table 6.1. Following the recommendation of Van de Ven and Drazin
(1985: 350) the ideal type patterns of each of the variables were
theoretically derived from the existing literature.

Different scales have been used to measure the intensity of the different
items considered. For that reason, scores within brackets in Table 6.1
represent standardized values ranging from –1, meaning low intensity, a
weak presence of the practice or simply an end point of a particular value,
to +1, indicating a high level, a strong presence of that practice or just the
other end point of a specific variable in a particular employment system.

6.4.2 Contingency arguments: specific employment systems as supporting instruments for the implementation of particular business strategies

Next, following contingency arguments, we will review the different
employment systems and their linkage to business strategies – defined in
section 6.3 – they tend to support. The theory-based ideal profiles of each
of the work organization practices, HRM policies, and other
organizational characteristics composing the six different employment
systems will be explained in detail. The outcome of our analysis will be
specific hypotheses that will later be empirically tested.

Cost leadership strategies and transactional employment systems

Following previous work in the field of SHRM (Arthur, 1992; Delery and
Doty, 1996) we argue that transactional employment systems are the most
appropriate ones to support a cost leadership strategy. Companies
competing through cost leadership require their employees to perform a

simple, repetitive and consistent job, work individually, care mainly for quantity produced, take low risk in the activities they carry out, give strong attention to results, and prefer certain routines in what they perform to achieve high levels of productivity. Therefore, we assign to transactional systems the lowest levels of job enrichment. All, work organization practices such as job rotation, empowerment, and teamwork, were given the minimum value of –1, according to our scale. With respect to HRM policies, transactional systems should not offer job guarantees (–1) which fits well a focus on short-term output level and minimum overheads required by cost leadership strategies.

At the same time, Cost Leaders usually have important economies of scale and high levels of productivity in each of the activities and processes performed. Transactional systems should be appropriate to achieve these objectives, since they induce high levels of individual output and productivity. As is showed in the second column of Table 6.1, these systems promotes high variable pay (with 30% considered a maximum in the case of Spain), compensation would be primarily based on market salary, individual output, and the level of skills employees shown in their job (–1). We can say, then, that in transactional systems what is being paid is the person and the way he or she performs the job and not the job *per se*. Additionally, we state that internal recruitment and careers are almost non-existent in transactional employment systems (–1). This makes sense for cost leadership strategies that search for short-term efficiencies and low costs, which in turn favors the hiring of the most efficient and cheapest human resources available in the external labor market. As we mentioned before, tasks and activities to be performed under a cost leadership strategy are quite simple and they are usually individually performed. Thus, employees with no previous job experience (–1) and little teamwork exposure (–1) might be preferred. These, in turn, are exactly two of the features that characterize transactional contracts.

Low employee qualification required for simple and repetitive tasks should make firms adopting a cost leadership strategy avoid the costs of training and only the basics should be provided to employees. Most of the knowledge employees possess will be rapidly accumulated through an on-the-job learning-by-doing type of process. Transactional employment systems should show then low levels of training (–1) both in general and firm-specific skills (0).

Other organizational characteristics such as personalized counseling and mentoring and extensive use of communication channels are almost non-existent (–1) in transactional employment systems. This is largely consistent with the required cost leaders' high turnover rates, individually performed work, and, consequently, the need to avoid high implementation costs of mentoring and communications programs.

Table 6.1 Ideal profiles of WO, HRM practices and other organization characteristics

Work organization practices	Transact.	Balanced	Relational	Mkt. E.	Org. E.	Best P.
1 Job rotation index (1 = Low; 7 = Extensive). Average of: • Level of rotation within area or department • Level of rotation outside area or department	1 (–1)	5.5 (+0.5)	2.5 (–0.5)	7 (+1)	7 (+1)	7 (+1)
2 Empowerment index (1 = Low; 7 = Extensive). Average of: • Participation in job design • Autonomy in the determination of the sequence of tasks to be performed • Decision-making over methods of work	1 (–1)	5.5 (+0.5)	2.5 (–0.5)	7 (+1)	7 (+1)	7 (+1)
3 Teamwork index (1 = Low; 7 = Extensive). Average of: • Participation in quality and control teams • Participation in problem resolution-oriented teams • Participation in self-directed work teams	1 (–1)	4 (0)	4 (0)	7 (+1)	7 (+1)	7 (+1)
Human resource practices Job security						
4 Job security index (1 = Low; 7 = Extensive). Average of: • Degree to which employees can stay in the company indefinetely • Degree to which it is uncommon to dismiss an employee	1 (–1)	4 (0)	7 (+1)	1 (–1)	1 (–1)	7 (+1)
Compensation						
5 Incentive pay as percentage of total pay (0% = low; 30% = high)	30% (+1)	15% (0)	0% (–1)	30% (+1)	30% (+1)	30% (+1)
6 Compensation criteria index (–7 = based on market salary, individual/group performance, skills acquired; 7 = based on tenure, corporate performance position)	–7 8-1	0 809	7 (+1)	–7 (–1)	–7 (–1)	0 (0)
Recruitment and promotion						
7 Source of recruitment index (1 = External; 7 = Internal). Average of:	1 (–1)	4 (0)	7 (+1)	1 (–1)	4 (0)	7 (+1)

	C1	C2	C3	C4	C5	C6
• Degree to which employees are internally recruited						
• Degree to which internal careers exist						
8 Level of experience/skills in recuiting index (1 = Low; 7 = High). Average of:	1 (–1)	5.5 (+0.5)	2.5 (–0.5)	7 (+1)	7 (+1)	7 (+1)
• Degree of employees' previous experience (1 = External; 7 = Internal)						
• Level of employees' skills at hiring (1 = External; 7 = Internal)						
9 Level of teamwork abilities required at recruitment level (1 = Low; 7 = High)	1 (–1)	4 (0)	4 (0)	7 (+1)	7 (+1)	7 (+1)
Training and development						
10 Breadth of training index (1 = Low; 7 = Extensive). Average of:	1 (–1)	2.5 (–0.5)	5.5 (+0.5)	1 (–1)	7 (+1)	7 (+1)
• Level of training to improve current performance in the job						
• Level of training to improve future performance in the job						
• Level of training to develop employee's skills for lateral mobility						
• Level of training to develop employee's skills for promotion						
11 Generality of the skills covered by training (–6 = Firm-specific; 6 = General) Substraction of scores on "Emphasis on general skills" minus score on "Emphasis on firm-specific skills"	0 (0)	3 (0.5)	–6 (–1)	0 (0)	6 (+1)	0 (0)
• Emphasis on firm-specific skills (1 = Low; 7 = Extensive).						
• Emphasis on general skills (1 = Low; 7 = Extensive).						
Bonding and linking mechanisms						
12 Level of personalized training like counseling and mentoring (1 = Low; 1 = Exten.)	1 (–1)	2.5 (–0.5)	5.5 (+0.5)	1 (–1)	7 (+1)	4 (0)
13 N. of communication channels between the firm and its employees (0 to 6)	0 (–1)	3 (0)	3 (0)	0 (–1)	6 (+1)	4.5 (0.5)
Sum of numbers of existing communication channels in the firms:						
• Newsletters						
• General meetings between managers and employees						
• Personal meetings between managers and employees						
• Level of training to develop employees' skills for promotion						
• Surveys						
• Grievance and conflict resolution procedures						

Speed–variety/static efficiency strategies and balanced employment systems

According to some authors (Kanter, 1985; Schuler and Jackson, 1987b), firms that tend to increase the variety of the products they offer and the speed at which those products and services are launched and delivered to customers must create an environment for collective creativity and distinctive ways of working. In this study, we argue that when the type of innovations firms pursue represent incremental changes – static efficiency – in their products, technologies and business processes, balanced employment systems would be the most appropriate ones to support the implementation of their competitive strategy.

Balanced systems blend elements from both transactional and relational systems (Ricart and Portales, Chapter 1), which we will refer to later on. As we will see, they represent a middle-of-the-road approach toward people management since in many of the 13 practices considered in this study they mix an external labor market orientation with some of the internal labor market features. The extensive utilization of work organization practices and, therefore, the high ideal values assigned to job rotation (+0.5), empowerment (+0.5), and teamwork (0) is the only major area in which balanced contracts present their own distinguishing features and do not just represent a combination of transactional and relational systems. Through the deployment of these practices, balanced systems develop people's initiative to consistently seek innovative problem identification, problem-solving and develop proposals for changes in products, technologies or business processes, required by speed–variety/static efficiency strategies. Flexible job assignments are expected to encourage creativity (Tornatzky, 1983) and teamwork is seen as a method of identifying new opportunities. The intensity with which these practices are implemented is not as high, however, as in the case of firms adopting speed–variety/dynamic efficiency strategies where the innovation process is much more radical.

In general, ideal values for HRM policies, as we mentioned before, were in between transactional and relational systems. An ideal value of 0 was assigned to job security in the balanced system. This is consistent with the need of companies following a strategy based on variety and speed and, at the same time, adopting a static efficiency approach. Their incremental modification of existing products, technologies and internal processes requires firm-specific skills and, therefore, some employment stability for those employees who develop and utilize those skills. In other words, employees should be experts in what the company is currently doing in order to generate those incremental innovations. To achieve that they in turn need some level of employment guarantee. At the same time, companies adopting speed–variety/static efficiency strategies need to encourage employees to propose and implement ideas for new and improved ways of performing their activities, manufacturing their products or delivering their services. Balanced systems may be adequate for these purposes. They include both some degree of variable pay (15% of total salary) and compensation based on market salary, individual performance and also tenure (0). These two policies may jointly promote an innovative attitude among employees and, at the same time, should motivate people to stay with the organization for some time. Balanced employment systems can also be considered a mechanism for obtaining new product and market ideas, required by speed–variety/static efficiency strategies (Peck, 1994). Acquiring employees who have experience with a variety of organizations in a variety of situations encourages new ways of considering opportunities. Accordingly, balanced systems were assigned intermediate ideal values for the degree of internal recruitment (0), and the level of experience and skills (+0.5) and teamwork ability (0) at hiring. Continuous innovation would also require some amount of training with emphasis on general skills – not as high, however, as we will see in the case of organizational employability systems. This may allow firms adopting variety–speed/static efficiency strategies to incorporate general knowledge into firm's innovation of existing set of products, technologies and business processes. This is reflected in Table 6.1 where the breadth of training in the balanced system was assigned an intermediate value of –0.5 and generality of skills covered by training shows an ideal value of 0.5.

Balanced employment systems are usually characterized by small amounts of personalized training (–0.5) and the implementation of a few communications channels (0), as is showed in Table 6.1. These organizational characteristics will help firms adopting speed–variety/static efficiency strategies to achieve some level of employee retention, in conjunction with some kind of employment guarantees mentioned before, and, therefore, allow their employees to innovate around the existing domain of products, technologies and operations. Similarly, they can increase the level of socialization inside the organization and, as a consequence, might foster collective creativity that is needed to develop incremental innovations.

Quality–brand name/static efficiency strategies and relational employment systems

Organizations competing by quality and brand name should foster an environment in which employees are constantly generating good ideas for product quality and brand reputation. Thus, employees in this type of organization need to have a high concern the whole process: how the products and services are manufactured or delivered (Schuler and Jackson, 1987b). They must show consistent behavior because errors should be minimized in order to preserve quality and a strong brand name. We argue that when firms pursue a strategy of quality–brand name/static efficiency in their products and services, relational employment systems would be the most adequate ones to successfully implement their business strategy.

Incremental changes – static efficiency – in quality improvement often mean changing the processes of production in ways that require workers to have some degree of involvement and flexibility in their jobs. In many cases, however, quality problems within the domain of existing products, technologies and operational processes are better resolved individually. Moreover, the search for quality and stronger brand reputation most of the time needs relatively repetitive and predictable behaviors. Relational systems are the most adequate to provide those organizational elements since they consider (as is show, in Table 6.1) some level – even though modest – of job rotation (–0.5), empowerment (–0.5) and teamwork (0) – mainly through quality circles. Employees, for example, are usually allowed to inspect their own work and do preventive maintenance in addition to running the machines.

HRM policies considered by relational systems might also be appropriate to support quality–brand name/static efficiency strategies. In these organizations people need to care about quality and the firm's reputation. Quality and reputation, in turn, require employees to be highly involved and committed to the organization. The achievement of product quality and the development of a strong brand image are processes that require a firm's long-term commitment to the organization itself, its customers and suppliers. In order to do that, these companies need to have a stable pool of employees who actually are the ones who manage and sustain those relationships. Relational systems provide a maximum level of job security (+1) and a long-term perspective, which is precisely what organizations adopting a quality–brand name/static efficiency need. Incremental improvements in quality and brand name are achieved through repetitive, consistent and low risk-taking activities. Thus, the ideal value for variable pay in relational systems is 0%. In fact incentive pay is not so relevant since job stability is the most important incentive for employees. At the same time strategies based on quality–brand name/static efficiency would be better implemented if employees have a long-term commitment with the firm. Accordingly, they show a high concern for the quality of every process (how the goods or services are made or delivered) that is developed inside the company. Accordingly, compensation in relational employment systems is strictly based, in turn, on tenure, corporate performance, versus individual output, and employee's position within the organizational hierarchy (+1). At the same time, the required long-term employer–employee relationship may be better achieved by recruiting people inside the organization. Moreover, internal development of promoted employees can increase their level of organizational commitment.

Relational systems might well satisfice these needs since they heavily emphasize internal recruitment of people (+1) with low levels of experience for the new job (–0.5) and some experience in teamworking (0) due to the existence of quality circles and other groups in charge of quality control processes. In turn, the amount of training is quite high (+0.5) and it is almost exclusively centered in firm-specific skills (–1) since employees need to constantly improve the quality of the company's existing products, technologies, and business processes.

Personalized training programs and internal communication channels are part of relational systems with assigned ideal values of +0.5 and 0, respectively. They, in turn, may increase employee commitment to organizational values and business methods required by strategies emphasizing quality–brand name/static efficiency.

Speed–variety/dynamic efficiency strategies and market employability systems

Organizations focusing on the speed and variety of their product development and delivery where at the same time the innovation process is radical – dynamic efficiency – contrast sharply with the three previous types of firms described in this chapter. Their focus on radical innovation in products, markets, technologies and operations creates an environment which is too unpredictable and dynamic to make developing human resources, through relational systems, a feasible strategy. Investment in developing employees, characteristic of relational systems, is difficult if one cannot predict future needs with any degree of confidence. This argument is also consistent with the observation of some researchers (Hirsch, 1987; Pfeffer and Baron, 1988; Bennett, 1990; Cappelli, 1999) that as the overall business environment becomes more dynamic, organizations are more likely to adopt external labor market oriented HR strategies. If the organization cannot predict future HR requirements, investment in developing employees is a risky proposition. At the same time, the intensity by which many of the practices are applied in balanced systems supporting speed–variety/static efficiency is not enough in a setting where innovation is radical and change is extremely dynamic.

Thus, we proposed that when a company's strategy is based on speed and variety and the type of innovations it follows represent radical departures from its existent set of capabilities – dynamic efficiency – the market employability system would be the most adequate one to help the implementation of that business strategy.

In order to support a collectively developed radical innovation process companies might require maximum levels of job rotation (+1), empowerment (+1) and teamwork (+1), that characterize market employability systems. At the same time highly skilled people are attracted to work for these firms since, through these work organization practices, they offer the most interesting and challenging jobs in the industry. In fact, employability guarantees not the continuity of employment with one company, as in the case of relational systems, but a commitment to enhancing the skills and competencies of the employees. In this way they can protect, and indeed, continuously improve, their options for gainful employment (Ghoshal *et al.*, Chapter 4).

Employees in firms implementing speed–variety/dynamic efficiency strategies do not have long-term relationships with their organizations. Market forces impose on these companies a need for greater organizational flexibility. Constant changes in the market place require continuous rearrangement of firm's products and technologies. In this sense, market employability systems might be very appropriate since they offer employees minimum levels of job security (–1), as it can be observed in Table 6.1. At the same time, these employment systems provide extremely high incentives for radical innovation given that 30% of employees' total pay is variable. Moreover, compensation for a particular job is increasingly shaped by both the market wage and individual performance (–1), and not by how that position fits into the structure of an internal compensation system. Companies adopting a speed–variety/ dynamic efficiency strategy change their people every time a new set of skills or capabilities is required. A good number of employees are employed on a project basis. Market employability systems provide support for this strategy since most of the people are recruited externally (–1). In addition, these employment systems promote the acquisition of employees who have experience with a variety of organizations, in a variety of situations (+1), and with great teamwork experience (+1). Moreover, firms' dynamic innovation imposes high turnover rates that make it impossible to recuperate investments in employees' training. In turn, this strategic need is well supported by market employability systems because no training is provided (–1) neither in general nor in firm-specific skills (0). Employees must take on more responsibility for their own training and for managing their own careers.

Other organizational features composing a market employability system are also consistent with short-term and project-based labor relationships that are established by speed–variety/dynamic efficiency strategies. In this sense, the level of personalized training is very low (–1) and internal corporate communication channels are extremely limited (–1) due to the small need for social attachment between employees and their organization.

Quality–brand name/dynamic efficiency strategies and organizational employability systems

Firms emphasizing dynamic efficiency need to constantly rearrange their products, technologies, and business processes and, at the same time, they require long, deep periods of development to improve products and strengthen their brand reputation. Organizational employability systems might be the most adequate approach to implement this type of strategy since they promote radical innovation processes. At the same time they retain employees not by offering job guarantees but through linking and bonding mechanisms that create a coherent and exciting internal organizational environment that bond employees to each other and to the firm (Ghoshal *et al.*, Chapter 4).

Work organization practices promoted by organizational employability systems are extremely appropriate to support quality–brand name/ dynamic efficiency strategies. As is shown in Table 6.1 teamwork is especially important (+1) for firms competing on quality and also emphasizing dynamic efficiency. This is so because individuals' general knowledge and skills must be combined – for example, through project development teams – to create fundamentally different high-quality products and services compared to the ones available. Concurrently, individuals working in companies pursuing quality and brand image need to show a high degree of empowerment (+1) in decision making and flexibility – job rotation – in their assignments (+1).

As we mentioned before, no employment security (–1) is offered by organizational employability systems. Like in the case of market employability systems, dynamic efficiency is promoted through high variable pay as a percentage of total salary (30%). Similarly, compensation is based on external market salary, individual/group performance, and the level of skills showed by employees (–1). It differs from this other form of employability in that organizational employability promotes an intermediate level of internal hiring and careers (0). This is possible because in firms following a quality–brand name/dynamic efficiency strategies innovation occurs through the combination of internally developed employees' general knowledge. Like market employability, however, it emphasizes high levels of both technical (+1) and teamwork experience (+1) at hiring because knowledge requirements at entry level are very high. To continuously enhance a firm's general skills required by quality–brand name/dynamic efficiency, organizational employability systems emphasize continuous training programs (+1), particularly in general skills (+1).

Firms implementing quality–brand name/dynamic efficiency strategies need to establish long-term relationships with their employees, without resorting to job security policies. Organizational employability systems might foster those employer–employee relationships given the high ideal values they show for linking and bonding mechanisms such as personalized training (+1) and a great number of communication channels inside organizations (+1).

The main purpose of this chapter has been to present both the contingency and the universalistic hypotheses that will be tested later. Following the contingency view toward SHRM, we should expect a number of firms showing an alignment between the business strategy chosen and the specific employment system implemented to support those strategies. Specifically, our contingency hypotheses, shown in Figure 6.2, will be that:

1. firms following a cost leadership strategy would tend to be more inclined to adopt a transactional employment system;
2. firms that pursue a differentiation through product variety and speed/static efficiency strategy would be inclined to implement a balanced system;
3. firms following a differentiation through quality and brand image/static efficiency strategy would support their strategy by implementing a relational employment system;
4. firms implementing a product variety and speed/dynamic efficiency strategy would prefer to adopt a market employability system; and
5. firms following a product quality and brand image/dynamic efficiency strategy are likely to adopt an organizational employability system.

Figure 6.2   Contingent employment contracts

		Product/market	
Capabilities development	Transactional	Balanced	Relational
		Market employability	Organizational employability

6.4.3 Universalistic arguments: best practices employment system as a key supporting instrument for the implementation of any business strategy

In this chapter, besides the contingency hypotheses, an additional hypothesis is proposed to test the relationship between this best practices employment system and the business strategy types. As is shown in Table 6.1, the best practices employment system is a combination of the five previously described systems. The last column of Table 6.1 shows the ideal values assigned for each of the 13 practices considered in our study. These values were derived from the literature following the universalistic approach toward SHRM (e.g. Osterman, 1994; Pfeffer, 1994, 1998; Huselid, 1995). Work organization practices are assigned their maximum possible scores (+1). The idea behind this is to provide the best possible jobs in the industry. Job security is also very strong in these types of systems (+1). The same occurs for variable pay (30% of total pay). The best practices approach uses mixed criteria to determine compensation (0). Most employees are hired outside (+1) and the "best people" in terms of their skills and teamwork experience are recruited (+1). Employees' capabilities are continuously upgraded through extensive training (+1) in both general and firm specific skills (0). Finally, some initiatives are taken in terms of personalized training (0) and communication channels (0.5) in order to provide linking and bonding between the firm and its employees.

In contrast to the contingency view, following the universalistic arguments we would expect that no matter what business strategy a firm implements it will always tend to support those strategies with the same type of employment system. In particular we should expect that, in contrast to the contingency view, firms following either:

1. cost leadership;
2. differentiation through product variety and speed/static efficiency;
3. differentiation through quality and brand image/static efficiency;
4. product variety and speed/dynamic efficiency; or
5. product quality and brand image/dynamic efficiency to adopt the same best practices employment system.

6.5 METHODS

Our sample was drawn from the Dun and Bradstreet database, containing 250,000 Spanish – including foreign owned – firms. Only medium and large firms with more than a hundred employees were included. Holding companies were excluded. Considering these criteria, 1300 firms were selected representing all major industries with the exception of agriculture, fisheries and mining.

Two questionnaires were sent to each company seeking information for 1997. The first one was sent to the CEO soliciting general information about business strategy, organizational design, and performance of the entire company. The second one was mailed to the senior human resource manager in each firm. They were asked for detailed information about HRM policies, work organization practices, and other organizational arrangements being applied to "core employees" only (Osterman, 1994). Core employees were defined as non-managerial employees directly involved in making the product or providing the service, and are the most difficult ones to outsource since they play a key role in the successful operation of the business. The questionnaires were carefully designed. We conducted interviews with corporate managers in eight firms (none of which were included in the final study) to identify the relevant topics. A review of salient literature was done to find questionnaire instruments appropriate for our study. We then pre-tested the survey items with eight management professors to assess content validity. A pilot study was also implemented in which pairs of questionnaires were mailed to CEOs and human resource professionals from 10 firms (again, not included in the final survey), 280 firms submitted both questionnaires, from which we obtained 218 pairs of usable responses (response rate of 16.7%).

Table 6.2 shows the distribution by size of these 218 usable responses. In general, firm size was well represented, with large firms slightly overrepresented in our usable responses.

Table 6.2   Sample distribution by size

	Usable responses		Firms in Spain in the sector considered	
Size	N.of firms	(%)	N. of firms	(%)
Medium (more than 100 and less than 500 employees)	93	42.66%	5.778	56.53%
Large (500 employees or more)	125	57.34%	4.444	43.47%
Total	218	100.00%	10.222	100.00%

Source: DIRCE-INE (1997)

Table 6.3   Country of origin in the sample

Country of origin	N. of firms	% of total
Spain	141	64.7%
Subsidiaries or multinational from:		
Belgium	1	0.5%
France	13	6.0%
Germany	14	6.4%
Holland	8	3.7%
Italy	2	0.9%
Japan	2	0.9%
Luxemburg	1	0.5%
Mexico	1	0.5%
South Africa	1	0.5%
Switzerland	3	1.4%
United States	16	7.3%
United Kingdom	15	6.9%

Table 6.4   Industry distribution in the sample

Economic activity	Usable responses		Firms in Spain in the sector considered	
	N. of firms	(%)	N. of firms*	(%)
Food, beverage and tobaco	16	7.3	545	7.3
Paper, publishing and graphic arts	8	3.7	113	1.5
Chemical and pharmaceutical industry	17	7.8	336	4.5
Rubber and plastic materials	3	1.4	162	2.2
Other non-metallic mineral products (cement, ceramics, glass)	8	3.7	223	3.0
Metallurgy and metallic products	9	4.1	439	5.9
Machinery and mechanical equip. for construction	7	3.2	217	2.9
Electrical, electronic and optical equip. and materials	16	7.3	246	3.3
Automobiles, material for transportation	18	8.3	259	3.5
Other manufacturing industries (textiles)	5	2.3	144	1.9
Production and distribution of electricity, gas, steam and hot water	5	2.3	108	1.4
Construction	6	2.8	760	10.2
Wholesale and retailing; repairing and maintenance of motor vehicles	22	10.1	1.283	17.2
Hostelry	8	3.7	546	7.3
Transportation, storage and comunication services	13	6.0	440	5.9
Financial services	28	12.8	422	5.7
Accounting, consulting, technical research, security and temporal work services	29	13.3	1.216	16.3
Total	218	100.0	7.459	100.00

Note: They represent 73% of total medium–large firms in Spain.
Source: DIRCE-INE (1997)

In terms of country of origin, Spanish firms accounted for 65% of our usable responses, as is shown in Table 6.3. The rest of the companies answering our survey were mainly subsidiaries of European and American multinational corporations.

Table 6.4 shows the distribution of our sample by economic activity. As can be observed, it was close to the distribution at a national level.

Among the 17 sectors considered only three sectors, electrical, automobiles, and financial services, were overrepresented in our usable responses. Additionally, only two industries in our sample, construction and wholesale and retailing, showed lower figures compared to the national distribution.

6.6 MEASUREMENT

6.6.1 Business strategy measures

In section 6.3 we argued that two dimensions, instead of the traditional one employed in previous empirical research, were going to be considered in order to define the competitive strategy of a firm.

The first dimension reflects Porter's (1980, 1985) product and market aspects of companies' strategic positioning. Within differentiators we will distinguish between those emphasizing speed–variety and those enhancing quality–brand name of their products. The second dimension was associated with the type of efficiency – static or dynamic – that a firm is pursuing.

Thirteen different questions were asked to companies' CEOs about the various aspects of strategy mentioned before.

As a first step, a factor analysis was conducted to test whether an overlap among these different strategic dimensions existed or if, in contrast, they represented independent aspects of firms' competitive strategies.

Four factors emerged from this analysis. Table 6.5 shows the 13 items used to measure business strategy and the way they were grouped into these four different factors.

Table 6.5   Matrix of rotated components

	Components			
	1	2	3	4
Product breadth	0.87	−0.09	0.15	0.18
Quantity of new products	0.83	−0.15	0.20	0.02
Market breadth	0.80	−0.07	0.02	0.14
% of sales spent on R&D	0.80	0.07	0.14	−0.06
Quality	−0.05	0.89	0.10	0.12
Brand name	−0.06	0.86	0.05	0.14
Value	−0.11	0.81	0.09	0.19
% of sales spent on marketing and advertising	0.02	0.75	0.05	−0.22
Radical innovation in business/operational processes	0.00	−0.02	0.86	0.10
Radical innovation in technologies	0.23	0.16	0.83	−0.05
Radical innovation in products and services	0.25	0.14	0.82	0.01
% of sales spent on infraestructure	0.03	0.03	0.01	0.93
Price	0.44	0.31	0.09	0.66

Note: Extraction method: principal components analysis. Rotation method: Varimax normalization with Kaiser.

The 10 questions measuring Porter's strategy typology were grouped into three different factors. The last two items in the list, percentage of sales spent on infrastructure and price of products, represent Porter's cost leadership strategy. In contrast, the first eight questions on the list can be associated with Porter's differentiation strategy. These eight items measuring Porter's differentiation strategy are divided into two different factors. The first four questions – product breadth, quantity of new products in last year, market breadth, and percentage of sales spent on R&D – represent the variety–speed strategy toward differentiation. The next four questions – quality of firm's products, importance of brand name, value, and percentage of sales spent on marketing and advertising – can be associated with a differentiation strategy characterized by the pursuit of quality and brand name building. Therefore, through factor analysis we confirm two distinctive modes of differentiation: one emphasizing product breadth and time to market; the other one characterized by the quality and strong brand image of a firm's products and services.

Finally, the remaining three questions – degree of radical innovation in business/operational processes, and products and services – are bundled in a fourth factor that describes whether firms follow a static or a dynamic efficiency toward innovation in their resources and capabilities.

Porter's competitive strategy dimension was measured utilizing items introduced by Govindarajan in 1988. He developed an instrument based on Porter's conceptual discussion of low-cost and differentiation generic strategies (1980, 1985). We asked respondents to rank their products or services relative to those of main competitors in the following 10 dimensions:

1. variety of products;
2. variety of clients;
3. number of new products launched last year;
4. product quality;
5. product selling price;
6. product value;
7. brand name;
8. percent of sales spent on marketing and advertising expenses;
9. percent of sales spent on research and development; and
10. percent of sales spent on equipment and infrastructure.

A seven-point Likert scale was used with values ranging from "significantly lower" to "significantly higher." An index was constructed with the sum of the scores for the ten items (Figure 6.3). Values above the mean (44.79) on this index indicated a strong Differentiation strategy (156 firms) whereas companies that ranked below were classified as cost leaders (62 firms).

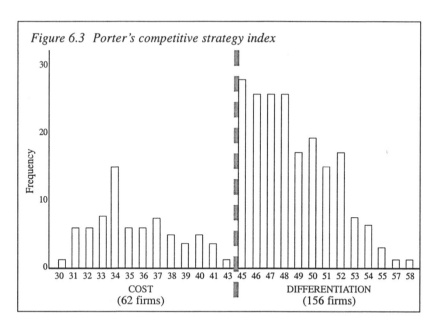

Figure 6.3 Porter's competitive strategy index

We then asked CEOs to indicate the importance of some key competitive methods to their firms' overall strategy to assess the construct validity of Porter's competitive strategy index. A seven-point Likert scale was used, with values ranging from "not important" to "extremely important." Questions were asked about the importance to their competitive strategy of:

1. low price;
2. number of new products delivered during the year;
3. quality; and
4. brand name.

As expected, Table 6.6 shows that results were consistent with Porter's strategy index.

Table 6.6 Construct validity of Porter's competitive strategy index

Correlations importance of	Porter's index
Low price	-0.66^{**}
Number of new products	0.48^{**}
Quality	0.40^{**}
Brand name	0.40^{**}
$^{**}\ p < 0.01$	

The convergent validity of our Porter's competitive strategy index was assessed by asking CEOs to indicate the percentage of their firm's 1997 sales (pesetas) that came from a low cost strategy and, on the other hand, that were a result of a differentiation strategy. Responses for each variable were additively combined to form the index. High values of this question indicated differentiation (156 firms), and low values indicated cost leadership (62 firms). Answers to this question correlated positively with values for the Porter's competitive strategy index ($r = 0.67$, $p< 0.01$).

A reliability test for the Porter's competitive strategy index reveals a significant interrelation among the included variables. The Cronbach's alpha score is 0.74 for the Porter's competitive strategy index.

We then wanted to distinguish, among differentiators, which companies were following a speed–variety strategy and which ones were emphasizing a quality–brand name approach. For each of the 156 companies adopting a differentiation strategy we first added the scores obtained in the four items bundled in the factor related to speed and variety. We then added, again for each of these 156 companies, the scores obtained in the questions included in the factor associated with quality and brand name. The second of these two scores was subtracted from the first one and in this way an index (Figure 6.4) indicating the type of differentiation followed by each firm was constructed. In other words, the

type of differentiation index =
(score in speed–variety) – (score in quality–brand name)

indicated if a particular firm was classified as following a speed–variety strategy when scores were above 0 (61 firms) or a quality–brand name strategy when values in the type of differentiation index showed a negative figure (95 firms).

In order to operationalize our second strategic dimension we translated the concepts of static and dynamic efficiency into the notions of incremental and radical innovation respectively. Incremental innovation consists in small extensions of existing products or services, technologies, and business and operational processes. In contrast, discontinuous innovation is defined as the implementation of new business and operational principles that drive the development brand new products, technologies and business and operational processes.

We developed an innovation index by asking the CEO of each firm, using a seven-point Likert scale, how radical were firm's:

1. products and services;
2. technologies used to manufacturing those products or delivering the services; and
3. business and operational processes.

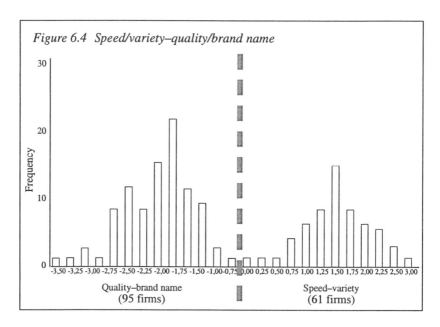

Figure 6.4 Speed/variety–quality/brand name

The scores on these three different questions constructed the index and it is shown in Figure 6.5. Values below the mean (10.07) on this index indicated a strategy of static efficiency (165 firms)[1]. In contrast, a high score indicated a strategy focused on dynamic efficiency (53 firms).

A reliability test for the innovation index showed a significant interrelation among the included variables. The Cronbach's alpha score is 0.79 for this index.

The construct validity of the innovation index was assessed by asking respondents to indicate the importance of three key organizational aspects of their businesses:

1. presence of loose controls and some chances for errors;
2. degree of operative decision making at low levels in the organization;
3. degree of strategic decision making at low levels; emphasis on vertical communications; and importance of informal networks and horizontal communications.

We expect all these aspects to correlate positively with the scores obtained in the innovation index. A seven-point Likert scale was used, with values ranging from "not important" to "extremely important." Correlation between the innovation index and these five organizational dimensions, as showed in Table 6.7, were all positive.

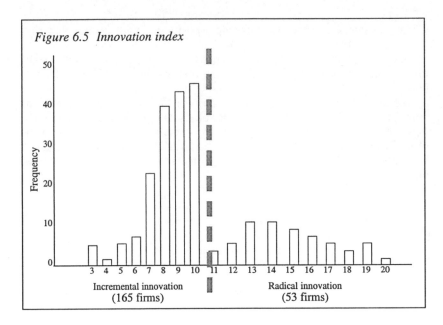

Figure 6.5 Innovation index

Table 6.7 Construct validity of innovation strategy index

Correlations, importance of	Innovation strategy index
Loose controls/errors allowed	0.34**
Operative decision-making at low levels	0.46**
Strategic decision-making at low levels	0.42**
Hierarchical communications	0.39**
Informal networks/horizontal communications	0.46**
** p<0.01	

The convergent validity of the innovation strategy index was assessed by asking CEOs, using a seven-point Likert scale with values ranging from "significantly lower" to "significantly higher", to rank how radical were the changes in their firm relative to their main competitors in three areas:

1.   their line of products or services;
2.   the technologies they use; and
3.   the business and operational processes that support their activities.

With these three responses we constructed a change index, which we expected to correlate positively with the innovation index. As expected,

CEOs' answers on change correlated positively with values for the innovation index (r = 0.68, p < 0.001).

After classifying each of the companies according to the two strategic dimensions adopted in this study we summarize in Figure 6.6 the final classification of the 218 firms of our sample.

To check whether our own classification of the 218 companies was an appropriate one we conducted a cluster analysis considering the 13 items defining firms' business strategy. Then, correlation between our own classification and the category of each firm was classified after the cluster analysis is showed in Table 6.8. Correlation between these two classifications was significant.

Figure 6.6   Classification of firms in the sample

	Product/market		
Capabilities development	Cost leadership **62**	Variety–speed static efficiency **40**	Quality–brand name static efficiency **63**
		Variety–speed dynamic efficiency **21**	Quality–brand name dynamic efficiency **32**

Table 6.8   Correlation between our own classification of firms and hierarchical cluster analysis

Importance of	Hierarchical cluster analysis
Our own	0.77**
** p < 0.01	

6.6.2 Employment systems measures

Employment systems variables were described in detail in Table 6.1. They were divided, as was explained before, into three different groups of practices. The first group three variables, work organization practices, refer to the way the different activities and tasks and decision-making processes are organized within the firm. A second group of eight variables correspond to standard human resource practices: job security, compensation, recruitment and promotion, and training and development. Finally, a third group including two practices represents some aspects of organizational design related to communication, information and some forms of socialization inside the firm.

As a next step, we conducted cluster analysis to check whether our theoretically derived employment systems existed or not in the Spanish business context. At the same time we wanted to test if the six clusters arising from the cluster analysis correspond to our six theoretically defined employment systems described earlier in sub-section 6.4.1. Table 6.9 contains a summary of the theory-based ideal profiles for each of the 13 work organization practices, HRM policies and other organizational characteristics described in detail in Table 6.1.

Table 6.9   Center of ideal type employment systems

Variables	Transactional	Balance	Relational	Market empl.	Organizational empl.	Best eractices
Rotation	1	5.5	2.5	7	7	7
Participation	1	5.5	2.5	7	7	7
Teamwork	1	4	4	7	7	7
Job security	1	4	7	1	1	7
Variable pay as % of total pay	30	15	0	30	30	30
Tenure, corporate performance and position-based compensation	–7	0	7	–7	–7	0
Internal recruiting	1	4	7	1	4	7
Experience at hiring	1	5.5	2.5	7	7	7
Teamwork skills at hiring	1	4	4	7	7	7
Breadth of training	1	2.5	5.5	1	7	7
Generality of training	0	3	–6	0	6	0
Bonding mechanisms	1	2.5	5.5	1	7	4
Linking mechanisms	0	3	3	0	6	4.5

Cluster analysis was used to derive four, five, six, and seven-cluster analysis. We applied both K-means and hierarchical clustering methods. Results obtained a high level of convergence among both the K-means and the hierarchical clustering procedures. According to our analysis, from the 218 firms in the sample, 46 firms implemented transactional systems, 65 had balanced systems, and 54 supported their business strategies with relational systems. We also found that a smaller number of firms implemented the so-called new employment forms: 14 companies implemented market employability systems, 16 had organizational employability systems, and 23 firms relied on best practices employment systems to support their competitive strategies. These findings are consistent with a generalized opinion within the field of SHRM which argues that the shift from traditional employment relations to employability systems is not a general or even a widespread phenomenon due to their complexity and difficulties in their implementation (Osterman, 1994).

Means from the six-cluster solution are presented in Table 6.10, since they can be readily interpreted. Cluster 4 emerging from the analysis was close to the ideal profile assigned to the transactional employment system. Cluster 2 closely resembles the theoretical profile of the balanced employment system. Cluster 6, in contrast, has a profile similar to the one previously assigned to relational employment systems. Cluster 1 in our analysis was close to the ideal profile defining market employability systems while values in cluster 5 were similar to the theoretical values assigned to organizational employability systems. Finally, cluster 3 emerging from our cluster analysis was close to our previous definition of best practices employment systems.

Comparison of ideal profiles in Table 6.9 and real profiles in Table 6.10 shows that clusters obtained from the analysis closely resemble the ideal types for transactional, balanced, relational, market employability, organizational employability and best practices employment systems theoretically defined in sub-section 6.4.1.

Table 6.10 Center of final cluster representing employment systems

	Cluster					
	4	2	6	1	5	3
	Transactional	Balance	Relational	Market empl.	Organizational empl.	Best practices
Variables	n=46	n=65	n=54	n=14	n=16	n=23
Rotation	1.47	4.08	2.67	5.00	5.19	5.41
Participation	2.09	4.91	3.54	5.43	6.08	6.31
Teamwork	2.28	4.22	4.21	5.21	6.23	6.25
Job security	3.33	4.91	6.56	2.68	2.72	6.67
Variable pay as % of total pay	22	14	5	20	22	22
Tenure, Corporate performance and position-based compensation	−4.68	0.15	5.72	−5.21	−5.59	−4.26
Internal recruiting	2.28	4.21	5.72	2.11	4.16	6.26
Experience at hiring	3.49	5.23	4.06	6.54	6.75	6.65
Teamwork skills at hiring	3.43	4.97	4.78	6.57	6.81	6.87
Breadth of training	2.70	3.77	5.18	2.86	6.22	6.42
Generality of training	−0.04	0.75	−2.96	−0.07	3.31	−0.13
Bonding mechanisms	2.15	3.82	4.59	1.93	6.31	6.48
Linking mechanisms	3.24	3.82	3.52	2.21	5.38	4.35

To confirm the similarities between theoretically derived employment systems and the real employment systems emerging from the cluster analysis we calculated the Euclidean distance between them. The resulting distance variable, therefore, represents a measure of the multivariate distance of each ideal employment system with each of the employment systems that emerged from the cluster analysis. This distance takes into account the overall effect of deviation on all the 13 work organization practices, HRM policies, and other organizational characteristics.

In Table 6.11, the smallest distances in all cases are the ones between each ideal employment system – horizontal axis – and its corresponding employment system resulting from the cluster analysis – vertical axis. For example, the distance between the ideal profile of the transactional system and cluster 4 emerging from our cluster analysis – which apparently looks like the transactional system – is 1.06. It is by far the shortest distance from the theoretically defined transactional system to any one of the clusters resulting from our analysis. The next closest system is the market employability one with a distance of 1.92. This in fact makes sense because the market employability system shares some of the market-oriented practices with the transactional system. Thus, the market employability system might be close to the ideal type of the transactional system although not as close as the "real" transactional system that resulted from the cluster analysis.

Similarly, the distances between each of the systems emerging from our cluster analysis and their corresponding ideal types are the lowest ones. The distances between both ideal and "real" balanced, relational, market employability, organizational employability, and best practices are 0.52;

Table 6.11 Distance between centers of ideal type employment systems and centers obtained from a cluster analysis of the sample

		Transactional	Balanced	Relational	Market empl.	Organizational empl.	Best practices
	Transactional	1.06	1.14	1.78	1.88	2.19	2.16
	Balanced	2.00	0.52	1.33	1.70	1.62	1.31
	Relational	2.33	1.23	0.55	2.39	2.21	1.60
	Market employability	1.92	0.82	2.07	0.88	1.56	1.57
	Organizational employability	2.57	1.30	1,98	1.71	0.77	1.13
	Best practices	2.81	1.38	1.74	2.01	1.26	0.68

Centers obtained from cluster analysis. Centers of ideal type employment system.

Note: This is a matrix of disimilarities.

0.55; 0.88; 0.77; 0.68, respectively. These values, appearing in the diagonal of Table 6.12, represent the shortest distances between each of the ideal employment systems previously defined and any one of the clusters emerging from the cluster analysis. The only exception might be the distance between the theoretical market employability system and the one emerging from the analysis – cluster 1 – is 0.88. It seems that the ideal type of the balanced system is also quite close (0.82) to cluster 1 – labeled transactional system – that emerged from the cluster analysis. This is in fact possible since both type of systems, balanced and market employability tend to foster speed–variety strategies although through different types of innovation processes. Thus, results shown in Table 6.12 indicate that the employment systems found in the Spanish business context closely resemble the theoretical systems previously defined.

Table 6.12 Relationship between competitive strategy and employment systems (number of firms in each category)

Competitive strategy	Employment system						Total
	Transac.	Balanced	Relational	Market employ.	Organizational employ.	Best practices	
Cost leadership	25	12	21	1	–	3	62
Variety–speed/ static efficiency	4	25	2	1	2	3	37
Quality–brand name static efficiency	13	18	24	2	1	4	62
Variety–speed/ dynamic efficiency	1	8	–	8	2	5	24
Quality–brand name dynamic efficiency	3	2	7	2	11	8	33
TOTAL	46	65	54	14	16	23	218

6.7 RESULTS: RELATIONSHIP BETWEEN COMPETITIVE STRATEGIES AND EMPLOYMENT SYSTEMS

At this point we have classified each of the 218 firms in our sample according to both their business strategy and the employment system they have implemented. The association between firms' business strategies and employment systems is shown in Table 6.12. In this two-by-two matrix we can see the number of firms following each of the business strategies and, at the same time, the employment system these companies adopted to support those competitive strategies. We can see that the majority of firms following a particular business strategy choose the predicted employment system that, according to theory, would better support that competitive strategy.

In particular, out of 62 firms following a cost leadership strategy, 25 of them (40%) supported that strategy by implementing a transactional employment system. The second most adopted employment system among cost leadership followers was the relational system with 21 firms representing 34% of the total. Along the same lines, from the 37 companies adopting a variety–speed/static efficiency strategy, 25 (68%) implemented a balanced employment system. Similarly, from the 62 companies that follow a quality–brand name/static efficiency strategy, 24 of them (39%) supported that strategy with a relational employment system. In the case of the 24 firms adopting a variety–speed/dynamic efficiency strategy, their preferences for a supporting employment system were divided. Eight companies (33%) following this strategy were inclined to adopt a market employability system and another group of eight (another 33%) chose a balanced system. Among the 33 organizations that adopted a quality–brand name/dynamic efficiency business strategy, eleven of them (33%) decided to implement organizational employability systems.

In contrast, best practices systems were adopted by fewer firms. Among the 218 companies surveyed, only 23 (11%) of them implemented the best practices employment system, showing no particular association with any one of the strategic business types defined in this study. Thus universalistic hypotheses are not supported by our data. This fact may reflect the small benefits that companies see in implementing these types of systems either because they simply don't fit well with their business strategy implementation process or due to their high implementation costs (Osterman, 1994; Ichniowski *et al.*, 1996).

Thus, the predicted employment systems were by far the most often adopted ones by firms following strategies best supported by these systems. As can be seen, the higher values for every type of strategy lie along the diagonal of Table 6.12. In aggregate terms we can say that out of our 218 companies, 93 of them (43%) implemented the employment system that, according to theory, best supports the particular business strategies these companies adopt.

These results indicate that business strategy has a significant relationship to the type of employment system adopted by firms. In addition to business strategy, other variables may have an effect on the type of employment system adopted by firms. The industry in which a particular company competes may influence the selection of employment systems. Similarly, a firm's size may also have an impact on the employment system it adopts. However, these other variables show no statistically significant association with the kind of employment systems firms use to support their strategies. Correlation between the type of employment system implemented and the industry in which the firm competes (–0.23) is non-significant. Correlation between employment system and the firm's size (–0.56) is also non-significant.

Although this study has not discussed the effect on performance of an adequate fit between business strategy and supporting employment systems, some of our preliminary results indicate that those companies showing an appropriate fit between these two organizational aspects obtain performance levels that are consistently above their corresponding industry average. In particular, our preliminary data from our 218 companies indicate that firms in which employment systems are aligned with their competitive strategy show returns over investment (ROI) that are between 9% and 26% above the average of the sector in which these firms are competing.

In contrast, companies that adopted the best practices employment system that, according to universalistic arguments, should show superior performance are in fact very close to the industry mean in which these firms operate. Specifically, average ROI of companies implementing best practices system was only 3% above the average ROI of industries considered.

6.8 CONCLUSIONS

In this chapter we have investigated two hypotheses left unresolved by research within the field of SHRM. The first one, following a contingency approach, argues that depending on the type of the strategy firms adopt, they should implement specific employment systems to support those strategies. The second hypothesis is derived from a more universalistic approach and states that organizations should always adopt a best practices employment system irrespective of the competitive strategy adopted.

Our analysis of business strategies and employment systems in a significant number of firms supports the argument that a contingent strategic choice framework provides a powerful perspective for understanding current labor relations diversity within Spanish industries. Business strategy followed by firms appears to have a strong influence on the type of employment systems firms implement to support their strategy. The study shows that even where companies compete in the same industry with similar product and market environment, there is substantial diversity in the type of employment system they select to support the implementation of their business strategies.

Similarly, our work indicates that, in contrast with the important role business strategy plays in employment systems' selection, other variables such as firms' size do not have an influence in the type of work organization practices, HRM policies and other organizational characteristics companies decide to implement. Thus, when deciding what type of labor relationships they want to adopt managers should pay close attention to the type of business strategy they are intended to support. Other variables such as the sector in which the firm competes or the company's size are less relevant for decisions about employment systems adoption.

Although an increasing body of theoretical studies exists, past research on the relationship between the business strategy followed by firms and the employment system they implement to support that strategy has been inconclusive. In part this is due to the small amount of empirical research that has been conducted within the field of SHRM. Studies outside the US or the UK are even scarcer with no empirical research available.

This study has made considerable progress in supporting contingency arguments. It has shown the strong association that exists among competitive strategies and supporting employment systems. Although an increasing body of theoretical literature argues that people and the way they are managed in organizations should provide strong support in the strategy implementation process, very little empirical work has supported this widespread view. In contrast, we found that among 218 medium and large Spanish firms competing in a wide variety of economic sectors, around 43% of them adopted specific employment system that, as predicted by theory, were specially suited for implementing the business strategy they adopted. Moreover, preliminary results from our data show that this fit has in turn effects on the company's performance. Returns over investment between 9% and 26% above industry average were found for those firms capable of aligning their strategy and employment system.

In contrast, in this study we found no support for the universalistic arguments. Our data show a weak presence of companies adopting the so-called best practices employment systems. Only 23 out of 218 firms (10%) implemented that system. Moreover, firms following competitive strategies based on dynamic efficiency mainly adopted this universal employment system. Therefore, firms adopting cost leadership and static efficiency strategies did not support their competitive position with the best practices approach. Thus, it seems that this system is not as universal as it is proposed by the SHRM literature. Even in performance terms, best practices systems do not outperform other employment systems. Based on data collected for the 218 firms in our study, companies implementing this "universal system" are achieving performance levels that are only slightly superior (3%) to industry averages calculated for the economic sector each of these firms operate in.

Our results suggest that organizations tend to align the employment systems they implement with the competitive strategy they intend to pursue. Given the increasing levels of competition in almost every industry, firms try to improve their competitive position and result through an increasingly efficient process of skills and capability allocation. In particular many companies understand that resources should be concentrated in successfully implementing their competitive strategies. Thus, managers should try to achieve an adequate fit between business strategy and employment systems. Through this type of strategic action they should obtain important increases in financial performance levels compared to their competitors. In contrast, copying what in a particular economic sector are considered best practices for managing would add no value to the firm. Moreover, in many cases this best practices approach may even have negative returns.

This work may also provide some methodological contributions. This is the first study that uses both a more comprehensive typology of business strategies and an enriched framework to study employment systems. Previous research has usually operationalized business strategy using either Porter's (1980, 1985) or Miles and Snow's (1978) strategic types. In contrast our research incorporates two different independent dimensions in the study of business strategies. The first one corresponds to the traditional product and market positioning developed by Porter. The second dimension has to do with the type of innovation firms decide to follow: incremental versus radical, which in fact may present similarities with some of the aspects considered by Miles and Snow in their typology. In some way we incorporated elements of both typologies in our own classification of firms' strategies. A series of analyses showed that our classification makes sense, it covers a wider range of strategic dimensions and, therefore, it may be implemented in future empirical research within the management field.

Our study also shows that diversity in the way organizations manage their work relationships to better support their competitive strategies can be empirically described by a limited number of distinct employment systems. They go from traditional transactional, balanced, and relational employment systems to newer forms of managing people such as market and organizational employability, and best practices systems. In fact, our typology of employment systems is consistent with our empirical findings. Each of the employment systems we included in our typology was found in the Spanish business context.

Of course, employability systems were less in number compared to the more traditional ones. We expected this since the whole idea of employability is quite new and has only recently been adopted not only in Spain but also in the rest of the world economies. So, Spain is not as different as some people say in the sense that certain particularities of Spanish labor markets and business culture might preclude the adoption of those employment systems proposed by American researchers. It is possible to think, then, that these six employment systems are not specific to the American business context but, in contrast, they can be quite universal in the sense that they are applicable in multiple and quite diverse labor environments.

The inconclusive empirical results existing within the SHRM field are in part a consequence of unsatisfactory operationalization of the business strategy and employment systems concepts. Both our strategy typology and the employment system categorization we used may help in improving the way we operationalize concepts derived from theory.

Finally, the results obtained for the Spanish business context will enrich an already existing wide body of accumulated research that is primarily Anglo-Saxon based. Being the first comprehensive study within the field of SHRM outside these two contexts, results obtained could serve as a first step to continue extending our knowledge of strategic human resource management to a wider variety of business contexts.

NOTES

1   These 156 firms following a static efficiency approach include all 63 companies following a cost leadership strategy. As we expected all firms adopting a cost leadership strategy also pursued a static efficiency approach, with none implementing a dynamic efficiency type of competitive strategy.

REFERENCES

Arthur, J. B. (1992). The link between business strategy and industrial relations systems in American steel minimills. *Industrial and Labor Relations Review*, 45: 488–506.

Arthur, J. B. (1994). Effects of human resource systems on manufacturing performance and turnover. *Academy of Management Journal*, 37 (3): 670–87.

Bailey, T. (1993). *Discretionary Effort and the Organization of Work: Employee participation and work reform since Hawthorne*. Working paper, Columbia University, New York.

Baird, Ll. and Meshoulam, I. (1988). Managing two fits of strategic human resource management. *Academy of Management Review*, 13 (1): 116–28.

Bennett, A. (1990). *The Death of the Organization Man*. New York: William Morrow.

Brown, S. L. and Eisenhardt, K. M. (1998). *Competing on the Edge*. Boston, MA: Harvard Business School Press.

Cappelli, P. (1999). *The New Deal at Work*. Boston, MA: Harvard University Press. See also Chapter 5 in this book.

Chandler, A. (1962). *Strategy and Structure*. Cambridge, MA: MIT Press

Delaney, J. T., Lewin, D. and Ichniowski, C. (1989). *Human Resource Policies and Practices in American Firms*. Washington, DC: US Government Printing Office.

Delery, J. E. and Doty, D. H. (1996). Modes of theorizing in strategic human resource management: tests of universalistic, contingency, and configurational performance predictions. *Academy of Management Journal*, 39 (4): 802–35.

Dess, W. L. and Davis, P. S. (1984). Porter's (1980) generic strategies as determinants of strategic group membership and organizational performance. *Academy of Management Journal*, 27: 467–88.

Dewar, R. and Werbel, J. (1979). Universalistic and contingency predictions of employee satisfaction and conflict. *Administrative Science Quarterly*, 24: 426–48.

Dunlop, J. T. and Weil, D. (1996). Diffusion and performance of modular production in the US apparel industry. *Industrial Relations*, 35 (3): 334–55.

Dyer, L. and Holder, G. W. (1988). A strategic perspective of human resource management. In L. Dyer (ed.), *Human Resource Management: Evolving roles and responsibilities*: 1–46. Washington DC: ASPA-BNA.

Fisher, C. D. (1989). Current and recurrent challenges in HRM. *Journal of Management*, 15: 157–80.

Galbraith, J. R. and Kazanjian, R. J. (1986). *Strategy Implementation: Structure, systems, and process*. St. Paul, MN: West.

Ghemawat, P. and Ricart, J. E. (1993). The organizational tension between static and dynamic efficiency. *Strategic Management Journal*, 14 Special Issue: 59–73.

Ghoshal, S. and Bartlett, C. A. (1997). *The Individualized Corporation*. New York: Harper Business. See also Chapter 4 in this book.

Hambrick, D. C. (1983). High profit strategies in mature capital goods industries: a contingency approach. *Academy of Management Journal*, 26: 687–707.

Hirsch, P. (1987). *Pack Your Own Parachute*. Reading, MA: Addison-Wesley.

Huselid, M. A. (1995). The impact of human resource mnagement practices on turnover, productivity, and corporate financial performance. *Academy of Management Journal*, 38 (3): 635–72.

Ichniowski, C., Kochan, T. A., Levine, D., Olson, C. and Strauss, G. (1996). What works at work: overview and assessment. *Industrial Relations*, 35 (3): 299–333.

Ichniowski, C., Shaw, K. and Prennushi, G. (1997). The effects of human resource management practices on productivity. *American Economic Review*, 87 (3): 291–313.

Kanter, R. M. (1985). Supporting innovation and venture development in established companies. *Journal of Business Venturing*, Winter: 47–60.

Kerr, J. L. and Slocum, J. W. (1987). Linking reward systems and corporate cultures. *Academy of Management Executive*, 1 (2): 99–108.

Kochan, T. A. and Katz, H. C. (1988). *Collective Bargaining and Industrial Relations*, 2nd edn. Homewood, IL: Irwin.

Lengnick-Hall, C. A. and Lengnick-Hall, M. L. (1988). Strategic human resource management: a review of the literature and a proposed typology. *Academy of Management Review*, 13: 454–70.

MacDuffie, J. P. (1995). Human resource bundles and manufacturing performance: organizational logic and flexible production systems in the world auto industry. *Industrial and Labor Relations Review*, 48 (2): 197–221.

Miles, R. H. and Snow, C. C. (1978). *Organizational Strategy, Structure, and Processes*. New York: McGraw-Hill.

Miles, R. H. and Snow, C. C. (1984). Designing strategic human resource systems.

Organizational Dynamics: 36–52.

Milgrom, P. and Roberts, J. (1995). Complementarities and fit: strategy, structure, and organizational change in manufacturing. *Journal of Accounting and Economics,* 19: 179–208.

Mintzberg, H. (1978). Patterns in strategy formation. *Management Science,* 24: 9.

Osterman, P. (1987). Choice of employment systems in internal labor market systems. *Industrial Relations,* 26 (1): 46–67.

Osterman, P. (1994). How common is workplace transformation and who adopts It? *Industrial and Labor Relations Review,* 47 (2): 173–88.

Ostrow, M. H. (1992). The relationship among competitive strategy, human resource management practices, and financial performance. Unpublished doctoral dissertation, University of Maryland, College Park.

Peck, S. R. (1994). Exploring the link between organizational strategy and the employment relationship: the role of human resources policies. *Journal of Management Studies,* 31 (5): 715–36.

Penrose, E. T. (1959). *The Theory of the Growth of the Firm.* Oxford: Basil Blackwell.

Pfeffer, J. (1994). *Competitive Advantage Through People.* Boston, MA: Harvard Business School Press.

Pfeffer, J. (1998). *The Human Equation.* Boston: MA: Harvard University Press.

Pfeffer, J. and Baron, J. N. (1988). Taking the workers back out: recent trends in the structuring of employment. *Research in Organizational Behavior,* 10.

Porter, M. E. (1980). *Competitive Strategy: Techniques for analyzing industries and competitors.* New York: Free Press.

Porter, M. E. (1985). *Competitive Advantage: Creating and sustaining superior performance.* New York: Free Press.

Purcell, J. (1989). The impact of corporate strategy on human resources management. In J. Storey (ed.), *New Perspectives in Human Resource Management.* London: Routledge.

Quinn, J. B. (1978). Strategic change: the logic of incrementalism. *Sloan Management Review,* 28, (Fall): 7–21.

Ricart, J. E. and Portales, C. (2000). Employment contracts, new organizational forms, and competitive advantage for continuous innovation. Chapter 2 of this book and paper presented at the 1st Iberoamerican Academy of Management Meeting, December 1999, Madrid, Spain.

Rousseau, D. M. (1995). *Psychological Contracts in Organizations.* Thousand Oaks, CA: Sage Publications.

Sánchez-Runde, C. (1996). Firm strategy and human resource management: A case-study approach. Unpublished PhD. dissertation, University of Oregon, Eugene.

Sánchez-Runde, C. (2000). Paper presented at the Annual Conference on Employment Creation, IESE, University of Navarra.

Schuler, R. and Jackson, S. (1987a). Linking competitive strategies and human resource management management practices. *Academy of Management Executive,* 1 (3): 207–19.

Schuler, R. and Jackson, S. (1987b). Organizational strategy and organizational level as determinants of human resource management practices. *Human Resource*

Planning, 10 (3): 125–41.

Schuler, R. and Jackson, S. (1988). Human resource management choices and organizational strategy. In R. Schuler, S. A. Youngblood and V. L. Huber (eds), *Readings in Human Resource Management,* 3rd edn: 24–39. St. Paul, MN: West.

Sivasubramaniam, N. (1993). Matching human resources and corporate strategy. Unpublished doctoral dissertation, Florida International University, Miami.

Smith, E. C. (1982) Strategic business planning and human resources. Parts I and II, *Personnel Journal,* 61: 606–10, 680–82.

Sonnenfeld, J. A. and Piperl, M. A. (1988). Staffing policy as a strategic response: a typology of career systems. *Academy of Management Review,* 13: 558–600.

Stalk, G. (1988). Time: the next source of competitive advantage. *Harvard Business Review,* July/August.

Terpstra, D. E. and Rozell, E. J. (1993). The relationship of staffing practices to organizational level measures of performance. *Personnel Psychology,* 46: 27–48.

Tichy, N. and Sherman, S. (1993). *Control Your Destiny or Somebody Else Will.* New York: Currency/Doubleday.

Tornatzky, L. G. (1983). *The Process of Technological Innovation: Reviewing the literature.* Washington, DC: National Sciences Foundation.

Van de Ven, A. and Drazin (1985). *Control Your Destiny or Somebody Else Will.* New York: Currency/Doubleday.

Walton, R. E. (1985). From control to commitment in the workplace. *Harvard Business Review,* 64 (2): 77–84.

Wernerfelt, B. (1984). A resource-based view of the firm. *Strategic Management Journal,* 5: 171–80.

Wright, P. M. and Snell, S. A. (1991). Toward an integrative view of strategic human resource management, *Human Resource Management Review,* 1: 203–25.

Wright, P. M. and McMahan, G. C. (1992). Theoretical perspectives for strategic human resource management. *Journal of Management,* 18 (2): 295–320.

7 The Adoption of Innovative Forms of Organizing in Europe and Japan in the 1990s*

Andrew Pettigrew and Silvia Massini

7.1 INTRODUCTION

In Western Europe at the end of the twentieth century the predominant form of organization amongst the very largest firms is multidivisional. Recent research by Whittington *et al.* (1999a) shows that the diffusion of the divisional structure has effectively suppressed indigenous forms in many European countries. Thus in the mid 1990s, 75% of the top 100 French firms, 70% of the top 100 German firms and 89% of the top 100 UK firms were divisionally organized.

However, behind and within this apparent homogeneity there is evidence of the emergence of innovative forms of organizing amongst large and medium sized firms in Europe and beyond? Perhaps buoyed up by the impending new millennium, some commentators have suggested a widespread sense of revolution in the form, character, and processes of contemporary organizations.

Thus we are variously persuaded of the rise of the network and cellular form (Miles *et al.*, 1997), the federal organization (Handy, 1992), the post-modern and flexible firm (Volberda, 1998) and the individualized corporation (Ghoshal and Bartlett, 1998). If there are doubts about whether these ideal type formulations truly capture the nature and extent of contemporary organizational change, there is now accumulating evidence of experimentation in the way firms are organizing themselves. Some authors have also been able to establish an association between innovative forms of organizing and company performance (Whittington *et al.*, 1999b). This innovation–performance link can thus underpin previous claims that competitiveness is now an innovation contest, where the inflexible and bureaucratic cannot succeed.

But why are organizations in transition? As ever, big questions are rarely answered by single causes. There appears to be a convergence of factors, economic, technological, informational and political driving the emergence of innovative forms of organizing. Heightened international competition in a globalizing economy is pushing firms to think and act globally and locally. There are efficiency drives to reduce costs, pressures to concentrate manufacturing resources regionally and to simplify complex matrix structures by de-emphasizing country organizations. Internationalizing firms are strengthening internal networks between functions, divisions, countries and regions in order to speed the transfer of knowledge and skill and are investing in alliances and other partnerships to compete through cooperation. Technological change is shortening product life cycles in many industries and pressurizing firms to build organizations with greater flexibility. Advances in information and communication technologies are enabling network formation and utilization and permitting a quantity and quality of hierarchical control and lateral knowledge sharing previously considered impossible. De-regulation has also been an enormous driver both of increased economic competition and of cultural and people change in organizations. New skills, knowledge, attitudes and standards are now required in industries and firms previously sheltered from competition.

The above drivers for organizational change are justifiably creating a new vocabulary to think and act about innovation in organizational arrangements. Such are the pressures for change that thinking about organizing has had to take on a more dynamic and strategic quality. There is now an understandable tendency to drop the noun of organization and to use the more dynamic verb of organizing to try and capture the realities of continuous innovation.

With this verb status, organizing is now seen much more clearly to be an instrument of strategic development. Organizing and strategizing are now recognized as truly complementary activities even to the point where the form of organizing may be synonymous with the strategy of the firm. There is also a new and more inclusive appreciation of the range of levers to pull in organizing. The general trend of the new forms of organizing literature places structure and design backstage, and strategy, processes, systems, boundaries and people front stage.

All of these changes leave the empirical researcher, manager and policy maker with a number of conundrums. The drivers for innovation in organizing are clear enough but the responses of firms less so. In their attempt to capture the new reality of organizational responses, some authors have retreated into the use of ideal types. So we are informed about the rise of the 'N' form, the cellular form, the boundaryless and individualized corporation. But thus far such claims (often expressed in apocryphal and dramatic language) have rested heavily on case studies of exceptional organizations, notably ABB and 3M (Bartlett and Ghoshal,

1993) or atypical sectors and regions, for instance, West Coast American high-tech (Bahrami, 1992).

The very character of the proposed changes, implying, as they do, not just changes in form or structure but dynamic adjustments in form, process, systems, boundaries and behaviour, means that the empirical capture of the changes is complex. Theoretical developments are also problematic when the appropriate analytical language is still emerging to capture empirical developments which themselves are also still in the process of evolution.

And finally, there are genuine questions to be asked about any differential content and pace of innovation in new forms of organizing in different parts of the globe. Europe is not the only continent facing industrial, economic, and organizational change. The 1980s, economic bubble in Asia has been deflated if not burst. Have the assumed pressures for organizational innovation in Europe been matched by equivalent pressures and responses in Japan? These are some of the central questions posed and answered in this chapter.

In what follows we outline the aims, methods and participants of the INNFORM program of research which comprises a large-scale standardized survey of new organization practices in Europe, Japan, and the United States. We define these innovative forms of organizing in terms of changes in structures, processes and boundaries, and then examine progress in the patterns of innovation in a large sample of European and Japanese firms. Comparisons are offered in Europe and Japan between 1992 and 1996.

Alongside this treatment of new forms of organizing in terms of changing structures, processes and boundaries we also ask and seek to answer a wider set of questions about the extent to which these new forms are supplementing or supplanting existing forms. In our survey instrument we asked our firms to indicate, again in 1992 and 1996, the extent to which they organized themselves in one or other of four logics of organizing: by product or service; by geographical region; by function; or by project form.

Presumably if we find that between 1992 and 1996 there was an overwhelming tendency for firms to reduce their attachment to the first three logics and move towards the project form this is evidence for older forms being supplanted. If the opposite is happening, i.e. the project form is being adopted more but alongside the continuing attachment to one or other of the other three logics, then this is some confirmatory evidence for new forms supplementing existing forms.

The final part of the chapter discusses the extent and speed of change in Europe and Japan and identifies some of the contradictions and challenges as firms manage their ever-changing competitive landscape.

7.2 MAPPING INNOVATIVE FORMS OF ORGANIZING: THE INNFORM PROGRAM

The INNFORM program is a research network of scholars from Europe, Japan, and the US. The focal research team providing leadership and coordination of the network is at Warwick Business School in the United Kingdom. The other research teams are located in Europe at Erasmus University (The Netherlands), ESSEC (France), IESE (Spain), Jönköping (Sweden) and St Gallen (Switzerland). The United States and Japanese teams are located at Duke University and Hitotsubashi University. The program has three main aims: to map the extent of development of new forms of organizing in Europe, Japan, and the US; to test for the performance benefits of such changes; and to examine the management processes as organizations move from more traditional to novel forms of organizing. The progress and performance aims are being addressed by a standardized survey of organizational innovations in Europe, Japan, and the United States. The processes of organizational innovation are being studied in 18 case studies carried out in Europe. This chapter reports findings on progress in innovative forms of organizing in Europe and Japan. Study findings linking new forms of organizing and performance in Europe have been published in Whittington *et al.*, (1999b). The first book length manuscript on eight of the European case studies was published in Pettigrew and Fenton (2000).

The INNFORM survey design began from an examination of the literature on new organizational forms and three mini-case studies of innovative organizations. We also benefited from the strengths and limitations of survey instruments developed to identify patterns of restructuring in European firms (Markides, 1996) in the late 1980s and early 1990s. Many of these instruments appeared ill-adapted to the new competitive landscape and in any case were not developed specifically to test for new forms of organizing. Accordingly, our own survey instrument was eclectic and adaptive in design.

The review of literature we did on new forms of organizing to prepare the INNFORM survey instrument revealed a wide list of indicators of organizational change.

We decided to cluster these indicators of contemporary change under the headings of "changing structures," "changing processes," "changing boundaries." Here we define these three main dimensions, draw out some of the significant interdependencies between them and also indicate the limited extent of systematic and large-sample surveys of innovative forms of organizing. Figure 7.1 summarizes nine areas of change measured in the INNFORM survey.

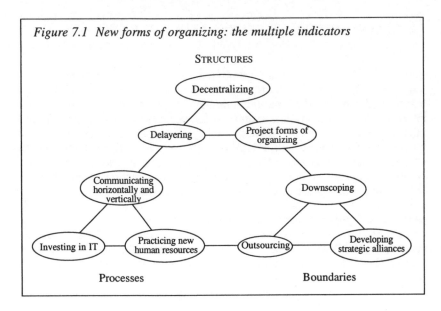

Figure 7.1 New forms of organizing: the multiple indicators

7.3 CHANGING STRUCTURES

The new competitive environment has put traditional hierarchical structures under dual pressures. First, the heavy hierarchical layers of middle managers have become too expensive; second, these layers have impeded the information flows and quickness of response necessary for flexibility and innovation. As a result, firms have apparently been resorting to widespread delayering in order to remove these expensive barriers to action.

The removal of layers has been accompanied by increased decentralization, operational and strategic. Increased operational decentralization – for example, in areas such as product design and marketing – has been necessary both to improve response times and to harness the on-the-ground knowledge of operating managers. Strategic decentralization, for example, increased responsibility for investment decisions, increases the profit orientation and accountability of business managers, incentivizing them in an increasingly competitive environment. ABB's business managers are even reported to be able to retain profits in their local balance sheets from year to year. Decentralization into smaller units promotes cross-functional and cross-boundary teams. In place of rigid traditional structures, organizations are increasingly shifting towards more flexible, project-based forms of organization. Structures are therefore taking on a more horizontal character, projects being the vehicle for bridging the "divisions" of traditional divisional organization (Ghoshal and Bartlett, 1995).

7.4 CHANGING PROCESSES

The flexibility and knowledge required in the new knowledge economy requires intensive interaction, vertical and horizontal. Learning organizations are communications-intensive, requiring new investments in information technology. These unite different parts of the organization in intense exchanges of information. A key dimension of these flows is horizontal, promoting "co-adaptive" exploitation of cross-business synergies. These flows of information are moving outwards as well, to embrace suppliers and customers through electronic data interchange (EDI) and similar initiatives. The new communication-intensive organization allows still further process innovation, in terms of participation, polycentricity, and flexibility.

For these processes to work, the hard infrastructure of IT needs to be underpinned by "softer" investments in human resources. As Ghoshal and Bartlett (1998) have insisted, the new strategies and structures require new ways of managing and new kinds of managers. Whittington and Mayer (1997) suggest that the human resources function has become central to making the new forms of organization work. These new HRM practices have two broad dimensions for the emerging model of organization: those concerned with supporting horizontal networking and those concerned with maintaining organizational integration.

The new HR fosters horizontal processes in a variety of ways. Growing use of corporate-wide conferences, seminars and similar events is reported, as companies seek occasions on which to bring together key personnel for exchange. Companies are increasingly seeing their key resources as their people and the knowledge they carry, so that corporate-wide management of careers across organizational boundaries is becoming important. These horizontal processes need integration too within a corporate sense of purpose. High profile leadership and corporate mission building are necessary to provide the sense of shared corporate identity on which exchange can be built. Investment in managerial development plays a key part in cementing a common purpose within a "boundaryless organization," as at GE. Here the deliberate cultivation of cross-unit teams and cross-unit communications are key functions (Nohria and Ghoshal, 1997).

7.5 CHANGING BOUNDARIES

Large scale drives high hierarchies; wide scope stretches horizontal relationships. Delayering and more interactive processes are likely to be accompanied, therefore, by decreased scale and increased focus on narrower spans of activities. This correlate of changing structures and processes is reinforced by increased competitive pressures forcing companies to focus on "core competencies," redrawing their boundaries around what constitutes or supports their true competitive advantage.

This pressure is reflected in the widely observed shifting of business toward smaller, decentralized units. Hierarchy and scale can hamper the strategic flexibility required for competing in increasingly hyper-competitive environments. The shift in scale is often reinforced by strategic downscoping and the abandonment of conglomerate strategies, leaving firms focused on areas of advantage (Hoskisson *et al.*, 1993). Even within particular product-market domains, firms appear increasingly to be outsourcing value-chain activities of low value or strategic significance, with a wide range of non-core activities from training to R&D subcontracted. Where superior skills or resources exist outside the firm, firms are making increased use of strategic alliances to supplement and sometimes enhance their own competencies. In sum, whether by alliances, outsourcing or downscoping, firms appear to be drawing in their boundaries around narrower spheres of activity.

The above review of trends in organizational change reveals a patchwork quilt of conjecture and pockets of evidence to suggest that some dimensions of change may be occurring faster than others. The distinctive contribution of our survey is first to measure all the indicators of change together; second to measure them over two time points (1992 and 1996), and third to examine the extent to which the dimensions cohere: were some firms innovating predominantly in the areas of structures, or processes, or boundaries? And what is the extent of these changes?

Unusually for a survey instrument of this kind, respondents were asked to compare their organization in 1992 with 1996. This is, of course, a limited time-scale within a process of organizational change which probably started some time previously and is continuing now. However, problems of reliable respondent recall precluded a longer period of retrospection, and the period 1992–6 certainly included considerable pressure for change in both Europe and Japan.

An initial questionnaire was tested with a large group of executive MBA students; a further refined version was piloted on a small sub-sample of large British firms. After certain adjustments, the questionnaire was mailed during 1997 to the chief executives of large medium-sized (i.e. with more than 500 employees), independent, domestically owned firms throughout Western Europe: for the UK, these were the largest 1500 independent businesses by employment; for the remainder of Western Europe, these were 2000 large and medium-sized firms sampled in proportion to home-county GDP. Although relying on single-respondents, our targeting of chief executives was designed to elicit as comprehensive a view as possible and is in line with widespread practice, given the difficulties of obtaining multi-respondent returns from large-scale surveys.

Except for the Dutch and Scandinavian samples, the Continental European questionnaires were translated into German, Italian, Spanish, or French as most appropriate, using native translators and checked for accuracy by local team members. We re-mailed to initial non-respondents and subsequently used telephone follow-ups. The overall response rate was 13.1%, comparable to other recent European surveys of organizational change.

Corresponding to their original sampling proportions, the largest groups of respondents were British (40.7%) and German (15.9%): no other country accounted for more than 10% of responses. Tests for the UK sample indicated no response biases for size, industry or profitability.

The Japanese survey instrument was translated into Japanese by colleagues from Hitotsubashi University. Only very minor changes were made in the survey instrument to reflect the Japanese context. In order to improve the response rate the survey was sent out with an appropriate covering letter by the Japanese National Institute of Science and Technology Policy (NISTEP). The questionnaire was mailed in 1998 to the chief executives of 1000 large and medium-sized companies with more than 500 employees/independent, domestically owned firms in Japan. The response rate for the Japanese survey was a commendable 25.7%.

There are no large-scale published surveys mapping the extent of development of new forms of organizing in Europe or Japan, and no studies comparing Europe and Japan. There are, of course, a number of good studies (particularly by Lincoln and his colleagues: Lincoln and Kalleberg, 1990) comparing US and Japanese organizations in the 1980s and then in the 1990s. These studies variously indicate that, compared to the US, Japanese manufacturing organizations have taller hierarchies, less functional specialization, less formal delegation of authority but more *de facto* participation in decisions by lower levels of management. The picture presented in these studies of Japanese firms is of a highly integrated and interdependent set of factors embedded in Japanese institutions, the interlinkages between large and medium-sized firms in the *Keiretsu* arrangements, and the form and processes within Japanese firms which cumulatively help to build a highly adaptive and flexible form of organizing in Japan. Thus in large Japanese firms life-term employment and promotion through seniority are said to provide a platform for the building of generalist skills which are enabled by frequent job rotation and regular training. Innovation in product development is said to be encouraged by elaborate processes of organizational and individual learning. Strong hierarchies are combined with equally strong processes of horizontal coordination which encourage both knowledge creating and sharing (Aoki, 1990; Nonaka and Takeuchi, 1995).

The above features of Japanese organizations lead us to expect that at least some of the features of structures, processes, and boundaries now said to represent new forms of organizing in Europe and the US were already present in at least some Japanese firms. But were the economic and business pressures in Europe in the 1990s pushing European firms towards greater change in their structures, processes, and boundaries? And what impact, if any, were equivalent pressures in Japan in the 1990s having on the context and pace of organizational change there? In the following sections of the chapter we draw on our survey results to seek answers to these and other questions. For example, what is the pace of organizational changes in large companies? Are these organizational changes adopted incrementally or more radically? And are there differences between European and Japanese companies in terms of extent of change in their organizational structures, processes, and boundaries?

In the next section we first introduce a picture of the adoption of organizational innovations in Europe and Japan for the two years 1992 and 1996. The aim is to understand their positions as measured at the start point and end point of our survey investigation, and to test for statistical differences. Next, we explore in more detail the extent of change in Europe and Japan, again testing for statistical differences. We then raise the important question about the extent to which innovative forms of organizing are supplanting or supplementing existing forms. The presentation of the results is followed by a discussion of the characteristics of Japanese organizations. The chapter ends with a brief summary and conclusion.

7.6 COMPARING FORMS OF ORGANIZING IN EUROPE AND JAPAN

This section deals with the empirical analysis of our survey results of organizational changes in Europe and Japan.

The answers to questions in the survey were structured in a five point Likert scale for both 1992 and 1996. For example, the question on the adoption of a project-based structure asked chief executives to indicate the extent to which the corporate structure was formally organized according to that form. The possible answers for both 1992 and 1996 were: 1 = None; 2 = Little; 3 = Moderate; 4 = Much; 5 = Great.

In general, the percentages for years 1992 and 1996 represent the proportion of organizations answering 4 or 5 in the five point Likert scale.

In Table 7.1 we show the percentages of adoption of organizational innovations by European and Japanese organizations. In order to draw sharper conclusions on the extent of the difference between the two regions some statistical tests on the adoption of organizational innovations in Europe and Japan, in 1992 and 1996, are also provided.

The results in Table 7.1 indicate that the percentages of European and Japanese companies adopting organizational innovations have increased between 1992 and 1996. In general Japanese organizations show higher percentages than their European comparators. Exceptions are found in the higher percentages for European organizations for the adoption of strategic decentralization and horizontal linkages in both 1992 and 1996, and engagement in strategic alliances for 1996.

Table 7.1   Incremental and radical changes in European and Japanese organizations, 1992–6 (%)

	1992			1996		
	Europe	Japan	Chi-2	Europe	Japan	Chi-2
Structures						
Layers: *Mean	3.5	4.1	60.0 (0.000)	3.2	4.0	82.9 (0.000)
Median	3.0	4.0		3.0	4.0	
Project form	13.5	24.9	6.9 (0.001)	37.9	48.8	11.9 (0.001)
Operation decentralization	40.7	59.1	19.6 (0.000)	61.0	67.4	2.6 (0.110)
Strategic decentralization	15.3	14.6	0.1 (0.815)	18.9	16.8	0.4 (0.517)
Processes						
Vertical linkages	10.3	21.0	14.9 (0.000)	31.8	32.3	0.0 (0.897)
Horizontal linkages	10.8	10.1	0.1 (0.790)	25.6	18.75	4.3 (0.038)
Information technology	7.2	17.5	17.2	38.8	76.7	91.8 (0.000)
New HR practices	N/A	N/A		34.9	35.4	0.0 (0.899)
Boundaries						
Strategic Alliances	10.2	18.5	4.9 (0.028)	31.1	25.0	1.4 (0.234)
Downscoping: Single core Businesses	34.3	35.9	0.2 (0.677)	23.7	35.4	10.1 (0.234)
Dominant core businesses	25.4	32.7	3.9 (0.049)	34.3	32.3	0.3 (0.598)
Set of related businesses	25.6	21.8	1.1 (0.238)	29.9	23.2	3.3 (0.069)
Wide range of businesses	14.7	9.5	3.4 (0.065)	12.1	9.1	1.3 (0.252)

Note: *Number of layers.
Given the nature of the question on outsourcing, it was not possible to include this kind of result for this indicator.
Source: INNFORM program survey

Table 7.1 also shows that there are several statistically significant differences between companies in the two regions in the adoption of organizational innovations in structures, processes, and boundaries.

The hierarchical structures of European and Japanese organizations are almost stable between 1992 and 1996, with a slight reduction in the average numbers of layers between the manager with the lowest level of profit responsibility and the chief executive, and constant medians, respectively at 3 and 4. The higher number of hierarchical layers in Japanese organizations is significantly different from the patterns in Europe and this difference is stable over the period of analysis. Significant differences were found in the adoption of project forms of organizing between Japanese and European organizations in both 1992 and 1996.

Operational decision making also increased in the study period: 40% of European organizations had decentralized their operational decision making in 1992 and 61% by 1996. However, only 15% of the organizations in 1992 and 19% in 1996 reported sub-units with large or total discretion in strategic decision making. In Japan almost 60% of the firms had decentralized their operational decision making in 1992, and a slightly higher percentage of firms (67%) had done so by 1996. The figures for strategic decentralization in Japan, 15% in 1992 and 17% in 1996, are just slightly smaller than those found in Europe. These results show a tendency to delegate more responsibility than authority in both European and Japanese organizations.

Our survey results also reveal increases in the adoption of process innovations for European and Japanese firms between 1992 and 1996. These innovations include practices to enhance vertical and horizontal communication, investments in IT, and adopting new HR practices.

Only one-tenth of European companies in 1992 gave much or great importance to both vertical linkages between corporate headquarters and sub-units and horizontal linkages between sub-units, but the percentages increased respectively to one-third and one-fourth by 1996. Table 7.1 shows a greater investment of Japanese firms in vertical linkages in 1992 but by 1996 equivalent investments now existed in European firms. For the importance of horizontal linkages a different trend emerges: in 1992 about 10% of Japanese companies gave great or large importance to horizontal linkages. This is similar to the European figure. But by 1996 only 19% of Japanese firms, compared with 25% in Europe, were adopting horizontal linkages.

There are remarkable changes in the adoption of IT between 1992 and 1996. In 1992 only 7% of the European companies put (much or great) emphasis on managing information, whilst in 1996 almost 40% did. If the adoption of information technology increased remarkably between 1992 and 1996 in Europe, the figures are even more marked in Japan. In 1992, 17% of Japanese companies (more than twice the European) declared a great emphasis on and investment in information technology. By 1996 this figure had risen to 77%, twice the figure for our European sample of firms.

Interestingly, by 1996, more than one-third of the companies in Europe and Japan indicated they were introducing new human resources practices. These included the development of internal labor markets, corporate-wide mission building, team development and building internal networks for knowledge transfer.

The statistical tests reveal significant differences between European and Japanese organizations in 1992 in the adoption of operational decentralization, vertical linkages and information technology. In all these areas European companies were lagging behind the Japanese ones. However, by 1996, the gap between European and Japanese organizations had reduced for operational decentralization and vertical linkages, i.e. no significant differences were found for these variables. However, the gap in information technology between Europe and Japan was still evident in 1996.

In 1992 no significant differences were apparent in strategic decentralization and horizontal linkages. By 1996 statistically significant differences were found between Europe and Japan only in horizontal linkages. Interestingly by 1996 Japanese firms had developed less formal horizontal linkages compared to their European comparators. No statistical difference in strategic decentralization are apparent in 1996 between the two regions.

Interestingly a significantly higher percentage of Japanese organizations (18.5%) engaged in strategic alliances in 1992 compared to the European organizations (10.2%). But by 1996 the percentage of European organizations engaged in strategic alliance had increased to almost one-third. This was higher, even if not significantly, than their Japanese comparators.

The evidence on downscoping is mixed. In general Japanese organizations show only very modest changes in their percentage profiles of the range of businesses between 1992 and 1996. Comparing the two regions in the period of analysis, it is noteworthy that in 1992 significantly more Japanese organizations (33%) were focusing on a dominant core business compared to the European ones (25%). On the other hand, a significantly higher percentage of European organizations had a wide range of businesses than the Japanese ones, respectively 15% and 9%. By 1996 significantly fewer European companies focused on a single core business (24%) compared to the Japanese organizations (35%) but significantly more European companies (30%) had a set of related businesses than their Japanese comparators (23%).

From the above analysis it is possible to derive a portrait of the relative position of European and Japanese organizations at the beginning of the period of analysis, 1992, and at the end, 1996. Some differences between organizations in the two regions existed in 1992 and still existed in 1996, for example the taller hierarchies and higher investments in IT in Japan.

Also, European organizations are increasingly adopting, and thereby catching up on, some organizational innovations which have traditionally characterized Japanese firms. These include organizational practices such as decentralization at both operational and strategic levels, the development of vertical linkages, the adoption of new human resource practices, and engagement in strategic alliances.

The general picture from our findings is that European and Japanese organizations are adopting comparable new forms of organizing. The direction of change is remarkably similar, but with different rates of change in our nine indicator multidimensional model. However, it is not possible to conclude from these results a simple convergence in organizational development between European and Japanese firms.

We now extend our analysis and explore the pace of change between organizations in the two regions and see whether changes in organizational practices are adopted in an incremental or a more radical way.

The literature on technological innovation characterizes radical innovations as fundamental and clear departures from existing practice. Incremental innovations are defined as minor improvements or simple adjustments in current technology (Dewar and Dutton, 1986).

In a similar way, we define radical organizational innovations as large changes from the existing practice, and incremental innovations as smaller adjustments. Our survey instrument has allowed us to calculate measures of incremental and radical change in our sample of European and Japanese firms.

We compared the percentage profiles of the changes in the adoption of organizational innovations during the period 1992–6. As we have seen, most organizations were moving toward an increasing adoption of the innovations measured in our survey. We defined the changes between 1992 and 1996 as follows: a negative value in the difference between the value reported in 1996 and the value in 1992 in the five point Likert scale corresponds to a reduction of the emphasis of certain organizational innovations. We denote this negative value as "against the trend". A positive difference of 1 in our scaled questions is an "incremental" change; and a difference greater than one is a "radical" change. "No change" indicates the percentage of companies which did not change the emphasis of the organizational indicators during the four years.

In Table 7.2 we compare the profiles of European and Japanese organizations over the period 1992–6 and test for statistically significant differences between the percentage profiles of each organizational innovation in Europe and Japan.

Table 7.2 indicates that all the innovation profiles (structures, processes, and boundaries) show statistically significant differences between Europe and Japan (see the Chi-2 at the bottom of each column). For example, in the case of delayering, half of our European companies did not change their hierarchical structures, 14% increased the number of layers and one-third created shorter hierarchies. This percentage distribution is significantly different from the Japanese profile, where three-quarters of organizations did not change the number of organizational layers, only 8% of the companies created taller hierarchies and only 14% reduced the number of hierarchical layers in their organizations.

Table 7.2   Incremental and radical changes in European and Japanese organizations, 1992–6

	Structure				Processes				Boundaries		
	De-layer	Proj. form	Oper. dec.	Strat. dec.	Vert. links	Hor. links	Info. tech.	New HR	Out-sour.	Strat. all	Down-scope.
Europe											
Against trend	14.3	6.1	9.6	6.9	2.9	2.9	2.1	6.0	5.5	1.7	19.2
No change	54.0	46.2	46.5	55.5	18.3	18.3	8.8	7.7	31.4	68.1	69.4
Incremental	18.6	23.3	21.4	25.8	57.4	59.9	39.4	47.9	53.0	23.8	2.3
Radical	13.1	24.3	22.4	11.7	21-4	18.9	49.7	38.4	10.1	6.4	9.1
Radic+Incr	*31.7*	*47.6*	*43.8*	*37.5*	*78.8*	*78.8*	*89.1*	*86.3*	*63.1*	*30.2*	*11.4*
Japan											
Against Trend	8.0	3.2	2.8	4.7	2.0	1.2	0.0	8.7	3.6	0.7	2.4
No change	77.5	63.6	81.5	80.6	40.6	40.6	8.2	20.1	34.0	89.0	94.5
Incremental	12.1	23.2	13.0	11.9	53.9	56.3	52.9	64.6	57.3	9.6	3.1
Radical	2.4	10.0	2.8	2.8	3.5	2.0	38.8	6.7	5.1	00	0.0
Radic+Incr	*14.5*	*32.2*	*15.8*	*14.7*	*57.4*	*58.3*	*91.8*	*71.3*	*62.4*	*9.6*	*3.1*
Chi-2	42.4	28.4	89.8	46.7	64.6	57.8	16.1	88.8	6.8	23.7	70.8
(prob)	(0.000)	(0.000)	(0.000)	(0.000)	(0.000)	(0.000)	(0.000)	(0.000)	(0.000)	(0.000)	(0.000)

Source: INNFORM program survey

The pace of change (as measured by the percentage profile of the extent of the differences between 1992 and 1996) in European and Japanese organizations differs for all the nine indicators defined here. In general Japanese organizations have lower percentage figures, indicating less change over the period than their European counterparts. This is evident, for example, in the "against the trend" figures for all the indicators, except for the adoption of new HR practices compared to European firms. Japanese organizations also show higher percentages for "no change" over the period, the only exception to this being in the adoption of IT. For IT investments the percentages of organizations displaying no changes is only slightly lower (8.2%) than in Europe (8.8%). It appears that investing in IT is the only indicator where Japanese firms reveal higher percentages of change compared to Europe.

Table 7.2 also indicates that European organizations had engaged in more incremental and more radical organizational innovations than Japanese firms over the period 1992–6. The exceptions to this trend are IT, new HR, and outsourcing. Thus more Japanese organizations have increased their investment in IT compared to European firms. Regarding the adoption of new HR practices, more Japanese firms are adopting incremental changes, but this is accompanied by a higher percentage of Japanese firms going against the trend or not revealing such changes.

It is in the process changes that we find the largest differences between Europe and Japan in pace of change. In particular, European companies are developing more vertical and horizontal linkages than Japanese firms, and are adopting more (radical) changes in new HR practices than their Japanese comparators. Japanese firms exceed European companies only in the speed of adoption of IT. These significant changes in processes are mirrored to a lesser degree in structures. Here, however, our survey results for Japanese organizations reveal much lower figures for radical and incremental changes and especially so for operational and strategic decentralizations and delayering.

Among boundary innovations a more differentiated pattern emerges among the three indicators of outsourcing, engaging in strategic alliances and downscoping. First, the highest changes in both regions are in outsourcing. Although there are no differences in the percentages of changes in outsourcing (respectively 63% and 63%) between the two regions, if we look at the percentages for incremental and radical changes we find clear differences. More Japanese organizations (57%) have opened their boundaries incrementally than the Europeans (53%), but only 5% of Japanese have made large increases in their outsourcing compared to 10% of European firms.

Second, only a few Japanese companies changed their proportion of total assets deployed in strategic alliances (10%) or their range of businesses (3%). This is in contrast with the patterns for Europe, where respectively 32% and 11% of companies increased strategic alliances and downscoping between 1992 and 1996. It is also noteworthy that no Japanese companies presented radical changes in downscoping or alliance developments within the period 1992–6.

Overall, our results indicate that European firms have significantly higher rates of adoption of organizational innovations in all the indicators in the survey, with the exception of the introduction of information technology indicator, for which Japanese organizations show higher percentages of adoption. The highest differences are in outsourcing, operational and strategic decentralizations, and vertical linkages.

There is now a well established literature in organization theory (Child, 1984) indicating that many large firms simultaneously adopt more than one logic of organizing in grouping their activities. Thus firms can be seen to be grouping their assets by product and service, geographical region, function and in terms of project-form. The INNFORM survey instrument included a question which asked our sample to indicate the extent to which their corporate structure was formally organized by product, geography, function, and project. Each organization was asked to compare 1992 with 1996 and indicate the extent of the emphasis on the four structural groupings on a five-point scale: none, little, moderate, much, and great. We took the project-based structure to be the closest to the characterization of innovative forms in the literature and were interested in the relative adoption of the four logics of organizing over the time period from 1992 to 1996. If we found over this period an overwhelming change towards the project-based structure this would represent at least some evidence for the new supplanting the old. If, however, any rise in the project form was occurring alongside the corresponding adoption of the other three logics of organizings then this was some evidence to support a more incremental innovation pathway: organizations would be supplementing the old with the new and not supplanting the old with the new. Tables 7.3, 7.4 and 7.5 represent some very interesting results about the extent to which innovative forms are supplementing or supplanting existing forms in Europe and Japan.

Table 7.3 shows the percentage of organizations adopting the four logics of organizing in Europe and Japan in 1992 and 1996. The table clearly

Table 7.3   Types of corporate structure in European and Japanese organizations, 1992–6 (%)*

	1992		Chi-2	1996		Chi-2
	Europe	Japan	Eur–Jap 1992	Europe	Japan	Eur–Jap 1996
Products & services	53.1	82.2	53.3 (0.000)	77.4	88.6	11.9 (0.001)
Geographical region	45.4	60.0	12.2 (0.000)	49.9	64.1	12.2 (0.001)
Functions	46.6	62.1	13.9 (0.000)	56.6	69.9	10.7 (0.000)
Project-form	13.5	24.9	6.9 (0.001)	37.9	48.8	11.9 (0.001)

Chi-2 on the profiles

3.271 (0.352)   1.480 (0.687)

Note: *Percentage of companies answering "much" or "great".
Source: INNFORM program survey

indicates that the four groupings are accepted more in Japan than in Europe in both 1992 and 1996. The statistical differences are significant for both regions in 1992 and 1996 for all four logics of organizing. However, there are no significant differences in the whole profile (Chi-2 on the profile), indicating that the profiles of the two regions of Europe and Japan do not vary at 1992 or at 1996. It can be seen both in Europe and Japan that product and service is the most adopted logic, project the least, and geography and function are in the middle for both regions. Table 7.3 also indicates that the proportion of adoption of all four logics increases from 1992 to 1996, thus providing some basic support for the supplementing proposition.

Table 7.4 reaffirms and consolidates the evidence for supplementing innovation. Here we report the percentage profiles of organizations increasing emphasis in one organizational logic or type, or two, or three, or four. We also report the percentage of companies that did not change or reduce the emphasis in the period 1992 to 1996. The categories are mutually exclusive (i.e. they add up to 100%). The tests on the differences of these proportions in Europe and Japan are statistically significant for both the whole profiles and on the individual logic or types.

In Table 7.4 we can find the strongest evidence of supplementing organizational innovation. This evidence is stronger for Europe, where only 23.5% of the organizations reduced the emphasis or made no change in their logic of organizing. Among the remaining 76.5%, 26.9% of the total increased the emphasis in only one type of logic (and either decreased or did not change the emphasis in the others), but 49.6% of the European organizations increased the emphasis in two, three or four of the logics of organizing. The evidence for Japanese organizations is weaker, as only 25.3% of the organizations in the sample increased the importance of more than one organizational logic. In Japan almost half the sample (47.9%) did not change at all or reduced the emphasis between 1992 and 1996.

Table 7.4   Increasing emphasis in organizational structural types in European and Japanese companies in the period 1992–6 (%)

	Europe	Japan	Chi-2
No changes or reduction of emphasis	23.5	47.9	44.004 (0.000)
Increasing emphasis in one organizational type	26.9	26.8	11.205 (0.001)
Increasing emphasis in two types	28.9	17.1	12.197 (0.000)
Increasing emphasis in three types	13.2	7.4	5.578 (0.018)
Increasing emphasis in four types	7.5	0.8	15.414 (0.000)

Note: Chi-2 on profiles   58.516 (0.000)
Source: INNFORM program survey

Table 7.5   Increasing emphasis in organizational structures in European and Japanese organizations: intentional choice or random adoption? %

		Europe			Japan		
		Actual changes	Expected changes	z (prob.)	Actual changes	Expected changes	z (prob.)
Individual logics	Product and services	41.2	–	–	17.4	–	–
	Geographical region	25.1	–	–	15.3	–	–
	Functions	26.8	–	–	14.3	–	–
	Project form	47.7	–	–	33.2	–	–
Adoption of two logics	Prod. & serv. + regions	16.2	10.3	4.021 (0.000)	5.1	2.7	2.375 (0.009)
	Regions + functions	12.5	6.7	4.871 (0.000)	5.1	2.2	3.120 (0.001)
	Functions + projects	18.7	12.8	3.712 (0.000)	9.3	4.8	3.445 (0.000)
	Prod. & serv. + functions	17.1	11.0	4.040 (0.000)	5.4	2.5	3.036 (0.001)
	Prod. & serv + projects	28.2	19.6	4.530 (0.000)	10.9	5.8	3.520 (0.000)
	Regions + projects	21.0	11.9	5.821 (0.000)	8.2	5.1	2.240 (0.013)
Adoption of three logics	Prod. & serv. + regions + functions	8.4	2.8	7.232 (0.000)	1.9	0.4	4.055 (0.000)
	Prod. & serv. + functions + projects	12.3	5.3	6.603 (0.000)	3.5	0.8	4.730 (0.000)
	Regions + functions + projects	10.5	3.2	8.667 (0.000)	2.7	0.7	3.750 (0.000)
Adoption of four logics	Prod. & serv. + regions + projects	12.1	4.9	6.920 (0.000)	2.3	0.9	2.477 (0.007)
	Prod. & serv. + regions + functions + projects	7.5	1.3	11.380 (0.000)	0.8	0.1	2.929 (0.002)

Source: INNFORM program survey

In Table 7.5 we report the percentage of organizations who actually increased the adoption of the different organizational logic in Europe and Japan compared with those which might have increased the emphasis by chance over the same period.

Table 7.6   Individual organizational innovations with regional and business contingencies in Europe and Japan 1996

	Europe					Japan		
	R&D intensity	Internationalization	UK	German speaking	Chi-2 (prob)	R&D Intensity	Internationalization	Chi-2 (prob)
Delayering	0.171 (0.143)	0.272 (0.138)	−0.037 (0.146)	−0.062 (0.171)	6.92 (0.140)	0.073 (0.207)	0.136 (0.212)	0.68 (0.712)
Products & services	−0.046 (0.155)	0.182 (0.152)	0.317** (0.151)	0.562 (0.194)	12.30 (0.015)	0.004 (0.216)	0.567** (0.251)	5.82 (0.054)
Regions	−0.092 (0.139)	0.289** (0.134)	−0.215 (0.139)	0.257 (0.166)	16.64 (0.002)	−0.139 (0.171)	−0.019 (0.178)	0.74 (0.691)
Function	0.098 (0.140)	– (0.136)	−0.264* (0.140)	0.325* (0.170)	18.15 (0.001)	0.004 (0.177)	0.126 (0.185)	0.50 (0.780)
Projects	0.277** (0.142)	−0.084 (0.139)	−0.400** (0.144)	0.735*** (0.169	56.11 (0.000)	0.280 (0.169)	−0.140 (0.174)	2.97 (0.226)
Operational decentraliz.	0.035 (0.140)	0.035 (0.136)	0.471*** (0.141)	0.354** (0.166)	14.62 (0.006)	0.184 (0.177)	0.293 (0.184)	4.59 (0.101)
Strategic decentraliz.	0.295** (0.154)	0.498*** (0.150)	0.014 −(0.168)	0.246 (0.183)	25.89 (0.000)	0.210 (0.192)	0.058 (0.200)	1.49 (0.475)
Vertical linkages	0.172 (0.142)	−0.128 (0.139)	0.026 (0.147)	0.340** (0.168)	6.97 (0.137)	0.010 (0.175)	0.370** (0.178)	4.59 (0.101)
Horizontal linkages	0.336** (0.149)	−0.373** (0.151)	0.074 (0.156)	0.433** (0.176)	15.37 (0.004)	−0.115 (0.196)	0.303 (0.196)	2.44 (0.295)
New HR – hrm	0.101 (0.143)	0.073 −(0.137)	−0.199 (0.143)	−0.244 (0.168)	3.61 (0.461)	0.226 (0.186)	−0.049 (0.196)	1.46 (0.482)
Information technology	0.160 (0.139)	0.084 (0.135)	−0.295** (0. 142)	0.178 (0.164)	14.38 (0.006)	−0.262 (0.185)	0.477** (0.205)	6.49 (0.039)
Outsourcing	−0.158 (0.144)	0.329** (0.141)	−0.063 (0.141)	0.452*** (0.178)	18.88 (0.000)	−0.040 −(0.172)	0.266 (0.180)	2.21 (0.331)
Strategic alliances	0.040 (0.145)	0.496*** (0.142)	0.003 (0.143)	0.102 (0.172)	16.05 (0.003)	0.268 (0.170)	0.414** (0.178)	9.91 (0.007)
Downscope	0.495*** (0.182)	0.150 (0.182)	0.691*** (0.196)	−0.059 (0.254)	22.86 (0.000)	– –	−0.187 (0.470)	0.17 (0.682)

Notes: *p < 0.1;   ** p < 0.05;   *** p < 0.01.
N Europe = 439;   N Japan = 257

Source: INNFORM program survey

The actual changes are located in that column and the expected changes capture the probability estimate over the same period for the adoption of multiple logics of organizing.

If the percentage changes in the actual column are greater than the expected column and these are significantly different (which they are), this indicates that the changes are adopted as an intentional choice rather than by pure chance.

Finally Table 7.6 presents the results of the probit models to analyze the effect of some business and regional contingencies on the adoption of organizational innovations in Europe and Japan in 1996. The contingencies considered are R&D intensity and degree of internationalization.

R&D is a binary variable with 1 for the organization spending more than 3% of their turnover in R&D (29% in Europe and 35% in Japan). Internationalization is also a binary variable with 1 for the organizations with operating businesses producing products and services in more than 10 countries (28% in Europe and 31% in Japan).

The regional contingencies in Europe are for British companies and German-speaking (German, Austrian and Swiss) companies. They are dummy variables and thus are compared against the rest of the sample, i.e. Northern European and Southern European companies. Thus the significant positive coefficient for UK in the adoption of organizing by products and services indicates that organizations in the UK are adopting this type of organizational structure significantly more compared to the companies in Northern and Southern Europe, which are our benchmark. It is interesting that British companies are also less likely to adopt an organizational structure based on functions and projects, but German-speaking companies are more likely to do so. Organizations in the UK and German-speaking countries are also more likely than those in the rest of Europe to adopt operational decentralization. German-speaking organizations are more likely to develop horizontal and vertical linkages and increase outsourcing. It is noteworthy that British organizations are investing less in IT than the rest of European organizations. They are also downscoping significantly more.

Comparing the business contingencies in Europe and Japan we find only one regional similarity: the effect of the degree of internationalization on engagement in strategic alliances.

We can also see in Table 7.6 how a high degree of internationalization affects the probability of organizing by product and services in Japan and of organizing by geography in Europe. In Europe highly internationalized organizations are less likely to organize by function. Highly internationalized organizations are also more likely to outsource and, like Japanese organizations, to engage in strategic alliances. In Japan highly internationalized organizations are also more likely to develop vertical linkages and to invest in information technology.

R&D intensity in Europe affects the adoption of organizing by projects, strategic decentralization, horizontal linkages, and downscoping.

Table 7.7   Similarities and differences between European and Japanese organizations

	1992	1996
Similarities in the adoption of organizational innovations	• Strategic decentralization • Horizontal linkages • Single core business • Set of related businesses	• Operational decentralization • Strategic decentralization • Vertical linkages • New human resources practices • Strategic alliances • Dominant core business • Wide range of businesses
Differences in the adoption of organizational innovations	• Lower hierarchical layers in Europe than in Japan • Lower adoption of project form of organizing in Europe than in Japan • Lower operational decentralization in Europe than in Japan • Lower adoption of products and services in Europe than in Japan • Lower adoption of geographical regions in Europe than in Japan • Lower adoption of functions in Europe than in Japan • Lower vertical linkages in Europe than in Japan • Lower information technology in Europe than in Japan • Lower strategic alliances in Europe than in Japan • Lower dominant business in Europe than in Japan • Higher wide range of businesses in Europe than in Japan	• Lower hierarchical layers in Europe than in Japan • Lower adoption of project form of organizing in Europe than in Japan • Lower adoption of products and services in Europe than in Japan • Lower adoption of geographical regions in Europe than in Japan • Lower adoption of functions in Europe than in Japan • Higher horizontal linkages in Europe than in Japan • Lower information technology in Europe than in Japan • Lower single business in Europe than in Japan • Higher set of related businesses in Europe than in Japan

Source: INNFORM program survey

7.7 DISCUSSION

In the previous sections we showed some empirical results from the survey on organizational innovations in Europe and Japan and the statistical tests on the significance of the differences between the two regions. The statistical analysis of the percentages of European and Japanese organizations adopting innovations in structure and processes in the years 1992 and 1996 provides interesting results in the two regions. Table 7.7 summarizes the main findings in terms of similarities and differences between European and Japanese organizations in the adoption of organizational innovations in 1992 and 1996.

In 1992, at the starting point of our analysis, Japanese organizations had taller organizations, higher operational decentralization and vertical linkages, higher use of information technology, more strategic alliances, and tended to focus more on a dominant business than on a wide range of businesses. We also found that Japanese organizations adopted all four logics of organizing more than their European comparators in both 1992 and 1996. Also in 1992, no differences between Japanese and European organizations were found in the use of horizontal linkages between sub-units and strategic decentralization, and in the proportions of companies having a single business or a set of related businesses.

Some of the differences between the two regions apparent in 1992 still persisted by 1996 (taller hierarchies and higher use of IT by Japanese companies). However, some differences in the proportion of adopters had disappeared by 1996 (operational decentralization and vertical linkages and strategic alliances), and new differences had also emerged by 1996 (increasing adoption of project forms of organizing in Japan; more European organizations developing horizontal linkages compared to Japanese organizations; fewer European organizations had a single business but more European firms developed a set of related businesses). For the decentralization of strategic decision making a similar pattern between the regions emerges in both 1992 and 1996. The introduction of new HR practices did not show any significant difference between the two regions in 1996.

Table 7.7 raises interesting questions about the nature and explanations for the revealed differences and similarities between European and Japanese organizations. For instance, did they start from the same level or did they present different levels of adoption of organizational innovation in the starting year 1992?

The analysis in the previous section revealed significant differences in the pace of change between European and Japanese organizations. Although the organizations in both regions moved in the same direction, Japanese companies changed more slowly or incrementally than their European comparators. Why did the European companies change more radically compared to the Japanese?

Are European organizations adopting innovations which make them more similar to Japanese firms? Is there a developing convergence between European and Japanese organizations? Or do these organizations in the two regions have different characteristics and belong to different cultural, social and economic contexts which make them act and think of organizational changes quite differently?

Clearly, from the results of our analysis, Japanese organizations showed different organizational characteristics and levels of adoption of organizational innovations in 1992. These characteristics included in the survey instrument are discussed now alongside additional information from research and writings by other scholars to derive a more extensive profile of Japanese organizations in the late 1980s–1990s.

The fundamental philosophy of Japanese organization and management culture is focused on people. In particular, Japanese management ascribes a big emphasis to organizational issues related to people, such as training, lifetime employment, job rotation, encouraging suggestions from workers at any level, and involving them in the decision making process. At the same time, Japanese workers are portrayed as being very dedicated to their jobs, cooperative, and hard working.

Japanese organizations also feature job rotation. Workers typically spend a few years in a position after which they are usually moved elsewhere within their organization. This process may create an attitude for change and a good degree of adaptability among workers. Such job rotations can also facilitate knowledge flows among people with different experience. It allows for the creation of informal worker networks and awareness of other people's skills and knowledge. Potentially, job rotation may also widen individual skills and expertise and provide wider experience of different functions in the organization. Workers can develop a capacity to adapt to changes in tasks and cope with unforeseen events as distinguished from the operational skills useful for performing routine tasks (Koike, 1994). Frequent changes of job within a company are consistent with the generalist-oriented Japanese career system which allows people to readily substitute for each other. This contrasts with the specialist career system more widespread in Western organizations. Also the bottom-up decision making process featured in Japanese firms supplements the job rotation practices and can facilitate integration among divisions and departments, and the creation of internal networks.

The results from our survey confirm the adoption of the project form of organizing by Japanese companies. Project forms had increased by 1996, alongside higher operational decentralization, and higher vertical linkages and IT investments in Japanese organizations compared to European companies. All these characteristics of Japanese organizations facilitate integration among divisions and departments, and assist the creation of internal networks.

Japanese organizations are also characterized by long-term employment, the philosophy of a "job for life," although only large firms can maintain these practices. Lifetime employment is neither a formal policy nor a contractual stipulation but it has important consequences for the strong feeling of belonging and commitment to the company. Life-time employment can create an atmosphere of cooperation and harmony, with limited insecurity for the future. From the company perspective it also provides the rationale for (expensive) training schemes, and people with improved skills do not usually leave the organization. Japanese organizations also invest heavily in information technology and training for newly recruited personnel to improve their IT skills. The importance of the day-to-day interaction between colleagues, high levels of intimacy, and shared decision making characterize the Japanese work relations (Briggs, 1991).

The informational structures used by various Japanese companies in coordinating operational decisions among interrelated units are often portrayed as being different from their Western counterparts. Some scholars have argued that an important internal characteristic of Japanese organizations is horizontal coordination between units based on knowledge sharing rather than skill specialization. This is in contrast to the Western hierarchical coordination and separation of planning and implementation, and the emphasis on specialization typical of the late 1980s and early 1990s (Aoki, 1990).

However, as our results show, European organizations are now adopting more horizontal linkages than their Japanese comparators. By 1996 one fourth of the European companies in our sample adopted "much" or "great" linkages between sub-units and three-quarters increased the extent of these linkages between 1992 and 1996.

Some authors have stressed the high degree of organizational flexibility and pragmatism developed by Japanese firms during the last few decades which has allowed them to react swiftly to market demands and to conquer key positions in the world markets (Richter, 1996). This is especially so in high and medium technology sectors, like electronics, automobiles, and steel. It has also been assumed that "the major elements of Japanese-style management – lifetime employment, seniority promotion, enterprise unions, keiretsu and subcontracting relations – arose primarily as a consequence of the rapid and high economic growth achieved through post-war industrialization, rather than as a universal formula for economic success or as a consequence of a unique cultural tradition" (Hasegawa and Hook, 1998: 3).

From the discussion above it is possible to identify a few key elements characterizing Japanese organizations. Thus, for example, flexibility and adaptability appear to be fundamental in building on the Japanese investment attitude to people in the organizations. The importance historically given to human resources, the training of people, their involvement in the decision making process, and internal communication, all create a special basis for the management of the knowledge-creating company. These characteristics of Japanese organizations are highly interrelated. For example, job rotation enhances generalist skills, knowledge of different functions and departments within the organization, and awareness of other people's skills and functions. Collectively these elements stimulate the creation of a highly adaptive work force which becomes accustomed to incremental and possibly continuous changes.

The adoption of new HR practices, internal labor markets, company conferences, and the creation of internal networks support the argument of the importance of people meeting to share experience and transfer tacit knowledge. According to Nonaka and Takeuchi (1995), it is the spiral process of interaction between explicit knowledge, which can be articulated in formal language or mathematical expressions, and tacit knowledge, which is hard to articulate with formal language, that generates organizational knowledge. Clearly a way to transmit tacit knowledge is to encourage people to interact and work together, thus sharing tacit skills which they have gained from different experience and career paths. The interaction of new pieces of knowledge, explicit and tacit, is likely to develop a process for creation of new knowledge.

Looking at the organizational aspect of learning processes, it is important to analyze the interrelation and interdependence of organizational learning and individual learning. There cannot be organizational learning without individual learning and at the same time individual learning can only emerge through the organizational identification of the best operational practice, its standardization and diffusion throughout the organization as routines that guide individual behavior (Cole, 1994).

The portrait of Japanese companies in our sample is a mixed one. There is evidence of a certain degree of structural rigidity, for example, in both 1992 and 1996, due to the tall hierarchical structure. However, these relatively taller hierarchies are accompanied by other characteristics in their structure (project form of organizing) and processes (IT, training, job rotation) which can provide a good degree of flexibility and adaptability to external pressures. As in the case of individual and organizational learning, it is possible to draw a relation between individual and organizational adaptability and flexibility: organizational flexibility is based on people flexibility and vice versa, at least for incremental changes.

On the other hand, even though the economic and competitive forces on Japanese firms may require rationalization (e.g., restricted recruitment, direct secondment to related companies or departments) at present there is only modest evidence of redundancies or lay-offs by Japanese firms (at least by European practices). Cost reductions are being achieved by Japanese firms by moving part of the production overseas, where the labor is cheaper. Examples of this include East Asia and China. Japanese firms may prefer a subcontracting system with sharper and slimmer hierarchies.

Given the life employment system, Japanese managers are motivated to diversify to keep employment constant. Traditionally, in the event of economic crises the reduction of the workforce is the last action taken, which would follow cuts to top executives' salaries, then managers' salaries, then reductions of the dividends. Only if these actions were not enough to cope with the economic crisis would companies then start to lay off their workforce. Until recently, Japanese organizations are preserving the traditional commitment to employees in career, status and compensation terms, and there is a long-term concern for employees' morale and cohesion, with younger people supervising older ones. Reducing the organizational levels of the hierarchical structure of Japanese organizations would put some senior workers at the same level as younger workers, thus stimulating dissatisfaction. Corporate organizational structures are also changing as a consequence of the spread of new technologies, like microelectronics and information technology (Okubayashi, 1998).

Recent studies (Lincoln and Nakata, 1997) provide some supporting evidence of the tendency toward the creation of more buffer groups of temporary or part-time labor, usually women and retired people. Personnel can also be transferred to affiliates, suppliers, and other partner firms, which enhances control over the affiliate. There are also early signs of a shift from age/seniority remuneration to job performance pay with larger merit increases. This is also accompanied by a reduction of the hierarchies. Procedures to assess individual performance, alternative to the seniority pay system based on the long-term association of the workers with the firm, are not easy: often job demarcation is rather blurred, with the lower levels in the hierarchy involved and responsible in the decision making, and lateral interaction. The assessment of competencies and allocation of rewards tend to be more group-based than related to individual efforts and success (Lincoln and Kalleberg, 1990). Long-term employment is accompanied by a seniority pay scheme that implies regular increments, although not very high, and provides an incentive to spend the whole working life within the same organization. However, good young graduates might be unhappy about a salary structure that puts blue-collar workers with few years of experience above them and might look for better positions in smaller firms (Lincoln and Nakata, 1997).

There is some interesting recent evidence on the evolution of Japanese white-collar human resources management which shows divergences from the traditional policies of long-term employment and seniority and skill development appraisal (Morishima, 1997). Japanese firms are facing pressures to reduce costs and introduce flexibility in their HRM practices. This is because of lower productivity and lack of performance measurement for white-collar employees; increases in the middle management ranks; slow growth and the heightened sensitivity to profit performance; and changing management values emphasizing performance over skills development. However, strong white-collar employment security and the typical work organization, with employee participation and decentralization in decision making, represent serious limits to the speedy implementations of these changes.

Based on a survey undertaken in 1993, Morishima (1997) shows that the majority of firms are still adopting the traditional HRM practices, characterized by the long-term employment and appraisal and reward schemes based on skill development. However, Morishima also identifies two other clusters of firms with divergent HR policies. One of these clusters maintains the traditional long-term employment but emphasizes highly competitive performance-based appraisal. The other abandons both the traditional internal labor market rules, by emphasizing employment externalization and highly competitive performance-based appraisal. Although this kind of evidence did not emerge in our survey it is important to be aware of these kinds of changes in traditional Japanese HRM practices.

Some scholars have stressed the importance of "complementary assets" between innovation and other capabilities or assets, like marketing, competitive manufacturing, and after-sales support for the successful commercialization of a new product (Teece, 1986). According to the systemic approach to innovation processes (Nelson, 1993), the company's complementary assets are likely to belong to different parts of the system. This implies changes in the existing company boundaries and developing strategic alliances in order to acquire manufacturing, marketing, and research knowledge at a low cost. Our findings suggest that this is particularly true for European organizations that increased their engagement in strategic alliances. The Japanese organizations in our sample were not building strategic alliances at anywhere near the same pace of change.

As international alliances show, complementary assets are not necessarily located within the same country. There is now an increasing occurrence of mergers with international companies and greater boundary openness, especially in terms of the development of strategic alliances and outsourcing. This has tended to occur more often in the European business context.

Our findings show noteworth changes in the scope of European businesses in the period 1992–6. However, the nature of and extent of downscoping is very different in the two regions. Japanese organizations have hardly changed their businesses, whilst European organizations have been moving from the two ends of the spectrum of business diversification towards the middle. Thus European firms are moving from the extremes of the single core business and a wide range of unrelated businesses toward a dominant business and a set of related businesses.

7.8 SUMMARY AND CONCLUSION

Research and writing on organizational change (some speculative and some more empirical) suggest the development of new forms of organizing to cope with a more competitive landscape. These changes include, for example, the contraction of hierarchies or delayering, decentralization of strategic and operational functions, developing horizontal and vertical networks, investing in IT and redefining organizational boundaries. This writing also points to a sense of revolution in the form, character, and processes of contemporary organizations.

But why are organizations in transition? There appear to be multiple, accumulating and interdependent drivers of these new forms of organizing. These include economic, technological, informational, and political factors. Increased global competition, the speed of technical and market change, and the rise of information and communication technologies are all driving the knowledge economy and firm. However, the pressures for organizational change seem easier to identify than the actual responses firms are making to those pressures.

Empirical evidence to understand the extent and direction of change has been rather limited. We have been variously informed about the rise of the "N" form, the cellular form, the boundaryless and individualized corporations, but this writing often rests heavily and uneasily on case studies of exceptional organizations or atypical sectors and regions. There is a need for mapping studies which offer time series data on a relatively comprehensive scale comparing the emergence of new forms of organizing across economic regions such as Europe, Japan, and the US.

European–Japanese comparisons are particularly valuable because most of the surveys on Japanese organizations are mainly restricted to US–Japanese comparisons. There has also been speculation that Japanese organizations have traditionally displayed many of the characteristics of new forms of organizing now said to be emerging in Europe. But are they? And are European firms catching up or is the direction of change in Europe different from Japan?

In this chapter we have posed a number of critical questions which have allowed us to make comparative analyses of European and Japanese firms. These questions have enabled us to offer a fuller portrait of the character of change toward new forms of organizing in the two regions at the 1992 and 1996 time points.

Thus we have explored such question as: Is the starting point for change different in the two regions? What is the evidence for similarities–differences in the direction of change across the nine indicators of innovative forms of organizing between 1992 and 1996? Is there a different pace of change in Europe compared with Japan, and if so, why? And are such organizational innovations supplementing or supplanting existing organizational forms in both regions?

At the starting point of our analysis, Japanese organizations had taller hierarchies, higher operational decentralization and vertical linkages, greater use of information technology, more strategic alliances, and tended to be less diversified than their European comparators. However, no differences between Japanese and European organizations were found in the extent of organizing on the basis of project form, the use of horizontal linkages between sub-units, and the existence of strategic decentralization.

During the period of analysis, some of the differences between European and Japanese organizations disappeared (operational decentralization and vertical linkages and strategic alliances). But new differences had also emerged by 1996 (increasing adoption of project forms of organizing in Japan, more European organizations developing horizontal linkages compared to Japanese organizations, and fewer European organizations had a single business but more developed a set of related businesses). The introduction of new HR practices did not show any significant difference between the two regions in 1996. Some of the differences between the two regions apparent in 1992 still persisted by 1996 (taller hierarchies and higher use of IT by Japanese companies).

Our finding on the changing pattern of adoption of organizational logic or types (product and service, geography, function, and project) indicate, quite clearly that any move towards project forms in Europe and Japan is not at the expense of attachment to other logics of organizing. The innovative forms of organizing are thus emerging in more of an incremental than a radical fashion. The new forms are supplementing the old rather than supplanting the old. This is a notable finding for scholars who have tended to perhaps overemphasize the speed with which new forms of organizing are emerging in Europe and elsewhere.

Our analysis also shows a faster pace of change by European organizations compared to the Japanese ones. With the notable exception of IT, Japanese firms when they are making changes tend to make them in a much more incremental way than their European comparators. However the 1998–9 recession in Japan may have destabilized Japanese employment patterns, and there is some limited evidence that Japanese firms may have recently accelerated their pace of organizational restructuring and change.

Although the direction of changes in the two regions is similar, the pace is different, and we avoid making any simple-minded convergence thesis between patterns and directions of change in Europe and Japan. European organizations have been adopting more radical organizational changes. Their radicalness is most apparent in the development of horizontal linkages, strategic decentralization, and engagement in strategic alliances. Some of these individual characteristics may not differ from their Japanese comparators over the period of analysis, but the resulting multidimensional organizational forms do. We are observing a complex pattern and process of change which is still emerging, and the resultant pattern which finally evolves cannot easily be predicted.

There are several limitations to this study. Although it is rare to have a two-point analysis in a survey instrument, 1992 and 1996 are two moments in a longer-erm process in an ever-changing context. Our findings are therefore time bound and context bound. The Japanese context may have changed in 1998 and 1999 but the data in this chapter refer to 1992 and 1996 and do not enable us to show any very recent transformation. A further survey early in the twenty-first century would allow us to verify and quantify the further emergence of the changes we identify in this study.

This chapter is also silent on the third objective of the INNFORM program of research, the need to understand the change process as firms move from more traditional forms of organizing. However, the INNFORM program is studying 18 case studies of European organizations undergoing organizational transformation. The first results of these process studies of new forms of organizing is published in Pettigrew and Fenton (2000).

It is now apparent from our case studies that firms are facing a range of dualities as they attempt to build more competitive forms of organizing. These include simultaneously building hierarchies and networks, attempts to centralise strategy and decentralize operations, and moves to create greater performance accountability upwards and greater horizontal integration sideways.

We have seen in this chapter that the challenge in creating more flexible and responsive firms involves making a series of innovations in structures, processes, and boundaries. Managing such a complementary change agenda is likely to take very considerable top management awareness, confidence, commitment and skill, qualities that our survey findings and case studies suggest may still be rare.

7.9 TECHNICAL APPENDIX FOR THE TABLES

- The percentages for years 1992 and 1996 represent the proportion of organizations answering at least 4 or 5 in a five points Likert scale, corresponding to "much" and "great", "increase" and "great increase", or "small growth" and "large growth".
- The percentages of the changes between 1992 and 1996 result from the positive difference between the answers in 1996 and 1992. In the following, when we use the word 'change' we always mean toward a larger adoption, or increasing importance or emphasis, in that indicator of organizational innovation.
- There are a few exceptions. Delayering is the difference in the number of organizational layers between the manager with the lowest level of profit responsibility and the chief executive in 1996 and 1992. The process variables are composite variables, which are built from a series feasible answers to each item in the question. Given the formulation of the question, we can only report the percentage of the changes for outsourcing. The indicator for strategic alliances is the percentage of total assets deployed in strategic alliances:
  1=1–10%, 2=11–20%, 3=21–30%, 4=31–40%, 5= >40%.

The percentages in Table 7.1 are the proportions of organizations answering more than 1. For downscoping we reported the whole percentage distributions of the range of businesses in order to provide a clearer analysis of the direction of change.

NOTE

* This research has been funded by the Economic and Social Research Council Innovation Program, PricewaterhouseCoopers, the consortium members of the Centre for Creativity, Strategy and Change, Warwick Business School, and the institutions of the participating researchers.

REFERENCES

Aoki, M. (1990). Toward an economic model of the Japanese firm. *Journal of Economic Literature:* 28: 8.

Bahrami, H. (1992). The emerging flexible organization: perspectives from Silicon Valley. *California Management Review,* Summer: 35–52.

Bartlett, C. and Ghoshal, S. (1993). Beyond the M-form, towards a managerial theory of the firm. *Strategic Management Journal,* 14 (Special Issue): 23–46.

Briggs, P. (1991). Organizational commitment: The key to Japanese success? In C. Brewster and S. Tyson (eds), *International Comparisons in Human Resources Management.* London: Pitman Publishing.

Child, J. (1984). *Organization: A Guide to Problems and Practice.* 2nd edn. London: Harper and Row.

Cole, R.E. (1994). Learning and incentive systems in Japanese industry. In M. Aoki and R. Dore (eds), *The Japanese Firm: The Sources of Competitive Strength.* Oxford: Oxford University Press.

Dewar, R. D. and Dutton, J. E. (1986). The adoption of radical and incremental innovations: an empirical analysis. *Management Science,* 32: 1422–33.

Ghoshal, S. and Bartlett, C. (1995). Changing the role of top management: from structure to process. *Harvard Business Review,* January–February: 86–96.

Ghoshal, S. and Bartlett, C. (1998). *The Individualized Corporation.* London: Heinemann.

Handy, C. (1992). Balancing corporate power: a new federalist paper. *Harvard Business Review,* November–December: 59–72.

Hasegawa, H. and Hook, G. D. (1998). *Japanese Business Management: Restructuring for Low Growth and Globalisation.* London: Routledge.

Hoskisson, R. E., Hill, C. W. L. and Kim, H. (1993). The multidivisional structure: organizational fossil or source of value. *Journal of Management,* 19 (2): 269–98.

Koike, K. (1994). Different quality paradigms and their implications for organizational learning. In M. Aoki and R. Dore, (eds), *The Japanese Firm: The Sources of Competitive Strength*. Oxford: Oxford University Press.

Lincoln, J. R. and Kalleberg, A. (1990). *Culture, Control and Commitment*. Cambridge: Cambridge University Press.

Lincoln, J. R. and Nakata, Y. (1997). The transformation of the Japanese employment system: nature, depth, and origins. *Work and Occupations*, 24 (1): 33–55.

Markides, C. C. (1996). *Diversification, Refocusing, and Economic Performance*. Cambridge, MA: MIT Press.

Miles, R. E., Snow, C. C., Mathews, J. A. and Coleman, H. J. (1997). Organizing in the knowledge area: anticipating the cellular form. *Academy of Management Executive*, 11 (4): 7–20.

Morishima, M. (1997). The evolution of white–collar human resources management in Japan. *Advances in Industrial and Labor Relations*, 7: 145–76.

Nelson, R. R. (ed.) (1993): *National Innovation Systems: A comparative analysis*. Oxford: Oxford University Press.

Nonaka, I. and Takeuchi, H. (1995). *The Knowledge-creating Company*. Oxford: Oxford University Press.

Nohria, N. and Ghoshal, S. (1997). *The Differentiated Network*. San Francisco, CA: Jossey-Bass.

Okubayashi, K. (1998). Small headquarters and the reorganization of management. In H. Hasegawa and G. D. Hook (eds) (1998). *Japanese Business Management: Restructuring for Low Growth and Globalization*. London: Routledge.

Pettigrew, A. M. and Fenton, E. (eds) (2000). *The Innovating Organization*. London: Sage Publications.

Richter, Frank-Jurgen (ed.) (1996). *The Dynamics of Japanese Organizations*. London: Routledge.

Teece, D. (1986). Profiting from technological innovation: implications for integration, collaboration, licensing and public policy. *Research Policy*, 15: 285–305.

Volberda, H. W. (1998). *Building the Flexible Firm*. Oxford: Oxford University Press.

Whittington, R. and Mayer, M. (1997). Beyond or behind the M-form: the structures of European business. In H. Thomas, D. O'Neal and M. Ghertman (eds), *Strategy, Structure and Style*. Chichester: John Wiley.

Whittington, R., Mayer, M. and Curto, F. (1999a). Chandlerism in post-war Europe: Strategic and structural change in France, Germany and the United Kingdom, 1950-1993. *Industrial and Corporate Change*, 8 (4).

Whittington, R., Pettigrew, A.M., Peck, S., Fenton, E. and Conyon, M. (1999b). Change and complementarities in the new competitive landscape: a European panel study, 1992–1996. *Organization Science*, 10 (4).

8. Impacts on Employment of New Forms of Organizing: an Evaluation from a Knowledge Requirement Perspective

Rafael Andreu and Sandra Sieber

8.1 INTRODUCTION

The new competitive landscape requires organizations to be more open and flexible than in the past, and firms have responded to these requirements by adopting new or at least different organizational structures. Following the knowledge-based view of the firm, we believe that the main driver for the adaptation of new organizational arrangements is an increased need for knowledge creation and deployment, as knowledge constitutes a prime source of sustained competitive advantage in turbulent environments. In this chapter we argue that emphasizing knowledge puts new demands on workers and employment in firms. Two well-differentiated types of knowledge are required in open and flexible organizations. First, firms need to acquire and develop technical excellence. Therefore, they must remain in constant contact with the environment. This has led to the widely studied phenomenon of workers' employability, in which employees constantly update their knowledge in a particular area of expertise and, thus, do not need traditional job security. They have a sort of "market security", and this "external employability" is beneficial for both the employee and the company. In addition, this means the company is in a better position to react rapidly to environmental changes and demands.

Nevertheless, the constant reshaping of the importance of particular businesses and the high degree of employee turnover poses severe threats to the organization's cohesiveness and sense of unity. Therefore, in order to make technical excellence and external employability viable in the long run, a second type of knowledge, a sort of organizational "glue", must be developed and deployed. This organization-specific knowledge which refers to the ability of giving context, integrating new employees within teams or providing them with a consistent strategic vision, is more valuable inside the organization than in the market and, therefore, leads to "internal employability" and job stability. Developing this kind of internal knowledge is much less environment-driven and pertains more to the realms of organizational routines, particular ways of operation and organizational "idiosyncrasy". Both types of knowledge are complementary and indispensable for an organization's success. We conclude by exploring the implications for employment.

Trends in today's environment such as globalization, technical evolution, and deregulation are changing the competitive structure of markets so as to obscure the effectiveness of traditional sources of competitive advantage. The main reason for this is that, increasingly, any firm can have access to physical or financial assets (and even to technology) in the same open market conditions.

Consequently, firms need to concentrate on the development of distinctive capabilities, a particular "way of doing things" which is difficult for competitors to imitate. Eventually, such capabilities end up being related to persons in these firms who develop, apply, and organize their capabilities in unique ways based on "what they know." This is why developing idiosyncratic knowledge that gives added meaning to the firm's own mode of operation is increasingly important (Bell, 1973; Drucker, 1993). This idiosyncratic knowledge tends to be difficult to imitate because it cannot be acquired in open markets; i.e., it must be learned, which requires time, effort, and in most cases a specific context (organizational, social, etc.). Such knowledge is path-dependent and, therefore, very difficult to reproduce in a firm that differs from the one in which the knowledge originated. In order to develop these knowledge-based capabilities effectively, appropriate organizational forms are needed. In this chapter we focus on the organizational forms – knowledge link – and suggest implications for employment in the new competitive environment from a firm standpoint. In short, we set out to:

1. analyze briefly why new forms of organizing develop in response to new competitive challenges;
2. discuss what type of knowledge needs to be developed in firms in order to make such new forms effective; and
3. suggest how this point of view can shed some light on the employment issue as seen from the perspective of job creation in firms.

The chapter's structure is as follows: in the next section we expand on the relationship between new organizational forms and competitiveness. We then enter into an in-depth analysis of knowledge as an important source for competitive advantage under the new environmental conditions. Next, we argue that two basic characteristics of new organizational forms will determine the type of knowledge firms need to develop in order to make those forms truly effective. Finally, we turn to employability, knowledge requirements and their relationship to employment. A section dedicated to concluding remarks ends the chapter.

8.2 NEW ORGANIZATIONAL FORMS AND COMPETITIVE ADVANTAGE

As stated above, we start with the consideration that, in order to be competitive, today's firms must develop difficult-to-imitate "ways of doing" or capabilities. As these capabilities are based on the firm's idiosyncratic knowledge and then developed and learned through path-dependent, context-specific processes, they will give rise to sustainable competitive advantages.[1] Our contention here is that new organizational forms (NOFs) represent one tangible and observable way in which firms can develop such capabilities. For this reason, we propose to analyze NOFs with the objective of discovering how they help firms respond to today's competitive challenges, what the associated knowledge requirements are, and, consequently, how potential impacts on employment can be deduced.

From one angle, the new competitive environment puts pressure on firms to be more efficient and agile. This means not only streamlining their internal business processes, but also sharpening their ability to incorporate relevant knowledge from the environment so as to offer potential clients the current market place "standards" (e.g., an automobile without airbags or ABS is not competitive in the same way that a classic mechanical scale is not, unless conceived of as an antique). NOFs attempt to provide at least a partial response to these needs.

From another angle, NOFs are presently seen as new, positive "standard" management practice, thus becoming a means for streamlining management processes. In part, they constitute answers to the environmental challenges already mentioned. But they also represent better ways to approach traditional management tasks, which cannot be ignored.

The main characteristics of NOFs can be summarized as follows: they tend to be flattened (Galbraith, 1995) and flexible (Volberda, 1996) structures, providing increasing autonomy in decision rights which are delegated increasingly in order to produce "entrepreunership-like" situations (Kanter, 1983; Bartlett and Ghoshal, 1993; Collins and Porras, 1994; DeGeus, 1996), an emphasis on teamwork (Wellins *et al.*, 1994; DeSanctis *et al.*, 1999), and improved interpersonal relations (Jones and George, 1998). The immediate implications involve a need for more and better task coordination and communication (to cope with task and decision making decentralization) and an increased relevance of the organizational culture and context aspects (in order to maintain organizations' cohesiveness in an increasingly decentralized environment).

We have studied different types of new organizational forms closely. Extensive research has uncovered the basic characteristics of the network organization (Miles and Snow, 1986). Handy (1992) centered on the federation, Davidow and Malone (1992) focused on the virtual corporation, and Pasternack and Viscio (1998) presented distinctive issues of the "centerless" corporation.

Ricart *et al.*, (1999) maintain that all these different configurations appear as a consequence of the increasing need of organizations to cope with two fundamental goals simultaneously: the drive for knowledge integration and the quest for flexibility. In this sense, they argue that the increasing uncertainty and volatility of the environment creates a need for quick adaptation, requiring firms to increase their flexibility. As a consequence, organizations are forced more and more frequently to concentrate only on core knowledge and capabilities. Thus, they argue that flexibility must be complemented by another dimension, that of knowledge integration. New organizational forms have a tendency toward cooperation, whether on a business, corporate or inter-organizational level, in order to capture the relevant knowledge necessary for the organization's survival and sustained competitive advantage.

Beneath this line of argument is the increased relevance of knowledge as a main source of competitive advantage. Flexibility and knowledge integration require effective knowledge flows, both within the organization and with respect to the environment (Kogut and Zander, 1996). For this reason, the role of knowledge is crucial for the competitiveness of today's firms.[2] In order to expand on this reasoning, we need to explore further the concept of knowledge.

8.3 THE "NEW" IMPORTANCE OF KNOWLEDGE IN THE ORGANIZATION

There are several definitions of knowledge, including classic and well-known ones such as "a justified true belief" (Nonaka, 1994) and other more recent and pragmatic ones, e.g., "A mix of experience, values, information and 'expertise' which serves as a framework useful to incorporate new experience and information, for action" (Davenport and Prusak, 1998). We maintain that knowledge has three fundamental characteristics:

1.   Knowledge is *personal*[3] in the sense that it originates and resides in persons who assimilate it as the result of their own experience (i.e., of

their own "doing", be it physical or mental) and incorporate it in to their "base" once they are convinced of its meaning and implications. At the same time, they articulate it in the context of an organized whole, which gives structure and meaning to its different "pieces" (Kolb, 1984).

2. The use of knowledge (which, incidentally, can be repeated without dissipating it) allows persons to "understand" the phenomena that they perceive (each one in his or her own way, according precisely to what their knowledge implies at a given point in time) and, also, to "evaluate" these phenomena by judging how good or convenient they are with respect to a given person at a given time.[4]

3. Knowledge serves as a guide for action by helping individuals decide what to do at a given time – because action is geared to improve the consequences of the perceived phenomena (even changing them, if possible and judged convenient by the individual).

These characteristics make knowledge a solid basis for competitive advantage. To the extent that knowledge is the result of experience accumulation within the individual, imitating it will be difficult unless precise representations exist to facilitate its transmission and sharing. The distinction between explicit and tacit knowledge (Polanyi, 1962) stems from this idea – in particular, the notion that explicit knowledge is "codifiable" so that information and communication technologies (ICTs) can be used to register, store, transmit, and share it efficiently.

Often (if not always) the process of personal experience accumulation which leads to new knowledge takes place within a given social or organizational context (Tyre and von Hippel, 1997; Pentland, 1995). In addition, such a process unfolds in each person differently and depends, among other things, on the person's previous experience and knowledge. Thus, knowledge is both path, and context-dependent. Because duplicating contexts and paths in this sense is difficult, knowledge imitation is costly, and competitive advantages based on it will thus tend to be sustainable (Teece *et al.*, 1997).[5] When this happens, the value of a given type of knowledge tends to be higher in the context in which it was developed (e.g., a firm) than it would be in a hypothetical open market. We will resume this argument later on.

In summary: today's competitive challenges compel firms to develop distinctive capabilities which require new ways of organizing the firms' activities. These capabilities seem to put increasing emphasis on knowledge, the characteristics of which are particularly appropriate for competing in new and changing businesses. Still, as we will demonstrate in the next section, the quest for flexibility and knowledge integration calls for the development and deployment of different types of knowledge, and this has consequences relating to employability and employment.

8.4 LINKING NOFs AND KNOWLEDGE: THE NEED FOR FLEXIBILITY AND KNOWLEDGE INTEGRATION

We argue that the two basic dimensions elaborated by Ricart *et al.*, (1999) of knowledge integration and flexibility are both closely linked to the line of argument presented in the preceding section. The concept of "knowledge integration" involves the willingness and ability to detect and incorporate knowledge that is available in the environment so as to make it readily usable in the organization's quest for offering products and services that clients demand. We call this knowledge *external knowledge* so as to convey the idea that it is commonly brought into a firm from the environment and that it is useful not only inside a particular firm but also "externally" in the environment (i.e., useful and valuable to a series of firms). The previous example of airbag or ABS technologies in the automobile industry is an apt demonstration of this point: a firm competing in this industry needs to be capable of incorporating such technologies effectively (i.e., with enough know-how to incorporate them into their products in a competitive way) in order to "remain in the market." Thus, "knowledge integration" is a competitive necessity – it will not distinguish a firm above and beyond its competitors but, without it, a firm will not be able to compete effectively. A pertinent issue here is that, naturally, there is an alternative means of incorporating knowledge from the environment, namely by developing it in-house. We will touch upon this issue next, but first we must underscore that some knowledge will always have to be incorporated from the environment, as no firm can develop all relevant knowledge internally. Furthermore, there will always exist some types of knowledge within a firm that will not represent the basis of its sustainable competitive advantages (precisely because it will be available in the same market (environmental) conditions to all competing firms in an industry or sector). Another related issue involves *how* knowledge is incorporated effectively into a firm and thereby made an integral part of its knowledge base. This issue, although extremely relevant, goes beyond the scope of this chapter, for it has to do with learning, both individual and collective (see Spender, 1996, or Andreu and Sieber, 1999).

Being "flexible" means being fast and effective in assimilating new knowledge and "placing it in the context of the organization" so that it can be deployed as quickly as possible in a market place that is supposed to evolve rapidly. This notion of flexibility has two equally important components. On one hand, it implies an organizational context or structure where new knowledge can be integrated and made readily available for actual use. Thus, the organizational context:

1. fulfills the role of a skeleton where new knowledge pieces are

attached so as to "make global sense" in the firm's tradition, culture, and "way of understanding things" (Spender, 1996); and

2. defines the way in which new knowledge will be put to work, hence giving it the "idiosyncratic firm's touch" that will probably distinguish its use from that of other firms. We call this context and skeleton *internal knowledge* to indicate its specificity to a given firm or organization. On the other hand, to the extent that the assimilation process is fast enough, it constitutes the basis for the continuous integration of new knowledge in the firm's knowledge base. In this way, even in the case of new knowledge becoming quickly obsolete, the firm can react effectively without being eliminated from the market. Finally, this flexibility characteristic is also instrumental in the process of incorporating new internal knowledge created within the firm and even in the process of creation itself.

In principle, these two basic characteristics give NOFs and the firms that use them the required potential to respond to today's competitive challenges. They basically call for alertness to new, potentially relevant knowledge and the ability to incorporate it effectively and quickly into the firm's knowledge base for implementation of actual work. This is more easily said than done, of course. The main difficulty stems from the involved nature of knowledge processes, which we will discuss next. Bearing in mind that knowledge is personal, we can anticipate that these processes are related to people and their relationships to their firms, and this naturally prompts us to think about employability and employment.

8.5 KNOWLEDGE INTEGRATION, FLEXIBILITY AND THE ROLE OF KNOWLEDGE: EXTERNAL AND INTERNAL EMPLOYABILITY

As we focus now on the processes that incorporate knowledge in to the knowledge base of an organization, a few relevant remarks should be made regarding the main characteristics of such processes. First, it is worth differentiating between two processes. We will talk about the process of bringing external knowledge into the firm and the process of developing internal knowledge within the firm. It is precisely the combination of these two kinds of knowledge which gives NOFs the potential to develop the sustainable competitive advantages discussed above. External knowledge alone is not enough. External knowledge is "standard" and easily accessible, while internal knowledge in isolation is like a true skeleton: dead for lack of contents.

Figure 8.1 is a schematic representation of the two processes. The process leading to knowledge integration requires a continuous scanning of knowledge, complemented by an integration activity which places external knowledge into context. The process that leads to flexibility requires the maintenance of an effective skeleton of (internal) knowledge which is specific to the organization and gives meaning and context to the use of the external knowledge judged relevant at any point in time.

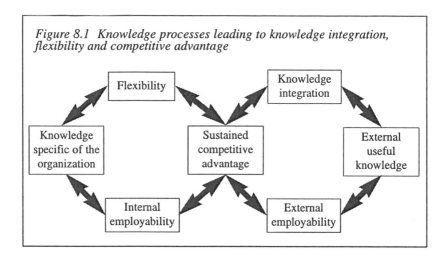

Figure 8.1 Knowledge processes leading to knowledge integration, flexibility and competitive advantage

Since knowledge is personal, we now turn to the persons involved in the processes, namely the employees in a firm. In the knowledge integration process or cycle, people incorporate external knowledge by learning or mastering it. This is achieved in several different ways depending on the type of external knowledge involved.

For example, explicit knowledge that can be encoded can be incorporated effectively through traditional training activities. Implicit or tacit knowledge can be incorporated by recruiting people who already possess it, although integrating it effectively into the firm-specific skeleton or base will then require an additional effort. The important aspect to consider in this process is that it results in a number of people possessing relevant external knowledge (useful not only within the firm, but also outside) which can nevertheless become obsolete quickly (both internally and externally). For precisely this reason of obsolescence, it becomes difficult to guarantee a long-term relationship between the firm and these people (i.e., to ensure them long-term employment). Hence, firms tend either to outsource access to this kind of knowledge if possible, or to motivate people to incorporate it by ensuring what has been called "employability" (see, for example, Chapter 5 by Cappelli and Chapter 4 by Ghoshal, Moran and Bartlett in this book), which in this chapter we call "external employability". The basic idea behind this is that the firm tries to represent the cutting edge in external knowledge so as to give its members the opportunity of finding another job outside should internal priorities change (or should these members simply desire to move to another firm).

There are plenty of examples of this dynamic, a common one being the specific or technical knowledge of a general character available in specialist consulting firms. Peter Cappelli provides an extensive discussion about the importance of external employability in Chapter 5 of this book, relating it to human resource management. He analyzes the nature of changing forces in human resource practices and suggests some new trends toward a new deal with employees.

However, knowledge integration as described above is insufficient to achieve a sustainable competitive advantage. We argue that a second cycle, the flexibility cycle, in which members of the organization develop internal knowledge, is needed as a complement. By definition, the flexibility cycle concerns knowledge developments within the organization. As this knowledge tends to have important implicit features, its development involves a lot of learning by doing and by "being there." Since this is very important for the firm's competitiveness and for achieving sustainability of its advantages, it tends to be true that as long as it has market appeal,[6] possession of internal knowledge gives the organization's members increased potential for "internal employability"[7] (that is, being guaranteed long-lasting relationships with the firm). An important component of internal knowledge involves providing the firm with a sort of "organizational glue" that ensures its cohesiveness in the face of potentially unstable environments.[8] Ghoshal, Moran, and Bartlett comment on this issue in Chapter 4, highlighting the importance of accumulating mechanisms which act on the knowledge integration cycle.

At the same time, they point out the importance of complementing accumulation with linking and bonding mechanisms for the creation of sustainable competitive advantage. This has implications for the type of professional careers or what we will call "learning trajectories" that are more appropriate for the development, both individual and collective, of a given organization's members.

8.6 EXTERNAL AND INTERNAL EMPLOYABILITY: KNOWLEDGE REQUIREMENTS AND EMPLOYMENT

It is now possible to turn our attention to the kind of knowledge processes that are needed in order to develop external and internal employability. External knowledge tends, by nature, to be technical and rather explicit.

Therefore, achieving excellence in technical skills is an important component of the associated knowledge processes. Excellence can be achieved relatively easily, either through well-known training procedures or by going to the market and recruiting individuals who already possess the relevant skills. On the other hand, some non-technical skills are also needed, such as the ability to work in teams or in a multicultural environment. This is also "general" knowledge, but it tends to be less explicit even though a few explicit rules may exist. Less conventional training efforts are needed for the purpose of developing this kind of knowledge, although it is relatively easy to find people and institutions who specialize at it.

Finally, there is the need to develop the ability to deploy external knowledge effectively so as to contribute to the firm's better operation and, eventually, to its success. This can be difficult, as it involves the synthesis of external and internal knowledge (see Figure 8.1). For those organizations whose members are willing to invest in the acquisition and development of internal knowledge (in exchange for a better chance at long-term employment opportunities), achieving this is easier. In the remaining cases, these same individuals will have to play an important role at the moment of synthesis or "intersection," as seen in Figure 8.1. Here, the integrators and "context-providers" have more to do with motivating and "situating" people.

Internal knowledge development and deployment is an altogether different matter. The issue here centers on achieving excellence in knowing "how to keep the organization together" and in developing mostly non-technical skills and capabilities. These include strong organizational learning, ensuring access to relevant knowledge of the day-to-day activities of the firm, effectively transmitting cultural values, and so on. For the most part, this knowledge is implicit and "non-codifiable," making its development and deployment very path- and context-dependent. The associated processes should therefore be conceived and implemented accordingly. This implies designing career profiles and "learning trajectories" very different from those that prove useful in the case of external knowledge.

Turning now to the implications for employment, we find it useful to distinguish between the two dimensions of knowledge presented in this chapter. First we examine the implicit or "non-codifiable" versus the explicit or "codifiable." Then we consider the task-related or external versus the organizational or internal; see Figure 8.2.

The message in Figure 8.2 is that there are situations where one can be relatively certain about the trends in employment. Jobs are likely to be on the decline for task-related activities involving codifiable knowledge, as these will probably be outsourced by firms. Thus, the trend seems to favor specialized, highly effective organizations to which other firms will subcontract activities based on what they consider "external" knowledge.

Since these activities involve mainly technical knowledge, coordination costs are likely to be low so that the outsourcing approach will evolve naturally.

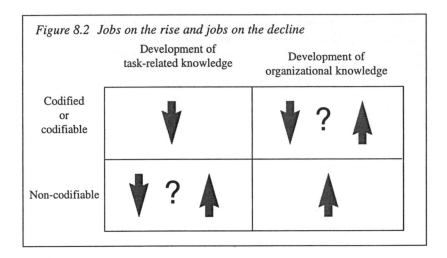

Figure 8.2 Jobs on the rise and jobs on the decline

Jobs involving task-related activities and non-codifiable knowledge are rare in general. Only cutting-edge, technology-based tasks tend to occupy this category, and normally these become codifiable rather quickly due to technological evolution and learning. Thus, in the cell of Figure 8.2 that pertains to this issue, our forecast would indicate a highly unstable situation involving a rather low number of jobs, the majority of them rapidly evolving to incorporate more explicit knowledge (with other jobs emerging due to technological innovation).

When we examine jobs involving organizational knowledge of the codified kind, we again see a trend in the direction of fewer jobs which, in turn, are continuously being taken over by technology applications. We also observe a permanent flow of new jobs that, in a transitory manner, change from involving non-codifiable knowledge to codifiable or explicit knowledge. The reason for this is that, by nature, the vast majority of internal or organizational knowledge is implicit and non-codifiable. When, for whatever reason, some of this knowledge becomes codifiable, the firm will have to develop new implicit knowledge in order to maintain its competitiveness and sustain its advantages. Thus, we see few jobs here, which will not be outsourced by companies because they are idiosyncratic.

Finally, the internal/organizational knowledge non-codifiable combination will involve a growing number of jobs. The main reason for this is covered at the beginning of this chapter, as these jobs are the ones at the root of a firm's sustainable competitive advantages in today's environment. Given the type of knowledge involved, these jobs will tend to emerge within individual organizations (as they cannot, by nature, be outsourced) and require very idiosyncratic "learning trajectories" or career paths.

Although somewhat speculative, the above discussion gives an indication of what types of jobs are likely to be on the rise in the foreseeable future, what types are on the decline and why (based on our analysis). Since this analysis has been highly conceptual, the next step would involve complementing it from an empirical standpoint.

8.7 CONCLUDING REMARKS

In this chapter, we have proposed a framework to analyze the impacts of NOFs on employment from a perspective based on their knowledge requirements. Distinguishing between the classical explicit and implicit knowledge types and between what we have called "external" and "internal" knowledge (both necessary in order to develop sustainable competitive advantages in firms), we have discussed why NOFs pursue the acquisition of knowledge integration and flexibility and what kind of knowledge this can imply. Focusing on the knowledge processes needed to satisfy those requirements, we have then suggested a framework in which the likely trends for employment can be analyzed and discussed. We think that such a speculative framework can be very useful in designing future research efforts of an empirical nature.

NOTES

1. This is the basic argument of the so-called resource-based view of the firm (Barney, 1991; Peteraf, 1993).
2. In the words of Connor and Prahalad (1996): "private knowledge is a basic source of competitive advantage."
3. Of course, there are knowledge representations which may not reside in persons (although not all knowledge can be put in this form so that, strictly speaking, the only general way of representing and storing knowledge is through persons). Such representations are fundamental when it comes to sharing and transmitting knowledge.
4. The result of such "understanding" and "evaluation" is additional knowledge, which is added to the global knowledge structure of a given person. Such a result can also be "negative" by making certain pieces of old knowledge "obsolete." This tends to be disregarded for future use and, therefore, takes away from the

new global knowledge structure.

5.   This has given rise to what several authors call the knowledge-based view of the firm (Grant, 1996).

6.   By "market appeal" of the internal knowledge we mean that the idiosyncratic "ways of doing" of the firm have a value for clients who are willing to pay for it – otherwise the firm would be unable to develop any advantage and would probably cease to exist. In the automobile industry example above, an internal knowledge with market appeal could for example be a brand name, a reputation for reliability backed by actual product quality, a mechanical guarantee, etc.

7.   This has traditionally been called internal employment. We prefer to use the term "internal employability" to make it clear that employment is a consequence of providing firm-specific relevant knowledge, and that, hence, the underlying reason for internal employment has changed.

8.   To stay with the same example, consider the sense of unity that an automobile firm must give to the potentially very different components of its distribution channel (dealers, etc.) – without implying that one is better than the other, it is obvious that there is a big difference between, say, Mercedes' and Fiat's dealerships; you could probably tell them apart easily, although the basic functions being performed in the two are similar.

REFERENCES

Andreu, R. and S. Sieber (1999). *Knowledge and Problem Solving: A proposal for a model of individual and collective learning.* Working Paper 1/99, Barcelona: IESE Publishing.

Barney, J. (1991). Firm resources and sustained competitive advantage. *Journal of Management,* 17 (1): 99–120.

Bartlett, C. and Ghoshal, S. (1993). Beyond the M-form: towards a managerial theory of the firm. *Strategic Management Journal,* 14, (Summer): 23–46.

Bell, D. (1973). *The Coming of Post-industrial Society: A venture in forecasting.* New York: Basic Books

Collins, J. and Porras, J. (1994). *Built to Last.* New York: HarperBusiness.

Conner, K. R., and Prahalad, C. K. (1996). A Resource-based theory of the firm: knowledge versus opportunism. *Organization Science,* 7 (5): 477–501.

Davenport, T. H. and Prusak, L. (1998). *Working Knowledge: How organizations manage what they know.* Boston, MA: Harvard Business School Press.

Davidow, W. H. and Malone M. S. (1992). *The Virtual Corporation.* New York: HarperCollins.

De Geus, A. (1996). *The Living Company.* Boston, MA: Harvard Business School Press.

DeSanctis, G., Staudenmayer, N. and Wong, S. S. (1999). Interdependence in virtual organizations. *Journal of Organizational Behavior,* 6: 81–104.

Drucker, P. (1993). *Post-capitalist society.* Oxford: Butterworth-Heinemann.

Galbraith, J. (1995). *Designing Organizations*. San Francisco, CA: Jossey-Bass.

Grant, R. M. (1996). Prospering in dynamically-competitive environments: organizational capability as knowledge integration. *Organization Science*, 7 (4): 375–87.

Handy, C. (1992). *Understanding Organization*. Cambridge, MA: Oxford University Press.

Jones, G. R. and George, J. M. (1998). The experience and evolution of trust: implications for cooperation and teamwork. *The Academy of Management Review*, 23 (3): 531–46.

Kanter, R. M. (1983). *The Change Masters*. New York: Simon and Schuster.

Kogut, B. and Zander, U. (1996). What firms do. coordination, identity, and learning. *Organization Science*, 7 (5): 502–18.

Kolb, D. (1984). *Experiential Learning: Experience as the source of learning and development*. Englewood Cliffs, NJ: Prentice-Hall.

Miles, R. E. and Snow, C. C. (1986). Organizations: new concepts for new forms. *California Management Review*, 28 (3): 62–73.

Nonaka, I. (1994). A dynamic theory of organizational knowledge creation *Organization Science*, 5 (1): 14–37.

Pasternack, B. A. and Viscio, A. J. (1998). *The Centerless Corporation: A new model for transforming your organization for growth and prosperity*. New York: Simon and Schuster.

Pentland, B. T. (1995). Information systems and organizational learning: the social epistemology of organizational knowledge Ssystems. *Accounting, Management and Information Technologies,* 5 (1): 1–21.

Peteraf, M. (1993). The cornerstones of competitive advantage: a resource-based view. *Strategic Management Journal*, 14 (3): 179–91.

Polanyi, M. (1962). *Personal Knowledge*. New York: Anchor Day Books.

Ricart, J. E., Sieber, S. and Svejenova S. (1999). *New Organizational Forms: What is new and why?* Working Paper 4/99, Barcelona: IESE Publishing.

Spender, J. C. (1996). Making knowledge the basis of a dynamic theory of the firm. *Strategic Management Journal,* 17 (Winter Special Issue): 45–62.

Teece, D. J., Pisano, G. and Shuen, A. (1997). Dynamic capabilities and strategic management. *Strategic Management Journal*, 18 (7): 509–33.

Tyre, M. J. and von Hippel, E. (1997). The situated nature of adaptive learning in organizations. *Organization Science,* 8 (1): 71–83.

Volberda, H. (1996). Toward the flexible form: how to remain vital in hypercompetitive environments. *Organization Science*, 7 (4): 359–74.

Wellins, R. S., Byham, W. C. and Dixon, G. R. (1994). *Inside Teams: How 20 world-class organizations are winning through teamwork*. San Francisco, CA: Jossey-Bass.

Williamson, O. (1981). The economics of organization: the transaction cost approach. *American Journal of Sociology,* 87: 548–77.

9. The New Employment Relationships: the Dilemmas of a Post-downsized, Socially Excluded, and Low Trust Future

Paul R. Sparrow

9.1 INTRODUCTION

This chapter analyses the new employment contract from a psychological perspective. It argues that we must consider some of the implications of the unfolding drama surrounding the future of work by looking beyond what is happening within organizations. Drama is an appropriate word to use, because the formation of the new employment contract is proving to be a very emotionally charged process. Some of these processes will be examined. The chapter explores some of the issues raised by changing perceptions of the employment relationship, the most notable of which include:

1. the downsizing phenomenon and its psychological consequences;
2. economic apartheid and problems of social exclusion;
3. managerial uncertainties and low levels of trust;
4. new generational perceptions of the employment relationship.

First, however, let us be clear about what is meant by the term the "new" employment contract. Organizational sociologists call it the "new capitalism." Emerging from 1980 onwards, it is based on stiff international competition, state deregulation of industry, institutional ownership of firms, rapid technological change, smaller firm size, structural simplicity, and flexibility (Budros, 1997). Labor economists view it in terms of the organizational internalization of product and labor markets (Cappelli, 1999, also this volume). Psychologists view it in terms of changes in the nature of trust, organizational justice, and reciprocal expectations and obligations (Sparrow, 2000). All would agree that competitive pressures have cut time to market and the obsolescence of fixed investments in capital (including human capital) has been accelerated. Information and communication technologies have replaced the coordination and monitoring tasks of middle managers, enabling a large range of business functions to be outsourced and creating the potential for radically different forms of work organization. Financial arrangements have made it possible to advance the interests of shareholders far ahead of other traditional stakeholders, increasing the squeeze on fixed costs. Finally, management techniques such as profit centers, external benchmarking, and core competences have exposed every business process and employee to market pressures. Market principles replaced behavioral rules of reciprocity, equity, loyalty, attachment, and long-term commitment. As these "old" rules have been challenged, psychologists have looked at the changing employment contract through new "lenses" or theoretical perspectives. These perspectives tend to raise emotive – and certainly moral – issues about the problems we face in coping with the new employment relationship and solving the problems it is creating. Consequently language has become important in how phenomena are presented. The use of bloodless terminology such as rightsizing, building down, re-balancing, re-focusing, reduction in force (RIF), or the creation of involuntary career events (ICE) has come to dominate the management press. Pascale (1995) puts the problems created by such rhetoric starkly. We are looking for a painless way out of dealing with the changes in self-esteem, community, and social identity that work is now creating, yet many of the changes are inescapably painful. We are facing complex changes, the consequences of which need to be fathomed quickly. It is clear that the broad redefinition of work that is taking place also impacts on society. Consequently the individual and the organization cannot resolve the resultant issues themselves. A new social context is necessary to legitimize the experiences associated with the loss and change to our working lives and make them acceptable. As researchers we must therefore ask deep and searching questions about the adequacy of our existing knowledge and theoretical frameworks, the assumptions we are making about the role of organizations, legitimate expectations about the employment contract, and the likely future behavior of employees.

Globalization, downsizing, and restructuring are creating deep shifts in the pattern of work and society, and the perceptions that employees and their managers have of work are being altered markedly. It is important to note that there are cross-national differences in the focus of popular literature on the nature of changes taking place in the employment relationship, and the level of optimism or pessimism contained within it. In the tighter labor markets of the US, Cappelli (1999) can focus discussion on poaching, transfer of whole teams across organizations, portfolio executive management careers, and retentive incentives. In the more protective labor markets of Europe, discussion still concentrates on the fundamental values-objections and societal health consequences of the new employment contract (Sparrow and Marchington, 1998). Indeed, national culture value orientations are not only reflected in the style in which we address discussions of the new employment deal, but they are predictive of much resultant organizational behavior. To date there has not been much work on the "psychological contract" based on non-US or non-UK samples. Rousseau and Tijoriwala (1998: 680) note that "cross-cultural differences exist in contracts but aren't well understood." However, there is good reason to assume that those individuals who remain hidebound by deep-seated cultural objections to changes in the employment contract may be unable to absorb or adapt to the new or desired behaviors. For example, Schuler and Rogovsky (in press) examined data from three international HRM surveys: the IBM/Towers Perrin world-wide study of HR practices, the International Social Survey Program (ISSP), and the Price Waterhouse/Cranfield project. Under the ISSP program data have been gathered for 11 countries covering the US and Europe. Standardized and stratified survey data for over 6600 employees allowed for sophisticated statistical analysis of work value and orientation data covering such components as high income, job security, and interesting work. By controlling for the effects of occupational grouping and demographic variables of age and sex, it was found that both line of country and the cultural value orientation prescribed by Hofstede (1980) for that country were the most significant predictors of work values. Their analysis found that national cultural values accounted for about 7% of the variance, for example, in the work value for high income. Sparrow and Wu (1998) similarly found that national value orientations were associated with three-quarters of individual preferences for a series of 55 HRM system design choices. Value orientations accounted for around 10% of variation in HRM preferences at the individual level. There is mounting evidence that stable sources of individual differences, such as value orientations, are predictive of reactions to some of the key elements of the new employment contract.

9.2 THE DOWNSIZING PHENOMENON

Flexibility, in its many guises, is one of these key elements. Although it has been a significant driver of change for the last two decades, it is only recently that organizations have attempted to introduce multiple flexibilities (numerical, functional, temporal, financial, organizational, geographical, and cognitive) as part of an integrated and urgent strategy. With numerical flexibility organizations seek more autonomy and control over the numbers of people they directly employ through initiatives such as downsizing, outsourcing, the pursuit of peripheral forms of employment, and the development of contingent relationships. At the organizational level, there is an important battle associated with this form of flexibility. It concerns the implicit ownership of the employment contract. Who has bottom line accountability for the consequences of employment? Who bears the social cost? Who pays if you become stressed? The trend has been for organizations to shift more social cost accountability onto the state or the individual, and to reduce the core of employees for whom they will accept accountability. Perceptions of ever-encroaching personal pain, unequal burden, and uncertain future durability of the new capitalism dominate the media.

The phenomenon of downsizing in the US and UK has been well documented, but it has now become a global phenomenon. Although the cost of firing a 45 year old manager with 20 years, service, and earning the equivalent of $50,000 varies markedly around the world (from $130,000 in Italy, $67,000 in Greece, $38,000 in Denmark, $25,000 in Germany, and $19,000 in the US and UK), reductions in force have not been the preserve of high labor cost countries alone. For example, in Brazil in 1998 some two million jobs were lost in Saõ Paulo alone, with for example Ford Motor Company cutting 2800 jobs. Nationally unemployment rose to a record 8%, or 24% if the under-employed are included (Margolis, 1999). In Hong Kong unemployment reached over 5%, up from a norm of 2%, and was expected to grow to 7% in 1999. German industry has pursued an aggressive policy of cost-cutting, with productivity rising by about a third from 1993 to 1998, unit labor costs falling by 15%, and middle management level employment falling by 20% (Ernsberger *et al.*, 1998). In an attempt to match "international standards" Elf Aquitaine of France reduced a seven-layer operation in Germany to three layers, and cut half of the 1600 jobs. There has been an associated rise in contingent workers, including independent contractors, some part-time roles, migrant, seasonal, leased, and temporary workers. In Japan, the appointment of Carlos Ghosn formerly of Renault France (known as "le cost cutter"), as CEO at Nissan has heralded plans for 21,000 cuts worldwide, the breakup of the *keiretsu* links with suppliers. No country it seems is immune.

9.3 MANAGING THE PSYCHOLOGICAL CONSEQUENCES

Baruch and Hind (1999) examine the new employment relationship critically and question how organizations should manage the processes concerned with motivating people within it when job security is no longer a valid concept. In a review of the literature, they show how a series of new concepts have been used to signal the realities of the new employment relationship. Handy (1989) brought the concept of "employability" into mainstream management thinking in the late 1980s. It refers to the absence of long-term commitments from the organization, but commitment to provide training and development that enables the employee to develop a portable portfolio of skills and find alternative employment when the relationship ends (Handy, 1989). By the mid 1990s the consequences of employability for careers took centre stage, with discussion of the "boundaryless career" (DeFillippi and Arthur (1994) and the "boundaryless organization" (Ashkenas *et al.*, (1995). The understanding that the employing organization is simply one of several stakeholders in an individual's career development led to new prescriptions for career behavior, incorporating the need for "intelligent careers" (Arthur *et al.*, 1995), "career resilient workforces" (Hind *et al.*, 1996; Waterman *et al.*, 1994), and "post corporate careers" (Peiperl and Baruch, 1997).

However, by the late 1990s some of the deeper psychological consequences of such shifts were being examined. Psychologists understandably concentrated on the reaction of employees, who, as surveys suggest, are not well disposed to the new employment contract, at least on the surface. The bottom-line question is, have the changes in the employment contract to date created any lasting damage to the nature of the relationship? Evidence on layoffs produces a complex and conflicting picture of change at the level of employee behavior. The negative impact on firm performance is increasingly evident (De Meuse *et al.*, 1994; Dougherty and Bowman, 1995). Singh (1998) supports the transformational view, arguing that there is much empirical evidence to show that layoffs have had a marked impact on the psychological contract. The popular perception is that the impact of downsizing has been diminished loyalty and perceptions of job security (O'Reilly, 1994; Seppa, 1996), reduced commitment in victims and survivors, guilt amongst the executioners, and higher levels of burnout (Smith, 1997), higher turnover intention (Brockner *et al.*, 1992), increased anxiety and stress, and in extreme cases, feelings of loss, grief and depression (Clark and Koonce, 1995).

There has been a debate amongst psychologists about whether the process used to manage downsizing can moderate the degree of "aftershock" (Baruch and Hind, 1999). In the non-unionized US environment, Mishra *et al.* (1998) highlight the need to use downsizing as a last resort, to tell the truth and over-communicate, to craft a credible business-case vision that shows that downsizing is not a short-term fix, to use cross-functional teams to identify targets, notify employees in advance, and sensitize them to the need for rationalization with prior work reorganization initiatives, offer employees time off as the announcement is made, provide outplacing counselling and job search help, be generous to leavers, allow voluntary separation, involve employees in implementation, and train the survivors. In this protracted process, the perception of fairness of decision making is a critical issue. Jackson (1997) has shown that the process of selection for those made redundant – preferably based on clear performance and operational related criteria – is indeed a significant moderator of subsequent dysfunctional behaviors. Managing such processes appropriately seems however to be an impossible task.

In a longitudinal study of employee perceptions surrounding enforced work role changes before, during and after the event, Hallier (in press) observed a temporary disturbance in employee behavior. The study showed that because employees were unable to arrive at convincing explanations of their organizational worth (or lack of it), there were clear changes in their information scanning behavior. Silence by management was seen as incompetence, lack of care, or hidden intentions. When communication took place it generally resulted in the perception of contradictory valuations by managers of employee worth. This lack of communication or misperceived communication does not just reflect ignorant and poor management skills, but often a lack of comprehension of the end solution or clear managerial strategy towards it, amongst managers who themselves are trying to find their way through a series of ambiguous, complex, and little understood changes. Most employers still place more emphasis on managing and legitimizing organizational changes rather than on the adaptation of employees.

Consequently, employees hone their coping behaviors and tactics accordingly. For Hallier (in press), contract breach should not be seen as a single episode attributable to specific signals sent by the employer. Rather, it operates as a longitudinal process of sense-making during which security is put into abeyance. Hallier uses the term "security abeyance" to depict a state of chronic concern about an individual's security which results from ambiguous organizational change. From 1990–95 Britain's top 12 companies reduced their workforces by 44%. Business process re-engineering (BPR) was often used to tidy up some of the confusion that resulted, but also tended to have a negative impact on employment. When Asea Brown Boveri introduced BPR into its headquarters, the number of HQ staff was reduced from 4000 to 200 employees with little additional employment created through decentralization. This type of flexibility is seen as a possible threat to organizational memory, with organizational cultures based on control. Clinical problems experienced by the survivors, executioners, and victims of downsizing have also been discussed.

9.4 CAPTURING THE COSTS OF DOWNSIZING

Therefore the true costs of downsizing might easily outweigh the efficiency gains. There are hidden social costs. These include recession fatigue – the point at which employee behavior shifts and employees no longer continue to do things because of fear, but decide that what will be will be, and therefore see no point in automatic conformity. Many unreported phenomena can pose a threat, such as higher levels of theft and shrinkage as employees recalibrate their ethics, or sabotage to databases and, creation of computer viruses by disgruntled employees. There are also reactive behaviors: the potential costs of higher stress, reduced effectiveness, absenteeism, and turnover. Payne (2000) provides the following analysis and evidence on the international situation regarding absenteeism. A survey of over 600 North American vice-presidents found that over half reported that the firms they managed were understaffed and that absence and turnover were up as a result (McShulskis, 1997). Indeed, unscheduled absenteeism in the US reached its highest level for seven years in 1998, reaching a rate of 2.9% Absences due to family problems accounted for 26% of this, and stress 16% (a figure up by a factor of three since 1995). Stress levels in Australia are seen as a significant issue. The Australian Industrial Relations Workplace Survey of over 18,000 workers from all levels found that between 40% and 65% of all levels of employees reported increases in the pace of work, the effort they had to expend to do the work, and reported increased stress levels. A survey by the Canadian Health Monitor suggests that although white-collar workers report greater levels of work stress, blue-collar workers are more likely to be absent due to stress. Over 50% of blue-collar workers and 33% of white-collar workers reported losing more than 13 days of work in 1997 (Fernberg, 1998).

Finally, there are the costs of non-conformance, such as unplanned recruitment and training costs if the downsizing equation has not been calculated correctly, the levels of rework due to poor organization or role confusion post-downsizing, and the development time needed to reach full productivity. Downsizing threatens the depth and quality of role understanding that the typical employee possesses, and generates issues surrounding skills and knowledge acquisition. In a typical middle management role, managers reach 80% proficiency after one year, but take three years to fully understand the role. The current rhetoric suggests that employees are moving towards a portfolio career which will consist of six significant role moves over a lifetime career. Indeed, the average tenure of a European employee is now seven years. In such circumstances, for at least 15% of the time spent in the role managers don't really understand what their job is!

It is not surprising then that the economic benefits of downsizing have been questioned. Organizational sociologists have pursued the central question of why firms continue to downsize when the economic benefits are not evidenced (Budros, 1997, 1999). Three dominant theories have been used to explain the attractiveness of downsizing strategies: economic, institutional, and socio-cognitive (Zhao *et al.*, 1997). The dominant theory has been the economic perspective, which sees downsizing as caused by a search for productivity and efficiency and as a response to organizational decline, or as an attempt to increase profitability, i.e. a rational attempt to manipulate performance. This stream of research has examined the financial outcomes of downsizing and established the link to productivity, profitability, and stock price (Bruton *et al.*, 1996; Worrell *et al.*, 1991). This perspective has been questioned as more evidence emerges that it has failed to deliver the financial benefits expected (De Meuse *et al.*, 1994; Mentzer, 1996). Institutional theory argues that it is social conventions that impel the pursuit of downsizing and view it as "good management" (McKinley *et al.*, 1995). Managers conform to this view in order to gain legitimacy (DiMaggio and Powell, 1983), and downsizing decisions are seen as cloned and learned responses to uncertainty, reinforced by the rewards that exist within the internal career systems and external professional networks for senior managers. US HRM professionals now show less objection to the pursuit of downsizing. The proportion who believe the process has "gone too far" fell from 52% to 39% during 1996–7 (International Survey Research Corporation, 1997). The socio-cognitive approach focuses attention on managers' mental models of downsizing and how these models are constructed (Zhao *et al.*, 1997). Managers' decisions to downsize are based on shared mental models that define the causes and effects of downsizing, and indicate that it is effective. However, downsizing strategies may then be based on false assumptions of efficiency and the view that conducting business better, faster and smarter is a sufficient organizational response.

9.5 CAPTURING THE CONSEQUENCES UNDER DISCUSSION OF A CHANGING PSYCHOLOGICAL CONTRACT

Building on, and in large part emerging out of, the work on the consequences of downsizing, psychologists have broadened their research in an attempt to capture the changes taking place in the emotionally charged, perception-based, mutual exchange "deal" that surrounds the employment relationship. The term "psychological contract" has been used to capture this relationship (Shore and Tetrick, 1994). Guest (1998) notes three reasons why the psychological contract has become a viable construct for capturing changes in the employment relationship:

1. it reflects the process of individualization of the employment relationship that has been taking place, in which the market philosophy views the individual as an independent agent offering knowledge and skills through a series of transactions in the market place;
2. it focuses attention on the relative distribution of power and the cost of power inequalities in the new employment relationship;
3. it has the potential to integrate research on a number of important

organizational concepts such as trust, fairness, and social exchange, and to add additional explanatory value to the prediction of a series of consequences such as job satisfaction, organizational commitment, sense of security, motivation, organizational citizenship, absence and intention to quit.

It represents an implicit and open-ended agreement on what is given and what is received and is therefore closely associated with the concept of trust (Sparrow and Cooper, 1998). It captures expectations of reciprocal behavior in the employment contract, covering a range of societal norms and interpersonal behavior and is based on changing perceptions of the employer–employee balance of power. It is also very emotive: academics argue that you only know what the contract was when you breach it. Highly idiosyncratic and situation-bound, it has none the less been used to capture recent changes in the new employment contract. A series of generic changes, summarized in Table 9.1, represent a quantum shift in the balance of this reciprocal agreement (Anderson and Schalk, 1998).

Table 9.1   Past and emergent foms of psychological contract

Characteristics	Past form	Emergent form
Focus	Security, continuity, loyalty	Exchange, future
Format	Structured, predictable, stable	Unstructured, flexible, open to (re)negotiation
Underlying basis	Tradition, fairness, social justice, socio-economic class	Market forces, saleable abilities and skills, added value
Employer's responsibilities	Continuity, job security, training, career prospects	Equitable (as perceived) reward for added value
Employee's responsibilities	Loyalty, attendance, satisfactory performance, compliance with authority	Entrepreneurship, innovation, enacting changes to improve performance, excellent performance
Contractual relations	Formalized, mostly via trade union or collective representation	Individual's responsibility to barter for their services (internally or externally)
Career management	Organizational responsibility, inspirating careers planned and facilitated through personnel department input	Individual's responsibility, out-spiraling careers by personal reskilling and retraining

Source: Anderson and Schalk (1998); after Hiltrop (1995).

Therefore much effort has been spent attempting to describe it, understand it, and predict its consequences (Coyle-Shapiro and Kessler, 1999).

It is the sense of mutuality implicit in the psychological contract that has proved a useful vehicle to capture the consequences of perceived imbalances of exchange in the new employment contract. Under the new psychological contract organizations build attachment to other proxies – such as the team – for whom employees will still perform. A cross-sectional analysis of a representative sample of 1000 UK employees showed that the state of the contract could be explained by the presence (or absence) of progressive human resource management practices, an organizational climate characterized as one of high involvement and partnership, and by future expectations of employment security (Guest, 1998). A positive psychological contract was associated with higher job satisfaction, higher organizational commitment, higher reported motivation, and a positive evaluation of employment relations, and lower intention to quit. Violation of the contract – an emotive and debated term in itself – has been linked to a number of consequences including: higher turnover (Guzzo *et al.*, 1994; Robinson and Rousseau, 1994; Schalk and Frese, 1997); lower trust and job satisfaction (Robinson and Rousseau, 1994); lower commitment to the organization (Guzzo *et al.*, 1994, Schalk and Freese, 1997); and lower levels of organization citizenship behaviors (Robinson and Morrison, 1995). Managers' loyalty to their employer seems to have declined (Stroh *et al.*, 1994) and commitment to type of work and profession appears to be stronger now than commitment to organization (Ancona *et al.*, 1996).

9.6 IS THERE A LONGER-TERM CONSEQUENCE?

Tensions in the employment contract surrounding the perception of trust can be expected to continue. American Management Association data show that 80% of US firms that downsized were still profitable at the point of downsizing, and that on the day of the announcement of rationalization stock prices typically rose by 7%. To test the proposition that victims of downsizing will be less likely to trust future employers than those who have not been laid off, Singh (1998) examined data from the 1993 General Social Survey, which assesses the general disposition, satisfaction, happiness, racial attitudes, and political views of 500 to 800 individuals representative of the US public. Items related to trust, and self–interest versus organizational interest were analysed for those in full-time employment and those who had had experience of being laid off. Victims represented over 6% of the general population, and were in fact significantly less trustful and had attitudes more inclined to self-interest.

Managerial attitude surveys also convey a sense of unease about the employment contract. However, they provide us with contradictory evidence about the level of trust that now exists and the likely consequences. When more reliable and representative surveys of the whole workforce are taken, the evidence suggests that there are far more limited levels of breach of psychological contract or trust than we might assume. Yet the general picture that emerges is one of uncertainty and the potential threat of future consequences. Three recent managerial surveys in the UK make the point:

1. Evidence from the national surveys carried out by Guest *et al.* (1996) for the British Institute of Personnel and Development (IPD) show that deterioration in the psychological contract is restricted to around 20% of the workforce, many less-educated employees in more peripheral jobs. Interestingly, even the larger unstructured surveys tend to come up with a figure of from 20% to 30% highly dissatisfied individuals perceiving dysfunctional consequences to the new employment contract (Davis, 1999). For the majority, however, change is far less stark than often suggested (Guest *et al.*, 1996). The IPD surveys showed that 79% of UK employees said that they still trusted management a lot; 25% had experienced some sort of redundancy in their lives; and 53% claimed to be working harder than before. However, 56% expected to be in their current jobs for the next few years.

2. A panel survey of 5000 British Institute of Management members by Worrell and Cooper (1998) found that 52% of managers feared that their company had lost essential skills and experience – up from 45% of managers in 1997; 41% of managers referred to a poverty of communication and consultation about strategic change in their organization. Attitudes to longer working hours were ambivalent: 45% of senior managers thought working long hours was acceptable, 22% of junior managers felt it unacceptable, but had no choice over the matter. 70% of managers reported working over 40 hours a week, 53% regularly work in the evening, and 34% regularly work over the weekend. 72% correctly sensed that working long hours affected their relationship with their partners. 55% perceive that long work hours damages their health; 55% feel it actually makes them less productive; and 49% feel that they suffer from information overload.

3. A *Management Today*/Ceridian survey of work–life balance of nearly 2000 managers (Davis, 1999) examined attitudes about what bothered managers in the new employment contract, what they would most like to change, and what the perceived consequences were. The conclusion was that British managers faced a "strain" as a significant proportion of senior managers made sacrifices in their personal lives to keep up with the "rat race." 49% thought morale in their organizations was low, 55% felt they faced frequent stress at work,

30% felt their health was suffering because of this, half felt they had no time to build relationships out of work, 20% admitting drinking to ease work pressure, and 8% had resorted to therapy. Now of course such surveys are not necessarily statistically representative – a point made later on the basis of the work of Guest *et al.* (1996) – but they capture a mood and a phenomenon that deserves further consideration. 40% were looking for a job over the next 12 months (whether they would get one is irrelevant: in their minds they were mobile). However, long work hours (12%), workload pressure (18%) and corporate culture (20%) were not the main drivers of this. Rather it was lack of challenge (44%), lack of recognition (37%), lack of money (36%), and poor work–life balance (35%). However, although 81% responded that "I am very loyal to my organization," 71% would seriously consider an approach from a head-hunter. Some loyalty!

Such surveys, then, show that emotions and rationality are currently rather confused. There will always be a limit to how much cross-sectional surveys can tell us about the changes taking place in the employment relationship. Surveys may simply pick up employee naivety – when faced with the enormous consequences of the radical economic and structural transitions taking place individuals act as though it will happen to others but not to them. For example, Hallier and Lyon (1996) found that middle management employees made responsible for downsizing lower echelons in their own organization still did not expect redundancy themselves, yet as we have seen this is a key target group. There is also the problem of what psychologists call perceptual framing (Hulin and Glomb, 1999). If times are tough, we learn to adjust our expectations downwards, reporting that perhaps things are not as bad as others make out. If the employee's frame is anchored in a context of no work, then even irregular work and income may be viewed positively. Therefore, some of the survey findings which show that reported levels of job satisfaction or trust are little altered might just be evidencing changes in the perceptual frame.

9.7 ECONOMIC REGENERATION VERSUS ECONOMIC APARTHEID: THE PROBLEM OF SOCIAL EXCLUSION

Not only are there questions about the loyalty of those still in core employment, there are new patterns of social exclusion being created within organizations which may also bring unexpected consequences. Psychologists have become concerned about the impact of inequality and social exclusion within organizations – defined as access to important resources, social networks, and intangible career opportunities. Barker

(1995) outlines the new behaviors being generated by the increasing differentiation between different layers of citizenship within an organization, and the associated privileges and exclusions that are embedded within each of these layers, in terms of access to facilities, training, or career enhancing experiences. Those with lower levels of citizenship accumulate deficits over their employment contract, and very probably new value sets that might shock those remaining in the core: "... contingent work may be the solvent that dissolves older forms of workplace privilege" (Barker, 1995: 50). Current models of socialization, commitment, and organization culture identification could well have limited utility for those organizations that will have a greater reliance on the contingent workforce.

Returning to the societal dimension of this, we see social exclusion on a global scale. We are faced with a paradox. Economic regeneration – and lest we allow discussion of the negative aspects of the new employment relationship to allow us to forget this, we should note that there is much of this taking place – is coming hand in hand with economic apartheid. For example, in the US in 1998, 385,000 manufacturing jobs disappeared, but more than 3 million new jobs were created. Key growth occupations include software programmers, management consultants, amusement park workers, mortgage lenders, and temporary employees. US unemployment has fallen to its lowest level (below 4%) since the 1960s (*Wall Street Journal*, 1999). Participation rates are growing (the workforce grew by 1% in real terms in 1998) and wage levels are rising by about 3% a year. But all is not well. It is often noted that during the decade of the 1980s nearly a quarter of all the US jobs created were part-time and of these 40% were filled by workers involuntarily (Appelbaum, 1992). More recent data suggest that the level of involuntary occupancy of peripheral work roles may have increased. Citing a US Department of Labor (1995) statistics survey of workers engaged in contingent and alternative work structures, Murphy and Jackson (1999) note that almost two thirds of respondents worked in such roles involuntarily and would prefer a more traditional full-time employment contract. Freeman's (1996) economic analysis of the dangers of an apartheid employment contract shows that the problem facing the US is not one of creating jobs, but is one of making work pay. He argues that comments about rising inequality, stagnant real wages, a declining middle class, high levels of child poverty, insecure workers, a waning union movement, homeless people in every city, bursting jails and prisons, and a fraying social safety net, are not the products of soapbox radicalism or neo-Marxian philosophy. They simply reflect characteristics of life in the United States as we move into the twenty-first century. From 1910 to 1973 the average employee enjoyed substantial gains in real earnings (wage increases of 2% per year leading to a doubling of generational income every 35 years) and leisure time. But from 1979 to the mid-1990s median earnings of male employees dropped by 13%.

Moreover, inequalities grew in this period. If the $2 trillion increase in GDP from 1980 to 1994 had been divided equally, each US family would have gained $2000. Instead, median family income was stagnant. The proportion of aggregate income for the top 5% rose from 15.3% to 19.1% from 1980 to 1993, while the proportion going to 80% of families fell. Nearly a decade of gains in GDP and in employment were accompanied by falling incomes for the bottom half of US families. The decline of trade unionism in the US from 30% to 11% of the private sector accounts for about one-fifth of the rise of inequality of earnings. Incarcerating a criminal costs roughly as much per year as sending someone to Harvard, and in California more money is spent on the prison budget than on higher education. There are notable international differences in the purchasing power of the lowest paid. US workers in the bottom 10% earn less real pay than in other countries: low-paid German workers earn 2.2 times more and low-paid Norwegians 1.8 times more. About one-third of US workers are paid less (in purchasing power units) than comparable workers overseas. Whether or not the continuance of what has become a low-cost structure and contingent workforce employment strategy will lead to a readjustment of expectations is a moot question.

The emotional and moral agenda cannot be ignored. Concern about apartheid economies and unproductive divisions across the employment relationship remains an international issue. It is sobering to consider the following United Nations (1998) analysis of the scale of social division and exclusion. Consumption in the world has doubled in the last 10 years, and has increased by a factor of six in the last 20 years. Amongst the wealthy nations only the US and Ireland suffer from higher levels of poverty than Britain (United Nations, 1998). International comparisons of poverty viewed on four measures (life expectancy, deprivation in knowledge, deprivation in income, and social exclusion) show that Sweden, Holland, and Germany have the best income equality in the West, whilst the Anglo-Saxon economies fill four of the six most unequal. The UK is the twelfth richest country in terms of average income per head, but in 1995 14% of the UK population lived in poverty (below the internationally recognised poverty line) and more than 20% of UK adults are functionally illiterate. The richest 225 people in the world have a combined wealth of $1 trillion, equal to the annual income of 2.5 billion people or the poorest 47%. Bill Gates, the Walton family of Wal Mart, and the investor William Buffett have assets greater than the poorest 48 least developed countries. Yet the additional cost of maintaining and achieving universal access to basic education, safe water, sanitation, basic health, and nutrition for all those deprived in the world, and to reproductive health care for women is roughly $40 billion a year. This is equal to $37 billion a year, which is the same amount of money spent on pet food, perfumes, and cosmetics in the US and Europe, or 4% of the income of the richest 225 people in the world.

9.8 ECONOMIC AND MANAGERIAL UNCERTAINTIES: THE END OF TRUST ?

In recent years changes in the nature of the employment relationship have generally received a negative press and has led to the lack of trust. Trust is a willingness to rely or depend on some externality such as an event, process, individual, group or system (Clark and Payne, 1997). It implies the ability to take for granted many features of the social order (Miles and Creed, 1995). The expectation is that actions will be beneficial rather than detrimental (Gambetta, 1988), though one can trust an enemy to behave consistently badly. Creed and Miles (1996) distinguish three different facets of trust:

1. *process-based* (personal experience of recurring exchanges which create ongoing expectations and norms of obligation about what is felt to be fair treatment);
2. *characteristic-based* (beliefs about another's trustworthiness that results from a perception of their expertise, intentions, actions, words and general qualities); and
3. *institutional-based* (trust in the integrity and competence of informal societal structures).

All three facets have been challenged recently, but the different HRM solutions to the breach and rebuilding of each facet is not as yet understood (Sparrow and Marchington, 1998). It is proving hard for managers to convince staff that they can be trusted to make decisions beyond short-term expedients. The behavior of social groups, and the trusted divisions between them, has been thrown into confusion. The new HRM philosophy challenges age-old and trusted divisions between employer and employee or between managers and unions. The trust that employees placed in the HRM paradigm of the 1980s and 1990s and their belief that it would deliver greater benefit than a reliance on "employee voice" achieved through formal union–management partnership has been questioned. The pursuit of flexibility has challenged the patterns of employee behavior that managers assumed characterized full-time workers or part-time workers, older employees or younger employees, men or women (Emmott and Hutchinson, 1998), and new social groupings of "victims," "accomplices," or "conscious believers" are emerging at work (Beardwell, 1998).

Sadly, there do not appear to be any fundamental certainties emerging even at the institutional level, and even the future end-point of the changes taking place is imbued with uncertainty. There is inherent instability in the economic structures that have driven the new employment contract. According to Klaus Schwab (1999), founder of the World Economic

Forum, globalization is no longer a process. It is a condition. Yet the sense among many economists and business analysts, worried by the global ramifications of recent mega-mergers and events in East Asia, Russia and Brazil, is that in a world that is becoming fast-paced, complex, intangible and boundaryless economically, we have to create new business boundaries. It is argued that we must develop a new set of procedural, legal, and institutional mechanisms aimed at coping with the "condition" that we are in. In a typical poacher-turned, gamekeeper analysis, George Soros, the currency speculator, argues that the whole global capitalist system came within days of meltdown in October 1998 for fundamental, structural reasons.

The global system is, according to Soros: "both at the height of its powers, but without reform is an 'endangered species' ... there is an urgent need to rethink and reform the global capital system ... the international financial system itself is the main culprit in the meltdown process ... Financial markets are inherently unstable ... how much instability can society take?" (Soros, 1999: 34–5). The World Economic Forum has given consideration to the need to create a global system of political decision making, the subordination of states' sovereignty to international law and institutions, and the re-regulation of large corporations in their wider social context, in order to ensure more transparent operations and greater corporate responsibility (Eigen and Rockefeller, 1999). If there are such uncertainties amongst the economists and business analysts, imagine the stirrings and dynamics within the mind of the typical employee.

At an anecdotal level, it is easy to suggest that there are growing levels of mistrust. How many people trust their president, politicians or political process? Do they trust major institutions such as the police or the independence of their judiciary? Do they trust many of the professions and scientific knowledge, such as food scientists or medical doctors? Do they trust the quality of information that they have to deal with at work? The television, the internet? There has of course always been distrust in the employment contract, a sense of us and them, but on the surface at least today we have growing levels of mistrust. The paradox facing HRM academics is that organizations are asking employees to trust in transition at the very time when the nature of employee trust is itself in transition (Sparrow and Cooper, 1998). The ability of organizations to re-establish high levels of trust after many of the changes that took place in the 1990s has to be questioned.

This raises an important issue, given the discussion of progress towards the network organization (see Pettigrew and Massini, Chapter 7 in this volume). Recent changes to the shape and design of organizations and jobs have either designed in or designed out trust. This occurs through the choices made by managers about empowerment and the design of control systems, coordination systems and associated business processes, and through the levels of information sharing and shape of reward systems associated with the operation of team working. Trust is a pervasive feature of organizational design and there is "a clear and compelling link" between the two. It is reflected in the control and coordination systems and the use of incentives to direct behavior. The higher the level of trust, the fewer the controls and therefore the lower the "transaction costs" that the organization has to incur. There are two important trust-related judgements that managers make when they redesign the organizational form: do they believe there is implicit employee "task reliability;" i.e. do they have the capabilities and potential to exercise responsible self-direction and self-control; and is there sufficient "values congruence" with the purpose of the organization; i.e. is there a dominant written and spoken philosophy that will guide the ultimate way in which employees will act? There is a clear conflict between the higher levels of trust that are both implicit in and a necessary ingredient of the operating logic of many of the new organizational forms (such as network organizations) and the levels of trust as reflected in the current attitudes and psychological contract of employees. Organizations will need to decide quickly whether they develop HRM systems to manage low-trust employees in high-trust, high-risk organizational designs, or whether they try to re-engage a sufficient proportion of people into a higher-trust employment relationship.

9.9 IS A NEW GENERATION X EMERGING?

Will they actually have a choice? What of the generation whose perceptions are first being formed now? What of future generations? Another area of debate has been about whether or not we will see generic adaptations in the way that people adjust to the new employment relationship, and whether or not a changed psychology across generational cohorts and across the work–life divide might occur in the future. If there is a shift in values, organizations might find it hard to cope with the new behaviors and rule sets that will govern the adaptive response of employees. The argument that we may see new patterns of employee behavior rests on three observations (Sparrow, 2000):

1. Employees now work in a state of permanent flux. Changes have no beginning or end point, and there is no oppportunity for individuals to internalize the usual sequence to transitions. There is no period of foreclosure and no refreezing of change. Consequently, the value systems intended to support organizational changes and supposedly generated by them do not necessarily become internalized.
2. The traditional period of engagement and disengagement with work and careers, beginning in the twenties and ending in the sixties, is now constricted to a shorter age range, and subject to several

stratified layers of employment contract. The needs and principles of motivation, value-sets, sources of satisfaction that applied to a life-long employment relationship should not be assumed to apply to this new pattern.

3. Many employees have now entered the workforce since changes to the employment relationship began in the 1980s – commonly referred to as Generation X. For this generation, there are no "former realities" to change.

What might be the impact of repeated exposure to people with transactional assumptions about their employment contract? Murphy and Jackson (1999: 358) conclude that if there is a continued and widespread erosion of the foundations of trust and relational expectations in the employment contract, then "at the societal level, such an effect could cause the psychological landscape of work to be so fundamentally altered that employment structures based on relational contracts may become increasingly difficult to retrieve." Cappelli (1999) supports this conclusion. His imaging inertia theory, based on the assumption that altered perceptions endure throughout generational cohorts, argues that employees do not make decisions or judgements purely on the basis of a rational cost-benefit model. They rely instead on recalling previous experiences in similar situations – imaging – and base their decisions on what happened then. People who experienced the hardships of the Great Depression often felt insecure throughout their lives even when they had become wealthy. The generation that grew up assuming their employer was responsible for careers may similarly never forget the waves of downsizing. Their children, the next generation of workers, may also never forget. Employers may find it difficult to go back to the old model because the new generation of employees will not go back to the old model. Their images of work may have been forever altered.

There is some emerging evidence to support this view. Work on the impact of layoffs on children's values (Barling *et al.*, 1998) and the impact of layoffs on third-party perceptions (Sharlicki *et al.*, 1998) suggests that a shift to more transactional contracts might indeed be taking place. Research into job loss also suggests that employees are adopting new beliefs or perceptions regarding their careers (Cavanaugh and Noe, 1999; Leanna and Feldman, 1994; Shore and Tetrick, 1994). Individuals who have experienced job loss believe that all subsequent employment opportunities are less secure and adopt a more transactional stance. Recent ethnographic research into the home–work interface in economic sectors characterized by "institutionalised instability" also appears to support this scenario. McKee *et al.* (1999) studied oil and gas families from three Scottish communities over a couple of years. Reflecting Cappelli's imaging inertia theory, when examining the experience of "instability survivors who surf the threat," the researchers found that the severe 1980s' recession had become a turning point and had permanently altered the mindset and family culture. Determined to "never again be left so vulnerable," families had more instrumental values. Whilst they still had short-term labor market power and good times, they were using the income to buy a big house and race towards safety in the future. The culture was one of never again becoming attached to the job.

Sparrow (2000) asks some questions that will arise if there has been a shift in values across the generations. Are higher levels of insecurity associated with a shift in the acceptable timeframe for rewards, with a tendency for more immediate reward and less deferred gratification? As employees make choices about the exchange of free time for consumerism, will they automatically trade-off or exchange more free time for less pay? What will be the impact of the increasing attractions of, the cost of losing touch with but desire to stay in touch with, a consumer society? Will the creation of increasingly productive households and processes of wealth creation outside employment (through the value of housing, inheritance of wealth from previous generations and so forth) lead to strategies of income substitution and blunt the value and incentives created by rewards from employment? Will the pursuit of job-pauperizing economic growth mean that traditional careers, progression systems, and rewards expectations become the interests of an ever narrower range of people, given that young employees enter the organization later and older employees leave it earlier? Is the pauperization of many areas of employment leading to large segments of the population becoming estranged from traditional social expectations of advancement and the historically validated exchange of financial security for compliance? In order to accommodate these potential shifts in behavior we see calls for more inventive work sharing, new forms of wealth distribution, alternative forms of work organization, and fundamental changes in work values.

9.10 CONCLUSIONS

In this chapter I have argued that changes surrounding the new employment contract are inextricably linked with emotional and moral processes. Globalization, and its associated downsizing and restructuring, is changing the perceptions that employees have of work. The construct of the psychological contract has been used to capture many of the phenomena at work, including the individualization of the employment relationship that is taking place, the changes in the balance of power and consequent inequalities at work, and changes in levels of trust, fairness, and commitment. Attention has been drawn to some areas where our knowledge is poor. One under-researched area is that of cross-national and cross-cultural differences in the psychological contract. The social construction of work and careers inevitably must mean that the loss or transformation of important aspects of it will be perceived differently, and likely be acted upon differently too. Most of our current understanding has been derived from the experience of managers in the US, the UK, and to some extent continental Europe. As globalization works its way through successive national business systems, we will need to map its impact in more subtle and culturally attuned ways.

Another under-researched area concerns our understanding of how organizations may go on motivating people in a world where job security is no longer a valid concept. There is much circumstantial evidence to suggest that for significant proportions of the workforce there has been some lasting effect generated by the experience of downsizing. The proportion of employees willing or indeed capable of rising to the challenge of boundaryless careers and the main precepts of the new psychological contract is likely to be small in the immediate future. Sadly, even where best practice in moderating the aftershock of downsizing can be made explicit, few organizations seem able to adopt it. One of the challenges faced by many people at work is that the truism that "change is continuous" actually means that they will be exposed to a work environment characterized by a protracted period of ambiguous, complex and little-understood changes. In this environment, there is little opportunity for individuals to internalize, absorb and learn from the transitions they are working through. The costs of such a difficult experience are hard to fathom. They will clearly be mediated by individual differences, but there is increasing evidence of an impact on well-being, absenteeism, and organizational citizenship behaviors. The moral dimension to the new employment relationship is triggered by two processes. First, there is an increasing stratification within work and division between those who have access to important resources, social networks and intangible career opportunities, and those who do not. Second, we see increasing economic apartheid at a societal level, with increasingly wide divisions in terms of earnings and wealth. There is also an important agenda relating to the issue of trust. At an anecdotal level it is clear that three important facets of trust – trust in processes, trust in others' trustworthiness, and trust in institutions – are each under threat. Most organizations are at a loss as to how to rebuild trust amongst their employees. We face an important juncture in our pursuit of new employment relationships. Do we accept that a lack of trust is inevitable, and build HRM systems that can cope with a future "trust no one" generation? Or do we try and re-engage individuals and find new bases of trust, or as the political scientists would argue, new communities of social capital? One way or another, we must decide quickly, because paradoxically most of the new forms of work organization (such as joint ventures, strategic alliances, virtual working, work share arrangements, etc.) actually build high levels of trust into them. Perhaps before deciding what would be the most appropriate strategy, we should fathom out the values of those who are moving into positions of power in these new organizations. What has been the reaction of the young generation to the new employment relationship? Here again, there is a pressing research agenda, but one that is made more pressing by the work of well-being psychologists, who see evidence of new value-sets amongst this generation; of ethnographers, who see a "never going back to such vulnerability" lifestyle pattern; and of labor economists, who see much inertia in the images we have of future work.

REFERENCES

Ancona, D., Kochan, T., Scully, M., Van Maanen, J. V. and Westney, D. E. (1996). *The New Organization,* Cincinnati, OH: South-Western College Publishing.

Anderson, N. and Schalk, R. (1998). The psychological contract in retrospect and prospect. *Journal of Organizational Behaviour,* 19: 637–47.

Appelbaum, E. (1992). Structural change and the growth of part-time and temporary employment. In V. L. duRivage (ed.), *New Policies for the Part-time and Contingent Workforce.* Armonk, NY: Sharpe.

Arthur, M. B., Claman, P. H. and DeFillippi R. J. (1995). Intelligent enterprise, intelligent careers. *Academy of Management Executive,* 9 (4): 7–22.

Ashkensas, R., Ulrich, D., Jick, T. and Kerr, S. (1995). *The Boundaryless Organization.* San Francisco: Jossey-Bass.

Barker, K. (1995). Contingent work: research issues and the lens of moral exclusion. In L. E. Tetrick and J. Barling (eds), *Changing Employment Relations: Behavioral and Social Perspectives.* Washington, DC: American Psychological Association.

Barling, J., Dupre, K. and Hepburn, C. G. (1998). Effects of parents' job insecurity on children's work beliefs and attitudes, *Journal of Applied Psychology,* 83: 112–18.

Baruch, Y. and Hind, P. (1999). Perpetual motion in organizations: effective management and the impact of the new psychoogical contracts on "survivor syndrome." *European Journal of Work and Organizational Psychology,* 8 (2): 295–306.

Beardwell, I. (1998). Bridging the gap? Employee voice, representation and HRM. In P. Sparrow and M. Marchington (eds), *Human Resource Management: The new agenda.* London: Financial Times/Pitman.

Brockner, J., Tyler, T. R. and Cooper-Schneider, R. (1992). The influence of prior commitment to an institution on reactions to perceived unfairness: the higher they are the harder they fall. *Administrative Science Quarterly,* 37: 241–61.

Bruton, G., Keels, J. K. and Shook, C. (1996). Downsizing the firm: answering the strategic questions. *Academy of Management Executive,* 10 (2): 38–45.

Budros, A. (1997). The new capitalism and organizational rationality: the adoption of downsizing programs, 1979–1994. *Social Forces,* 76 (1): 229–50.

Budros, A. (1999). A conceptual framework for analysing why organizations downsize. *Organization Science,* 10 (1): 69–82.

Cappelli, P. (1999). *The New Deal at Work: Managing the market-driven workforce.* Boston, MA: Harvard Business School Press.

Cavanaugh, M. A. and Noe, R. A. (1999). Antecedents and consequences of relational components of the new psychological contract. *Journal of Organizational Behaviour,* 20 (3): 323–40.

Clark, J. and Koonce, R. (1995). Engaging organizational survivors. *Training and Development,* August: 23–30.

Clark, M. C. and Payne, R. L. (1997). The nature and structure of workers' trust in management, *Journal of Organizational Behaviour,* 18 (3): 205–24.

Coyle-Shapiro, J. and Kessler, I. (in press). Consequences of the psychological contract for the employment relationship: a large scale survey. *Journal of Management.*

Creed, W. E. D. and Miles, R. E. (1996). Trust in organizations: a conceptual framework linking organizational forms, managerial philosophies and the opportunity costs of control. In R. M. Kramer and T. R. Tyler (eds), *Trust in Organizations: Frontiers of theory and research.* London: Sage.

Davis, E. (1999). Does your life work? The *Management Today* Work Life Survey. *Management Today,* August: 48–55.

DeFillippi, R. J. and Arthur, M. B. (1994). The boundaryless career: a competency-based prospective. *Journal of Organizational Behaviour,* 15 (4): 307–24.

De Meuse, K., Vanderheiden, P. and Bergmann, T. (1994). Announced layoffs: their effect on corporate financial performance. *Human Resource Management,* 33: 509–30.

DiMaggio, P. and Powell, W. (1983). The iron cage revisited: institutional isomorphism and collective rationality in organizational fields. *American Sociological Review,* 48: 147–60.

Dougherty, D. and Bowman, E. (1995). The effects of organizational downsizing on product innovation. *California Management Review,* 37: 28–44.

Eigen, P. and Rockefeller, D. (1999). New rules of the game. *Newsweek,* 133 (5): 50–51.

Emmott, M. and Hutchinson, S. (1998). Employment flexibility: threat or promise? In P. Sparrow and M. Marchington (eds), *Human Resource Management: The new agenda.* London: Financial Times/ Pitman.

Ernsberger, R., Warner, J. and Theil, S. (1998). A race won by the swift and the strong. *Newsweek,* Special Issue on Euroland, November: 42–8.

Fernberg, P. M. (1998). Stress: hidden source of lost time. *Occupational Hazards,* 60 (6): 76–80.

Freeman, R. B. (1996). Toward an aparteid economy? *Harvard Business Review,* September–October: 114–21.

Gambetta, D. (1988). Can we trust trust? In D. Gambetta (ed.), *Trust: Making and breaking co-operative relationships.* Oxford: Basil Blackwell.

Guest, D. (1998). Is the psychological contract worth taking seriously? *Journal of Organizational Behaviour,* 19, Special Issue: 649–64.

Guest, D., Conway, N., Briner, R. and Dickmann, M. (1996). The state of the psychological contract in employment. *Issues in People Management, n.* 16,

London: IPD.

Guzzo, R. A., Noonan, K. A. and Elron, E. (1994). Expatriate managers and the psychological contract. *Journal of Applied Psychology,* 79: 617–26.

Hallier, J. (in press). Security abeyance: coping with the erosion of jobs and conditions. *British Journal of Management.*

Hallier, J. and Lyon, P. (1996). Job insecurity and employee commitment: managers' reactions to the threat and outcomes of redundancy selection. *British Journal of Management,* 7 (1): 107–23.

Handy, C. (1989). *The age of Unreason,* London: Hutchinson.

Hiltrop, J. M. (1995). The changing psychological contract. *European Management Journal,* 13 (3): 286–94.

Hind, P., Frost, M. and Rowley, S. (1996). The resilience audit and the psychological contract. *Journal of Managerial Psychology,* 11: 18–29.

Hofstede, G. (1980). *Culture's Consequences: International differences in work-related values.* Beverly Hills, CA: Sage.

Hulin, C. L. and Glomb, T. M. (1999). Contingent employees: individual and organizational considerations. In D. R. Ilgen and E. D. Pulakos (eds), *The Changing Nature of Performance: Implications for staffing motivation and development.* San Francisco: Jossey-Bass.

International Survey Research Corporation (1997). Downsizing not such a downer. *HR Focus,* 74 (12): 6.

Jackson, P. R. (1997). Downsizing and deselection. In N. Anderson and P. Herriot (eds), *International Handbook of Selection and Assessment,* Chichester: John Wiley.

Leanna, C. R. and Feldman, D. C. (1994). The psychology of job loss. In G. R. Ferris (ed.), *Research in Personnel and Human Resource Management,* Vol. 12. Greenwich, CT: JAI Press.

Margolis, M. (1999). A tale of two countries. *Newsweek,* 133 (5): 38–44.

McKee, L., Mauthner, N. and Maclean, C. (1999). Organizational culture and change: a study of the male model of work and the psychological contract in the oil and gas industry. Paper presented at the British Academy of Management Conference, 1–3 September, Manchester.

McKinley, W. C., Sanchez, C. and Schick, A. (1995). Organizational downsizing: constraining, cloning, learning. *Academy of Management Executive,* 9 (3): 32–44.

McShulskis, E. (1997). Record numbers of companies say they are understaffed. *HR Magazine,* 42 (4): 26–9.

Mentzer, M. (1996). Corporate downzizing and profitability in Canada. *Canadian Journal of Administrative Sciences,* 13: 237–50.

Miles, R. and Creed, D. (1995). Organizational forms and managerial philosophies: a descriptive and analytical review. In L. L. Cummings and B. M. Staw (eds), *Research in Organizational Behaviour,* vol. 17: 333–72. Greenwich, CT: JAI Press.

Mishra, K. E., Spreitzer, G. M. and Mishra, A. K. (1998). Preserving employee morale during downsizing. *Sloan Management Review,* Winter: 83–95.

Morehead, A., Steele, M., Alexander, M., Stephen, K. and Duffin, L. (1997). *Changes at Work: The 1995 Australian Workplace Industrial Relations Survey.* Melbourne:

Longman.

Morrison, E. D. (1994). Psychological contracts and change. *Human Resource Management,* 33 (3): 353–72.

Morrison, E. W. and Robinson, S. L. (1997). When employees feel betrayed: a model of how psychological contract violation develops. *Academy of Management Review,* 22 (1): 226–56.

Murphy, P. E. and Jackson, S .E. (1999). Managing work role performance: challenges for twenty first century organizations and their employees. In D. R. Ilgen and E. D. Pulakos (eds), *The Changing Nature of Performance: Implications for staffing motivation and development.* San Francisco: Jossey-Bass.

O'Reilly, B. (1994). The new deal: what companies and employees owe one another. *Fortune,* June 13: 44–52.

Pascale, R. (1995). In search of "The New Employment Contract". Paper for *20th Anniversary Euroforum Conference,* September 15–16, Strategic Leadership Program, London Business School

Payne, R. (2000). Eupsychian management and the millennium. *Journal of Managerial Psychology.*

Peiperl, M. A. and Baruch, Y. (1997). Back to square zero: the post-corporate career, *Organizational Dynamics,* 25 (4): 7–22.

Robinson, S. L. and Morrison, E. W. (1995). Psychological contracts and organization citizenship behaviour: the effect of unfulfilled obligations on civic virtue behaviour. *Journal of Organizational Behaviour,* 16: 289–98.

Robinson, S. L. and Rousseau, D. M. (1994). Violating the psychological contract: not the exception but the norm. *Journal of Organizational Behaviour,* 15: 245–59.

Rousseau, D. M. and Tijoriwala, S. A. (1998). Assessing psychological contracts: issues, alternatives and measures. *Journal of Organizational Behaviour,* 19, Special Issue: 679–96.

Schalk, R. and Freese, C. (1997). New facets of commitment in response to organizational change: research trends and the Dutch experience. In C. L. Cooper and D. M. Rousseau (eds), *Trends in Organizational Behaviour,* Vol. 4. Chichester: John Wiley.

Schuler, R. S. and Rogovsky, N. (in press) Understanding compensation practice variations across firms: the impact of national culture. *Journal of International Business Studies.*

Schwab, K. (1999). The realities of globalism. *Newsweek,* 133 (5): 114.

Seppa, N. (1996). Downsizing: a new form of abandonment. *American Psychological Association Monitor,* 26 (5): 1.

Sharlicki, D. P., Ellard, J. H. and Kelln B. R. (1998). Third-party perceptions of a layoff: procedural, derogation, and retributive aspects of justice. *Journal of Applied Psychology,* 83: 119–27.

Shore, L. M. and Tetrick, L. E. (1994). The psychological contract as an explanatory framework in the employment relationship. In C. L. Cooper and D. M. Rousseau (eds), *Trends in Organizational Behaviour,* Vol. 1. Somerset, NJ: John Wiley.

Singh, R. (1998). Redefining psychological contracts with the US work force: a critical task for strategic human resource management planners in the 1990s. *Human*

Resource Management, 37 (1): 61–70.

Soros, G. (1999). The crisis of global capitalism. *Newsweek,* 133 (5): 32–7.

Sparrow, P. R. (2000). The new employment contract. In R. Burke and C. L. Cooper (eds), *The Organization in Crisis.* Oxford: Basil Blackwell.

Sparrow, P. R. and Cooper, C. L. (1998). New organizational forms: the strategic relevance of future psychological contract scenarios. *Canadian Journal of Administrative Sciences,* 15 (4): 356–71.

Sparrow, P. R. and Marchington, M. (1998). *Human Resource Management: The new agenda.* London: Pitman/ Financial Times.

Sparrow, P. R. and Wu, P. C. (1998). Does national culture really matter? Predicting HRM preferences of Taiwanese employees. *Employee Relations,* 20 (1): 26–56.

Stroh, L. K., Brett, J. M. and Reilly, J. H. (1994). A decade of change: managers' attachment to their organizations and their jobs. *Human Resource Management,* 33: 531–48.

United Nations (1998). *Human Development Report 1998.* New York: United Nations. http//www.undp.org/undp/hdro

US Department of Labor (1995). Contingent and alternative employment arrangements. *Bureau of Labor Statistics Report* no. 900. Washington, DC: US Department of Labor.

Wall Street Journal (1999). The outlook: the blessings of low unemployment. *Wall Street Journal,* 233 (55): A1.

Waterman, R. H. Jr., Waterman, J. A. and Collard, B. A. (1994). Toward a career-reslient workforce. *Harvard Business Review,* 72 (4): 87–95.

Worrell, D., Davidson, W. and Sharma, V. (1991). Layoff announcements and stockholder wealth. *Academy of Management Journal,* 34: 662–78.

Worrell, L. and Cooper, C. (1998). *The Quality of Working Life: The 1998 survey of managers' changing experiences.* Manchester: Institute of Management/UMIST.

Zhao, J., Rust, K. G. and McKinley, W. (1997). A socio-cognitive interpretation of organizational downsizing: toward a paradigm shift. Paper presented at the 23rd European International Business Academy Conference on Global Business in the Information Age, Stuttgart, December 14–16.

Index

absenteeism 221
absorptive capacity 92, 94, 97
achievement, need for 19
advanced general skills 90–93
  developing through accumulating
    mechanisms 93–5
Albrecht, K. 36
Albrecht, S. 36
Alderfer, C.P. 17, 19, 20
Allen, N.J. 26, 100
Altman, B.W. 62
American Management Association 224
Ancona, D. 224
Anderson, N. 223
Anderson, P. 83
Andreu, R. 3, 39, 206
Angle, H.L. 55
Aoki, M. 176, 192
Appelbaum, E. 227
appraisal systems 12, 13
Arthur, J.B. 5, 6, 9, 10, 11, 12, 13, 36,
    49, 59, 64, 67, 127, 128, 134, 136
Arthur, M.B. 219
Ashkensas, R. 219
Ashmos, D.P. 48
attachment to the organization 21, 36, 38
autonomy 19
Aycan, Z. 68

Bahrami, H. 171
Bailey, T. 124
Bain, J.S. 82
Baird, L.S. 6, 54, 55, 134
balanced contracts 27, 35, 37
balanced employment systems 140–41
Barker, K. 226–7
Barling, J. 232
Barnard, C.I. 22, 23, 67

Barney, J.B. 5, 82, 87, 97, 106
Baron, J.N. 66, 81, 82, 84, 85, 86, 87, 89,
    143
Bartlett, C.A. 2, 3, 12, 15, 81, 133, 169,
    170, 173, 174, 203
Baruch, Y. 218, 219
Bateman, T.S. 100
Batson, C.D. 21
Beardwell, I. 229
Beattie, D.F. 59
Becker, B.E. 6, 50, 60, 67
Becker, G.S. 86
Beer, M. 48
Begin, J.P. 11
"behavioural perspective" 6
Bell, D. 202
belongingness 20
Belous, R.S. 62
Bennett, A. 143
Besanko, D. 31, 33
best practices employment systems 10,
    127, 136, 146–7, 161
Blau, P.M. 7, 16
bonding mechanisms 98–100, 136, 138
Boudreau, J.W. 67
Boulding, K.M. 48
boundaries
  between jobs 63
  changing 174–7
boundary conditions 100–107
boundaryless careers 219, 234
boundaryless organization 219
Bowman, E. 219
Boxall, P.F. 6, 65
brand image 31, 36, 129–30
Brazil 218
Brewster, C. 68
Bridges, W. 63

Briggs, P. 192
British Institute of Management 225
British Institute of Personnel and
    Development 225
Brockner, J. 219
Brown, S.L. 132
Bruton, G. 222
Budros, A. 215, 221
Buller, P.F. 59, 65, 66
Burack, E.H. 53
Burnham, D.H. 19
Burns, T. 96
business process re-engineering (BPR)
    220
business strategies
    and employment systems 133-7
    typology 128-33
business strategy measures, in survey
    150-56
Butler, J.E. 11, 48, 54

Caligiuri, P.M. 58, 59, 60
capabilities 203
Cappelli, P. 2, 3, 11, 28, 37, 38, 40, 50,
    59, 60, 64, 79, 80, 82, 89, 143, 215,
    216, 232
Cardona, P. 7, 16, 17, 18, 28
career behaviour 219
Cascio, W.F. 18
Cavanaugh, M.A. 232
Caves, R.E. 82
cellular form 169
Ceridian 225
Chandler, A. 127
changing
    boundaries 174-7
    processes 174
    structures 173
Chatman, J.A. 54
Child, J. 49, 183
China 68
Clark, J. 219, 229
cluster analysis 157-9
codifiable knowledge 210-11
Cohen, W.M. 92, 97
Cohen, Y. 81, 83, 86
Cole, R.E. 193
Coleman, J.S. 79-80
Collins, J. 203

compensation 54, 117, 138
compensation policies 12, 13, 18, 117
competence, need for 19
competitive advantage 5, 79-84, 129,
    202
    in dynamic environments 88-100
    and employability 90
    and employment security 84-8, 88
    and flexibility 209
    and knowledge 205
    and new organizational forms 203-4
competitive strategies 30-39
    and employment contract alignment
        34-9
    and employment systems 11, 160-62
complementary assets 195
Conner, K.R. 82, 95
contingency approach to SHRM 11,
    50-61, 126, 127, 128, 134, 163
contingent employment contracts 35, 146
"contingent perspective" 6
Cool, K. 89, 97, 106
Cooper, C. 225
Cooper, C.L. 62, 223, 230
cooperation 22
core competencies 62
core employees 62, 63, 147
Cornfield, D.B. 103
corporate strategy, and HRM 58
corporate strategy models 59
corporate structure, Europe and Japan
    184-7
cost leadership strategies 30, 35-6, 39,
    129, 130-31, 161
    and transactional employment systems
        136-9
Coyle-Shapiro, J. 224
Crandall, R.E. 51
Creed, W.E.D. 55, 65, 229
Crocker-Hefter, A. 50, 59
Cronbach's alpha score 154
Cummings, L.L. 48, 52, 66
Cutcher-Gershenfeld, J. 6
Cyert, R.M. 67

D'Aveni, R.A. 62, 83
Davenport, T.H. 204
Davidow, W.H. 204
Davis, D.D. 62, 63

Davis, E. 225
Davis, P.S. 129
Davis-Blake, A. 62
De Cieri, H. 68
De Geus, A. 203
De Meuse, K. 219, 222
Dean, J.W. Jr 11, 59
decentralization 19, 175, 179, 180
Defillippi, R.J. 219
Delaney, J.T. 127
Delery, J.E. 6, 12, 13, 50, 67, 128, 136
DePree, H. 11
Deresky, H. 51, 52
DeSanctis, G. 203
Dess, W.L. 129
Devanna, M.A. 53
Dewar, R.D. 127, 181
Dierickx, I. 89, 97, 106
differentiation 35, 36–7, 39
  through product variety 131
  through quality and brand image
    131–2
differentiation strategies 30–32, 38, 129
DiMaggio, P.J. 66, 222
Dobbin, F. 66
Doeringer, P.B. 83, 86
Doty, D.H. 6, 12, 13, 50, 67, 128, 136
Dougherty, D. 219
Dowling, P.J. 68
downscoping 62, 180, 195
downsizing 80, 115–16, 216, 217–18
  costs 220–22
  economic benefits 221
  long-term consequences 224–6
  psychological consequences 218–20
  and the psychological contract 222–4
Doz, Y. 64
Drazin, R. 60, 136
Drucker, P. 202
Drucker, P.F. 36
Dunlop, J.T. 5, 10, 49, 50, 63, 128
Dutton, J.E. 181
Dyer, L. 6, 12, 13, 14, 50, 58, 65, 67, 128
dynamic efficiency 39, 130, 132, 143
  strategies 143–4

earnings 227–8
ecological perspectives 65
economic exchange 17–18, 26

efficiency 33–4, 35
Eigen, P. 230
Eisenhardt, K.M. 62, 132
electronic data interchange (EDI) 174
Emmott, M. 229
employability 3–4, 79–84, 88–100, 92,
    99, 100, 102–5, 201–2
  and competitive advantage 90
  concept 218–19
  external and internal 207–12
  organizational 2, 14, 134, 144–6
employability based contracts 38
employee behaviour 15, 16
  new patterns 231–2
employee commitment 117
employee performance 124
employee specialization 83
employee turnover 116
employment agreements 3
employment contract alignment, and
    competitive strategies 34–9
employment contracts 7, 8
  balanced contracts 27
  and exchange relationships 24–9
  market employability contracts 27–8
  new 62, 215–16, 219
  organizational employability contracts
    28–9, 38–9
  relational contract 26–7
  transactional contracts 26, 35, 36
employment relationship 2, 61–5, 79,
    84
  in a dynamic context 81–4
  and integrated models of firm strategy
    85
  new 61–5
  traditional 114–15
employment security *see* job security
employment system measures, in survey
    156–60
employment systems 6, 6–7, 11–16,
    127
  balanced systems 13–14
  and business strategies 133–7
  and competitive strategies 11, 160–62
  "market employability" system 14
  "organizational employability" system
    14–15
  and organizational strategy 10

relational system 13
transactional system 12–13
typology 133–6
empowerment 138
entrepreneurship 89, 90, 119–20
environmental uncertainty 55
Ernsberger, R. 218
Etzioni, A. 17
Europe
    corporate structure 184–7
    forms of organizing compared to
        Japan 177–89
    organizational change 197
    organizational innovations 189–90
Evans, P.A.L. 60, 64
evolutionary models 54
exchange relationships 16–23, 134
    and employment contracts 24–9
exchange theory 7
existence needs 17, 18
exploitation 33
exploration 33
external knowledge 207, 209
extrinsic needs 17

fairness 16, 27, 28
feedback 20
Feldman, D.C. 232
Fenton, E. 172, 194
Fernberg, P.M. 221
Ferner, A. 68
firm performance 11
    and HPWP 10
firm size, and work organization
        practices 163
firm-specific skills 90, 91, 118
Fisher, C.D. 48, 58, 59, 60, 127
flexibility 204, 207–9, 217–18, 229
    and competitive advantage 209
    and knowledge integration 206
Fombrun, C.J. 11, 51, 55
Freeman, R.B. 227
Freese, C. 224
Friedman, S.D. 59

Galbraith, J.R. 35–6, 59, 127, 203
Gambetta, D. 229
Generation X 232
generic strategies 59

George, J.M. 203
Georgopoulos, B.S. 18
Gerhart, B. 50, 60, 67
Gerstein, M. 51, 58
Ghemawat, P. 8, 33, 34, 130
Ghoshal, S. 2, 3, 8, 12, 15, 22, 29, 38, 81,
    83, 98, 133, 169, 170, 173, 174, 203
globalization 59, 216, 230, 234
Glomb, T.M. 226
Golden, K.A. 54, 65
Govindarajan, V. 6, 52
growth needs 19
Guest, D. 10, 222, 224, 225, 226
Gupta, A.K. 51, 52
Guzzo, R.A. 224

Hackman, J.R. 18
Hakim, C. 64
Hall, D.T. 62
Hall, R.E. 85
Hallier, J. 220, 226
Hambrick, D.C. 129
Hamel, G. 33, 62
Handy, C. 63, 169, 204, 218, 219
Hasegawa, H. 192
Heath, C. 79, 83, 101, 102
Heckscher, C.C. 63, 64
Helper, S. 49
Hendry, C. 59, 60
Herbert, T.T. 51, 52
Herzberg, F. 17, 19, 20
hierarchical structures 179
high performance work practices
    (HPWP) 6, 8
    and firm performance 10
Hill, C.W.L. 59
Hind, P. 218, 219
Hirsch, P. 143
Hitt, M.A. 62
Hofstede, G. 217
Holder, G.W. 12, 13, 14, 58, 128
Homans, G. 7, 16, 105
Hong Kong 218
Hook, G.D. 192
horizontal linkages 3, 21, 192
Horvat, B. 99
Hoskisson, R.E. 62, 175
Huber, G.P. 48
Hulin, C.L. 226

human resource management (HRM) 60, 82
  and corporate strategy 58
  policies 5, 6
  surveys 217
human resource management (HRM) practices 11, 47–8
  Japan 194–5
  new 174, 180
  strategic approach 49–61
  systems approach 48–9
Huselid, M.A. 5, 6, 10, 49, 64, 67, 127, 128, 135, 146
Hutchinson, S. 229

Ichniowski, C. 6, 10, 49, 128, 161
imaging inertia theory 232
In Search of Excellence 10
individual needs 7, 15, 16
individual-based models 51–3, 64
inequalities 227–8
information technology 179–80, 182, 192
INNFORM program of research 171, 198
  questionnaires 175–6
innovative work practices 64
institutional pressures 65
integration process 55
internal knowledge 207
internal labor market (ILM) systems 63
internal labor markets (ILMs) 85, 86, 87
International Survey Research Corporation 222
internationalization 188
IO-based theories 82
isolating mechanism 87
isomorphic processes 66
Itami, H. 94
Izumi, H. 49

Jackofsky, E.F. 48, 52
Jackson, P.R. 219
Jackson, S. 124, 127, 128, 134, 140, 141
Jackson, S.E. 5, 6, 11, 27, 58, 59, 82, 227, 232
Jacoby, S.M. 66, 67, 85
Japan 68, 176
  corporate structure 184–7
  forms of organizing compared to Europe 177–89

HRM practices 194–5
  organizational change 197
  organizational flexibility 193
  organizational innovations 189–92
  pay structure 194
job creation 202
job hopping 111–12
job rotation 19, 21, 135, 138, 191, 192
job security 79–84, 101, 102, 138, 146–7, 219, 234
  and competitive advantage 84–8
  and turnover 87
Jones, G.R. 51, 55, 203

Kalleberg, A. 176, 194
Kanter, R.M. 81, 92, 102, 140, 203
Katz, H.C. 49
Kazanjian, R.J. 127
Kerr, C. 49
Kerr, J.L. 6, 13, 48, 52, 128
Kessler, I. 224
Kim, W.C. 100
Kissler, G.D. 62
knowledge 201–2, 202, 204–6
  codifiable 210–11
  and competitive advantage 205
  definitions 204–5
  external 207, 209
  internal 210
  and new organization forms 206–7
  non-codificable 211
knowledge integration 207–9
  and flexibility 206
Kochan, T.A. 49, 64, 67
Kogut, B. 96, 98, 204
Koike, K. 191
Kolb, D. 205
Koonce, R. 219
Kotter, J.P. 51
Kuran, T. 33

Lado, A.A. 6, 82
Lake, D.G. 49, 66
Laubacher, R.J. 28, 29
Lawler, E.E. 17, 18, 20, 21, 49
Leanna, C.R. 232
Lengnick-Hall, C.A. 51, 58, 60, 127, 128
Lengnick-Hall, M.L. 51, 58, 60, 127, 128
Leonard-Barton, D. 89

Lepak, D.P. 62
Levinthal, D.A. 33, 92, 97
Levitt, B. 33
life-cycle model 56
lifetime employment 191–2
Likert scale 151, 153, 154, 155, 177, 181
Lincoln, J.R. 176, 194
linking mechanisms 95–8, 136, 139
Lorange, P. 64
low morale 39
loyalty 226
Lundberg, C.A. 59, 66
Lyon, P. 226

McClelland, D. 19, 20
McCormick, J. 49
MacDuffie, J.P. 5, 9, 10, 49, 50, 64, 127, 128
McEvoy, G.M. 18
McKee, L. 232
McKinley, W.C. 222
McLean Parks, J. 26
McMahan, G.C. 5, 6, 10, 11, 48, 127, 134
Macneil, I.R. 26
McShulskis, E. 221
Macy, B.A. 49
Malone, M.S. 204
Malone, T.W. 28, 29
management practices 106–7, 111–12
management processes 203
Management Today 225
manager-strategy matching models 51–2
Manz, C.C. 63
March, J.G. 33, 67
Marchington, M. 216, 229
Margolis, M. 218
market employability 2
market employability contracts 27–8, 35, 37–8
market employability systems 134, 143–4
Markides, C.C. 172
Martell, K.D. 11, 59
Martin, J. 66
Maslow, A.H. 17, 19, 20
Massini, S. 3, 14, 39, 62
"matching model" 6
Mathieu, J.E. 15

Mauborgne, R.A. 100
Mayer, M. 174
meaningful work 19
mentoring 116–17, 136
Mentzer, M. 222
Meshoulam, I. 6, 54, 134
Meyer, A.D. 62
Meyer, J.P. 26, 100
Meyer, J.W. 65, 66
Miles, R. 229
Miles, R.E. 49, 55, 56, 59, 65, 169, 204
Miles, R.H. 6, 11, 12, 13, 32, 127, 128, 164
Milgrom, P. 6, 9, 87, 127, 134
Milkovich, G.T. 60
Miller, D. 59
Mills, D.Q. 53, 62
mimetic processes 66
Mintzberg, J. 127
Mirvis, P.H. 59, 62, 65, 66
Mishra, K.E. 219
Mobley, W.H. 68
Montgomery, C.A. 83
Moore's Law 132
Moran, P. 2, 3, 22, 83, 98
Morhman, S.A. 49
Morishima, M. 68, 194
Morrison, E.W. 224
motivation 15–16, 17, 234
Mowday, R. 17
multidivisional organization 169
Murphy, P.E. 227, 232

Nakata, Y. 194
Napier, N.K. 59
Nelson, R.R. 97, 195
neo-contingency perspectives 49
network organization 230
networks 169
"new capitalism" 215
new deal 118–21
new employment contracts 62, 215–16, 219
new employment relationships, and strategic HRM system 61–5
new organizational forms (NOFs) 19
and competitive advantage 203–4
and knowledge 206–7
main characteristics 203

Noe, R.A. 232
Nohria, N. 174
non-codifiable knowlege 211
Nonaka, I. 176, 193, 204
North, D.C. 98

Okubayahsi, K. 194
Oldham, G.R. 18
Olian, J.D. 61
O'Reilly, B. 219
O'Reilly, C.A. 8, 54
Organ, D.W. 7, 15, 100
organization life cycle 51, 59
organizational change 169-70, 171,
    195-6
  indicators 172
organizational culture 66
organizational employability 2, 14, 134
  contracts 28-9, 38-9
  systems 144-6
organizational innovations 189-90
organizational learning 33, 193
The Organizational Man 115
organizational strategy, and ES 10
organizational theory 60, 65
organizing
  comparing forms in Japan and Europe
    177-89
  concept of 170
  innovative forms 172-3
Osterman, P. 5, 6, 9, 49, 50, 64, 127,
    128, 135, 146, 147, 161
Ostrow, M.H. 58, 127, 128
Ottensmeyer, E.J. 59
outsourcing 62, 63, 114, 175, 211

Paauwe, J. 67
Pascale, R.T. 33, 216
Pasternack, B.A. 204
Payne, R.L. 221, 229
Peck, S.R. 11, 127, 128, 134, 141
Peiperl, M.A. 56, 219
Penrose, E.T. 89, 130
Pentland, B.T. 205
perceptual framing 226
Pérez-López, J.A. 17
performance, and strategic HRM 67
periphery employees 62, 63, 64
personal responsibility 19

Peteraf, M.A. 83, 87, 89, 91
Peters, T.J. 10
Pettigrew, A.M. 3, 14, 39, 60, 62, 67,
    172, 194
Pfeffer, J. 5, 6, 8, 10, 12, 14, 40, 49, 50,
    66, 81, 82, 83, 84, 85, 86, 87, 89,
    127, 135, 143, 146
Piore, M.J. 83, 86
Piperl, M.A. 6, 128
poaching 118-19, 216
Polanyi, M. 205
Porras, J. 203
Portales, C. 2, 58, 126, 140
Porter, L.W. 18
Porter, M.E. 30, 31, 32, 56, 58, 82, 87,
    129, 130, 150, 164
Porter's competitive strategy index 152,
    153
Post, J.E. 62
poverty 228
Powell, W. 66, 222
Prahalad, C.K. 33, 62
process innovations 179
processes, changing 174
project forms 184, 191, 197
promotion 18, 114, 117-18, 119, 138
prospector organizations 59
Prusak, L. 204
psychological consequences of
    downsizing 218-20
psychological contract 222-4, 234
Purcell, J. 11, 58, 66, 128

quality 31, 36, 129, 130
quality circles 135
quality-brand name/dynamic efficiency
    strategies, and organizational
    employability systems 144-6
quality-brand name/static efficiency
    strategies, and relational
    employment systems 141-3
Quinn, J.B. 62, 127
Quintanilla, J. 62, 63, 66, 68

R&D 188
Ramanujam, V. 54, 65
Ramstad, P.M. 67
recruitment 54, 66, 93, 138
Reeves, T. 6, 50, 65, 67

Reisman, H. 51, 58
relational contracts 26-7, 35, 36
relational employment systems, and
    quality-brand name/static efficiency
    strategies 141-3
rent creation, and linking mechanisms
    95-8
resource conversion 89-90
restructuring 216
returns over investment (ROI) 162
Ricart, J.E. 2, 8, 33, 34, 58, 126, 130,
    140, 204, 206
Richardson, R. 67
Richter, F.-J. 192
Roberts, J. 6, 9, 87, 127, 134
Robinson, S.L. 224
Rockefeller, D. 230
Rogers, E.W. 67
Rogovsky, N. 217
Rothschild, W.E. 51
Rousseau, D.M. 7, 8, 17, 24, 25, 26, 27,
    62, 80, 217, 224
Rowan, B. 65
Rozell, E.J. 127
Rumelt, R.P. 87, 89, 95, 97, 106
Rynes, S.L. 61

sacrifice 94-5
safety networks 40
Salancik, G.R. 66, 86
Sánchez-Runde, C. 2, 62, 63, 65, 66, 128
Saxenian, A. 37
Schalk, R. 223, 224
Schein, E.H. 7, 15, 16, 17, 19, 20, 21
Schuler, R.S. 5, 6, 11, 27, 58, 59, 82,
    124, 127, 128, 134, 140, 141, 217
Schumpeter, J.A. 32-3, 89
Schwab, K. 229
Schwartz, S.H. 21
Schweiger, D.M. 52
Scott, W.R. 65, 66
security needs 17, 18
Segev, E. 59
self-esteem needs 19, 20
Seppa, N. 219
shared purpose 22
Sharlicki, D.P. 232
Sherer, P.D. 82
Sherman, S. 15

Sherman, W.C. 50, 60
Shore, L.M. 222, 232
short-term employment relationships 37
Shortell, S.M. 32
Sieber, S. 3, 39, 206
Silicon Valley 119, 120, 121
Simon, H.A. 80, 84
Sims, H.P. 63
Singh, H. 11, 60
Singh, R. 219, 224
Sivasubramaniam, N. 11, 58, 59, 128,
    129
skills
    advanced general 90-95
    firm-specific 90, 91, 118
Slocum, J.W. 6, 13, 128
Smith 219
Smith, B.J. 54, 55
Smith, E.C. 51, 52, 56, 59, 127
Snell, S.A. 6, 10, 11, 48, 54, 58, 59, 60,
    62, 67, 127
Snow, C.C. 6, 11, 12, 32, 49, 54, 56, 59,
    127, 128, 164, 204
social esteem 20
social exchange 20-23, 27, 29
social exclusion 226-8
social institutions 1
social needs 20, 21
social organizations 80
Sonnenfeld, J.A. 6, 56, 128
Soros, G. 230
Spain 125
Spanish firms
    survey 147-60
    results 160-162
Sparrow, P.R. 3, 40, 62, 215, 216, 217,
    223, 229, 230, 231, 233
Spender, J.C. 206, 207
Stalk, G. 30, 129
Stalker, G.M. 96
Standing, G. 62
static efficiency strategies 140-41
strategic approach to human resource
    management practices 49-61
strategic continuity 130
strategic human resource management
    (SHRM) 2, 5, 8-11, 54-5, 65, 124,
    125
    contingent approach 11

and new employment relationships 61–5
and performance 67
theoretical debate 127–8
Strategy and Structure 127
stress 221, 225–6
Stroh, L.K. 58, 59, 60, 224
structural grouping 184
structures, changing 173
substantive models 56, 59
Susman, I. 59
sustainable competitive advantage 79–84, 129
Sutton, J.R. 66
system-based models
  formal elaborations 55
  of strategy and HRM 53
  substantive elaborations 57
systems approach, to human resource management (HRM) practices 48–9
Szilayi, A.D. 52
Szulanski, G. 95

Takeuchi, H. 176, 193
Tampoe, F.M.K. 59
task identity 19
task significance 19
teams 224
teamwork 19, 135, 138, 140
technical excellence 201
technological innovation 181
technology 86, 115, 170, 194
Teece, D.J. 82, 97, 195, 205
Terpstra, D.E. 127
Tetrick, L.E. 222, 232
Thomas, A.S. 51, 52
Tichy, N.M. 15
Tijoriwala, S.A. 217
Tornatzky, L.G. 140
total quality management 135
trade unions 227, 228
training 54, 139
transactional employment contracts 26, 35, 36
transactional employment systems, and cost leadership strategies 136–9
trust 215, 223, 224–5, 229–31, 234
Tushman, M.L. 8, 83, 96
Tyre, M.J. 205

Ulrich, D. 49, 66
unemployment 218
  US 227
United Nations 228
universalistic, and contingency aproaches to HRM 60–61
universalistic approach 49–50, 126, 127, 128, 135, 146–7, 163
universalistic models 64
US, unemployment 227
US Department of Labor 227
Uzzi 62

Van de Ven, A.H. 60, 136
Van Dyne, L. 16
virtual employees 62
Viscio, A.J. 204
Volberda, H.W. 169, 203
Von Bertalanffy, L. 48
von Hippel, E. 205

Wachter, M.L. 87
Wade-Benzoni, K.A. 7
Walker, J.W. 10, 55
Wall Street Journal 227
Walton, R.E. 10, 12, 13, 14, 58, 128
Wang, Z.M. 68
Wanous, J.P. 54
Waterman, R.H. 10
Waterman, R.H. Jr 81, 219
Weber, M. 103
Weil, D. 5, 10, 49, 50, 128
Wellins, R.S. 203
Werbel, J. 127
Wernerfelt, B. 106, 130
Whittington, R. 169, 172, 174
Whyte, W.F. 20
Williamson, O.E. 86, 87
Wilson, M.C. 6, 82
Winter, S.G. 33, 83, 89, 91, 93, 94, 97
Wittington, R. 9, 12, 62
work exchange 18–19
work organization practices 124, 135
and firm size 163
work organization (WO) practices 5, 10
work practices 127–8
World Economic Forum 229–30
Worrel, L. 225

Worrell, D. 222
Wright, P.M. 5, 6, 10, 11, 48, 50, 58, 60,
    67, 86, 127, 134
Wu, P.C. 217

Zajac, D.M. 15
Zajac, E.J. 32
Zander, U. 96, 98, 204
Zhao, J. 221, 222